Privatization in Europe

Privatization in Europe

West and East Experiences

Edited by
Ferdinando Targetti

Dartmouth
Aldershot · Brookfield USA · Hong Kong · Singapore · Sydney

Published by
Dartmouth Publishing Company Limited
Gower House
Croft Road
Aldershot
Hants GU11 3HR
England

Dartmouth Publishing Company
Old Post Road
Brookfield
Vermont 05036
USA

A CIP catalogue record for this book is available from the British Library and the US Library of Congress

ISBN 1 85521 275 7

Printed and bound in Great Britain by
Billing and Sons Ltd, Worcester

Contents

PART IV: EASTERN PROCESSES

Foreword and acknowledgements

Most of the essays collected in this book were presented as papers to the Conference of the European Association for Comparative Economic Systems held at Trento University, Italy, on 1 - 2 March 1991.

The book also includes essays written by authors who did not attend the conference (Vladimir Andreff, Roman Frydman, Andrzej Rapaczynski, Brigita Schmögnerová and Eva Voszka) as well as others written at a later date by conference participants (Siro Lombardini and Robin Marris).

In writing my essay and editing this book I have benefited greatly from discussions with Roman Frydman, Andrzej Rapaczynski and Boguslawa Kinda Targetti. And equally stimulating have been my discussions with Alberto Chilosi, Bruno Dallago, Domenico Mario Nuti, Jerzy Osiatynski, Dariusz Rosati and Vittorio Valli. I would like to thank the Polish Minister for Privatization, Janusz Levandowski, for granting me so much of his time, the Central European University of Prague for having me as a guest at its seminars on privatization, Luigi Paganetto for inviting me to participate at the conference at Villa Madragone organized by him and for the opportunities he thus provided me for discussion on the theme of privatization on that occasion. I wish to thank Adrian Belton for helping me in my editorial work, and the Economics Department of the University of Trento for funding the Conference, the editorial expenses and my research.

F.T.

About the authors

Wladimir Andreff is Professor of Economics at the University of Paris 1 and director of R.O.S.E.S. (Reforming and Opening Economic Systems), Research Unit of the French *Centre National de Recherche Scientifique* (CNRS). His main areas of research are the following: comparative economic systems, the economies of Central and Eastern Europe, multinational corporations, and development economics. In these fields he has published or edited numerous articles and books, including *Les multinationales,* Paris, La Découverte, 1990, *La réalité socialiste* (co-authored with Marie Lavine: Paris, Ed. Economique, 1985) and *Réforme et échanges extérieurs dans les pays de l'Est* (Paris, Ed. L'Harmattan, 1990).

Will Bartlett received his training as an economist at the Universities of Cambridge, London and Liverpool. He is a Research Fellow at the School for Advanced Urban Studies, Bristol University, and works in the area of comparative economic systems and public policy.

Ivo Bićanić received his MA at Oxford University and his PhD from the University of Zagreb, both in Economics. His main fields of interest are the unofficial economy, economic equality, and the efficiency of centralized economic policy in crisis management.

Marie Bohatá holds a PhD from the Economic Institute of the Czechoslovak Academy of Sciences. She is currently Head of Department at the Central Research Institute of National Economy. Her main area of research is structural and industrial policies.

Roman Frydman is Associate Professor of Economics at New York University. He is the co-editor and co-author of a book and author of a number of articles on the foundations of market behaviour under uncertainty, and on domestic and international financial markets. He is the Chairman of the Advisory Board of the Economics Programme at the Central European University.

Branko Horvat, formerly Chief Methodologist at Yugoslavia's Federal Planning Bureau and Director of the Federal Economic Institute, is now

Professor of Economics at Zagreb University. He has been visiting professor at numerous universities around the world, and has published hundreds of books and articles in many different languages.

Siro Lombardini received his postgraduate training in Economics from the London School of Economics and the University of Chicago. He has published widely in the fields of monopoly theory, investment policies and development, economic planning, methodology and equilibrium theory. He was Italian Minister for State Firms in 1979-80, and is now President of the Italian Association of Economists.

Robin Marris graduated in Economics from the University of Cambridge, where he was Lecturer and then Reader in Economics until 1976. He then moved to the Department of Economics, University of Maryland, USA, and returned to the United Kingdom in 1981 to take up an appointment as Professor and Chairman of the Department of Economics at Birkbeck College, London University. In 1989-91 he was visiting professor in the Department of Economics, University of Trento. His many books include 'The Economic Theory of Managerial Capitalism', Macmillan, 1964; 'The Theory and Future of the Corporate Economy and Society', North Holland Press, 1979, 'Reconstructing Keynesian Economics with Imperfect Competition', Edward Elgar, 1991.

Alastair McAuley is Reader in Economics at the University of Essex, England, and Director of its Centre for Russian and Soviet Studies. He is interested in problems of income distribution and socio-economic problems in Soviet-type economies. He is the author of various books and articles in this field, including 'Economic Welfare in the Soviet Union', Wisconsin University Press, 1979.

Andrzej Rapaczynski is Professor of Law at Columbia University School of Law. He is the author of a book and a number of articles on political theory and constitutional law. He has served as an expert adviser to the Constitutional Committees of the Polish Parliament and the Supreme Soviet of the Russian Federation.

Dominique Redor is Associate Professor of Economics at the University of Paris 9. He is interested mainly in the theory of the market and comparison among economic systems. His book 'Pay Inequalities in East and West' has recently been published by Cambridge University Press.

Brigita Schmögnerová is a Senior Research Fellow and Head of the

Department of Microeconomics at the Institute of Economic Theory, Bratislava, Czechoslovakia. Her research has covered a wide range of topics, most recently industrial organizations and industrial policy in the transition from central planning to a market economy.

Marko Škreb received his PhD in Economics from the University of Zagreb, and has studied in the United States (University of Pittsburg). His main interests are the service economy and the transformation of post-socialist economies.

Roberto Tamborini received his PhD in Economics from the European University Institute of Florence. His research has concentrated in particular on the integration of world financial markets, the fluctuation of exchange rates, and balance of payments behaviour as regards both goods and capital. He has also addressed particular attention to the problem of the relation between micro- and macro-economics.

Ferdinando Targetti received his training as an economist at the Universities of Bocconi, Milan, and Cambridge, UK. Now he is Full Professor of Economic Policy at the University of Trento, Italy, after previously lecturing at the Universities of Bocconi, Brescia and Paris XIII. He has published books and articles on the subjects of value, growth, technical progress, development and the history of economic thought. His most recent book 'Nicholas Kaldor: The Economics and Politics of a Changing Capitalism' is about to be published by Oxford University Press.

Eva Voszka obtained her PhD from the Hungarian Academy of Sciences. She is senior researcher at Financial Research Ltd. and economic adviser to the President of Hungary. Her research interests are government-enterprise relations, changes in organizational and ownership structures, and the sociological aspects of privatization.

Ruben N. Yevstigneyev is Deputy Director of the Institute of International Economic and Political Studies, USSR Academy of Sciences. His research interests include the Soviet-type economy and the transition from a command to a market economy. He is the author of several books, including 'Economic Reforms in European Socialist Countries', 'New Trends in the Management of Economy', 'Socialist Economic Mechanism' (co-authored with L. Yevstigneyeva).

The privatization of industry with particular regard to economies in transition

Ferdinando Targetti

1. Socialism and state property

Together with centralized planning, the statization of the means of production was the economic dogma of real socialism. This dual process was supposed to achieve two objectives - equity and efficiency - and from a historical point of view it is possible to argue that for a limited period of time in the USSR, and only in the USSR, these objectives were indeed achieved. One may hold this view, however, only if the goal of equity is understood solely in terms of the distribution of money income and as distinct from the ends of freedom and democracy, and only if the goal of efficiency is restricted to the fulfilment of such targets as the rapid establishment of heavy industry in an economically backward country and the development of an arms industry able to secure victory for the USSR in case of war. Otherwise centralized planning and statization were a failure.

A great deal of literature, mainly influenced by neoclassical thought, has blamed centralized planning and the suppression of the market for the failure of the experiment of real socialism. From Lange onwards, many commentators have suggested that an alternative to capitalism (market plus private property) might be market socialism (market plus state ownership of the means of production). However, as Robin Marris reminds us in his contribution to this book, the alternative of market socialism was always and only theoretical in nature, and never found concrete form in any historically determined economic system. In theory, in the absence of externalities, the market would replace the plan because the latter was unable to gather the enormous amount of information it needed to maximize the social welfare function. The market, on the other hand, gave rise to as many Pareto equilibria as the possible distributions of the ownership of resources. Hence, the argument ran, the choice of the ownership system belonged to the sphere of equity and not to that of efficiency.

The argument was wrong. In fact, the stereotype of the Pareto-Lange model represented neither a capitalist economy nor a socialist one. The model was unable to represent the two economies because the hypotheses underlying its representation of the capitalist world were wrong. It envisaged a world of atomistic economic agents endowed with complete information and unbounded rationality; a topic which is given detailed treatment in this book by Roberto Tamborini. Equally mistaken were the base hypotheses which sought to depict the objective function of the socialist planner as a market simulator.

In contrast to the Pareto-Lange model, Marx maintained that the mode of production changes according to the differing relationship between the forces and relations of production. A more careful analysis of decision-making processes than that employed by the Pareto-Lange model shows that the structure of ownership of the means of production has significant effects on the productive allocation of resources. This is because capital accumulation and employment decisions are taken by those who are responsible for the running of enterprises (managers). These decisions depend on two factors: a) the type of dependence relationship between the managers and the owners of enterprises; b) the objective function of the owner himself.

From the historical point of view, the target of 'nationalization' has been the prime concern not only of communism as a political and cultural movement but, ever since the end of the last century, of the European socialist movement as well. In the years following the Second World War and especially during the 1950s and 1960s, from being one of the items on their political agendas, the socialist and social democrat parties of England, France and Italy turned nationalization into a concrete economic reality. However, in the second half of the 1980s the situation changed: denationalization was no longer the exclusive province of conservative parties, of which the Thatcher Government was the outstanding example, but also became a major objective of socialist governments like the second Mitterand Government in France and the Papandreu Government in Greece. In Italy, the *Partito Comunista* could never be described as having strenuously advocated a broad programme of nationalization (not even during the 1940s, as witness the preparatory work by the Constituent Assembly). And in recent years the *PCI* (and the *PDS*, the party into which the *PCI* has been transformed) has become even more lukewarm towards nationalization and the maintenance of firms in the state sector, after four decades in which its principal political rival, *Democrazia Cristiana*, has constantly formed, alone or in alliance with other parties, both Italy's political government and the government of its state-owned enterprises.[1]

2. Five theses in favour of privatization

The literature on 'state failure' (an expression coined in antithesis to 'market failure') is growing in quantity and importance. In his essay printed in this book, Alastair McAuley indicates the reasons why, according to the neoclassical theory of market failure and under the hypothesis of the cost-free nature of state intervention, the state replaced the market. He then indicates the costs that this measure can incur (even though they are difficult to quantify) and points out that a balance sheet of the costs of the property rights system is required. Without presuming to give an exhaustive account, I shall seek to draw up a check-list for use when identifying the possible inefficiencies of economic activities managed by the state. For simplicity's sake, I shall refer only to those economic activities which are not public utilities, which are not natural monopolies, and which do not display significant external diseconomies. I refer, that is, to those economic activities that constitute the bulk of the manufacturing activities of a mature economy.

I conduct my argument mainly within the framework of the 'motivations' that guide enterprise owners in their actions and as they evaluate these actions in terms of their relative success in achieving a social welfare objective.

I take the social welfare function to be simply the growth of output of a mature manufacturing economy operating within a context of international competition. Omitted, therefore, are equitable or redistributive targets; or, better, these are judged to be more appropriately pursued with other instruments like social services and progressive taxation.[2]

I shall consider, therefore, a number of theses which may be adduced in argument that the private system is preferable to the public. The first of these I call the 'subsidy' thesis. The government is more willing to grant subsidies and aid - and to soften the budget constraint of - the state-owned enterprise, which therefore does not minimize costs. This thesis holds under two conditions. One is that human, material and entrepreneurial resources must still be utilized, even in the absence of the state-owned enterprise, by an analogous national or foreign private enterprise (in the latter case, the trade balance remaining equal). The second is that the private enterprise must not be so large and uncompetitive as to constitute an equally if not more effective lobby in obtaining public aid and subsidies than that organized by the management of the state-owned firm.

A corollary to this thesis, which I call the 'outlaw' argument, maintains that state-owned enterprises, rather than setting a good example of respect for the laws of the state, are less afraid of administrative sanctions because controllers and controlled are all members of the same 'club'. Edward Phelps, for example, has argued that it is the activities of the public sector in New York that are mainly responsible for the city's air pollution.[3]

A second thesis, for which I shall use the label of 'political objective function', is based at the micro-level on the same arguments as used to explain the 'electoral cycle' at the macro-level. The manager of the state-owned enterprise obeys his minister-owner, who uses the state-owned enterprise in order to maximize, not some social welfare function, but an objective function of his own: ensuring re-election in a democratic-parliamentary government, or strengthening his power over other state bureaucrats in a government typical of the countries of real socialism.[4] Italy is a case, but not the only one, where these two objective functions interweave: its state enterprises fall within the sphere of influence of parties or party factions which vie against one other to increase their power bases despite the fact that they all belong to the same government alliance.

The thesis of the 'political objective function' is based on the assumption (which has not always been historically validated) that the manager is passively obedient to his minister-owner. In the reverse case, of what we may call 'state managerialism', the state manager uses the resources produced by the enterprise to condition the decisions made by his Minister. In the West, one of the most striking examples of this latter situation was Enrico Mattei's management of ENI, the second biggest Italian state-owned industrial holding. The financial resources Mattei was able to handle as chairman (and founder) of ENI allowed him to 'push' political leaders and government parties into adopting the policies he regarded most conducive to the development of the firm. Similar cases have occurred in the socialist countries: it has been shown, for example, that in socialist Czechoslovakia the Ministry of the Plan was strongly influenced in its decisions by the managements of large-scale enterprises, while small enterprises had no influence over the planner.[5]

A second assumption underlies the thesis of the 'political objective function': in its management of the state-owned enterprises, either the government is wrong to think of using the state-owned enterprise in order to achieve certain objectives like employment or economic democracy (objectives set for itself by the first Mitterand government, as Dominique Redor's essay in this book reports), or it is lying when it states that its intention is to pursue the goal of efficient management of the state-owned enterprises because it knows that this will harm its chances of re-election.

It is not difficult to contest either of these assumptions if they are presumed to have any general validity. A counter-example is provided by the objective of bringing the French state-owned enterprises first to the break-even point and then to profitability. That this proclaimed objective was subsequently achieved is demonstrated by the substantial number of French state-owned enterprises (the exceptions being Renault and EDF Chimic) which began to make profits after 1985 - as shown in Table 2 of W. Andreff's contribution to this book.[6]

A further limitation to this thesis is the fact that the realistic alternative to the state enterprise is not a Walrasian market without firms but a private firm. In the private sphere as well, there is a tendency towards the endogenous formation of institutions like firms with hierarchical-organizational features which may be detrimental (to achievement of a social optimum) and which have much in common with state-owned enterprises: bureaucracy, corruption, privilege-seeking by their members.[7]

A third thesis, which I call the 'non-innovativeness' thesis, concerns the entrepreneurship of the state-owned enterprise. By 'entrepreneurship' I mean the combination of two factors: the time-horizon used as a referent in assessing the viability of an investment, and the degree of risk involved in introducing innovation (technical, commercial, organizational). The argument is that the 'leave-well-alone' attitude of the bureaucrat is the antithesis of the 'animal spirits' of Keynes and Schumpeter.

Once again the validity of the thesis depends on the manager-owner relationship. (Siro Lombardini in his essay in this book points out a further element, namely the kind of technology used by the firm, and argues that an engineering technology, *ceteris paribus,* is more suitable to a state-owned firm than a commercial one). Under the assumption that both kinds of manager, private and public (I shall call the managers of state-owned firms public managers), are independent of their owners, there is no reason why one type of ownership should be preferred to the other (unless public managers reward their personal success in ways that differ from those of private managers, or unless there is an incompatible incentive system involved - stock options for example). It is even possible that a private manager may be closely constrained by the decisions of an owner who prefers the short-term maximization of his asset, while a public manager is free of this kind of constraint and can take innovative decisions which, in the long term, contribute more to the technological advancement of the overall industrial sector.[8] If, instead, the public manager does not enjoy this freedom and merely executes orders handed down by the minister, then we revert to the previous case of the 'objective function', where, it will be remembered, the success or otherwise of the state-owned enterprise depends on the objective function of the minister-government concerned.

One can, moreover, envisage a situation where a 'correct' objective is set by the government minister (that is, maximizing an intertemporal social welfare function of society instead of his own personal interests or those of his party or faction) but where the manager (endowed with broad autonomy) is unable to fulfil the task assigned to him. In this case, a fourth thesis - that of management and worker 'protection' - comes into play. This argues that whereas the owners of private firms can sack their managers and only incur economic costs, this is not the case in the public sector. If the government or parliament transfers or dismisses a manager, this is tantamount to sentencing him for treason. Public managers are therefore more closely protected, less subject to efficiency criteria, and more liable to be judged in terms of their political or, in the worst of cases, party loyalty. The protection theory also applies to workers: a private enterprise can close down plant or a whole factory even though this will put a large part of a town's population out of work, but no state-owned enterprise could undertake such action.

This fourth thesis also rests on underlying assumptions. The first holds that in the owner-manager relationship, pursuit of the owner's utility function is socially preferable to the manager's utility function. Bearing in mind what I said about the 'non-innovativeness' function, this is not always true. The second assumption is that the absence of constraints on plant closure or company failure is, in all cases, conducive to the optimal allocation of resources, even in the long term. The assumption holds as long as the labour, the skill, and sometimes the physical capital itself (unless it is obsolete, and the same goes for skill) can be used elsewhere; otherwise the guilty verdict requires more careful examination in terms of social costs and benefits.

The fifth and final thesis to consider I shall call the 'pluralism' thesis. This states that the dispersion of economic power acts as a counterweight to political power. A citizen who finds power distasteful knows that if he lives in a system with a private market economy, he will not be forced to depend on political power in order to support himself and his family. Here again there is an underlying assumption. The thesis is true to the extent that political power is concentrated and to the extent economic power is decentralized into multiple and competing activities. Since most developed countries display this pattern of political concentration and economic decentralization, the thesis acquires validity.

3. Privatization in capitalist economies and in economies in transition: a substantial difference

On the basis of the arguments set out in the previous section we may therefore state the following. Although there is no thesis that incontrovertibly demonstrates the superiority of private over public management, in many circumstances - those where the 'subsidy', 'outlaw', 'political objective function', 'non-innovativeness', 'protection' and 'pluralism' theses hold - a great deal of weight attaches to factors that militate in favour of the privatization of state-owned enterprises in sectors involving 'normal' activities. As regards the ownership system in the public utilities sector, however, matters become more complicated. Will Bartlett's essay in this collection analyses the privatization process in this sector begun by the Thatcher government in 1987. Bartlett concludes that, in this case too, assessment can only be framed in empirical terms and that it largely depends on how the competitive process works. In particular, whatever the increased efficiency generated by a competitive privatized arrangement, it must be measured against the greater costs that may accrue from privatization in the health provision sector and the greater inequalities that it may create in the educational sector. One can therefore certainly subscribe to Kaldor's statement quoted by Redor at the beginning of his essay in this volume: 'The choice between public and private enterprise cannot be analysed universally without taking into account the framework of political and social institutions, traditions and history, and the stage of economic growth of the particular country to which the analysis is applied'.[9]

Without presuming to ascribe the status of a 'law' to a general observation, one can nevertheless point out that the more mature the society, the less the state is required to govern by the direct management of productive activities, and the more it can provide rules and incentives for private enterprise. This, as I have said, is the reason why in many Western countries not only the political forces of the centre, but also those of socialist inspiration, have set themselves 'privatization' as a political objective.

It is also true, as Redor states in his essay, that the 'neutrality' criterion in the management of state-owned enterprises as defined by the European Economic Community tends noticeably to reduce the difference between the behaviours of the two kinds of enterprise.

Privatization in the ex-socialist countries with economies in transition (henceforth ET) has become a matter of necessity; especially in view of the fact that state management in these economic-political systems has shown itself to be particularly incompetent and now has practically non existent legitimacy in the eyes of the public. However, the privatization process is an extremely complex affair in these countries, as Ruben Yevstigneyev stresses in his contribution to this book, because it involves almost the whole of their economy and must proceed simultaneously with the transformation of a centrally-planned system into a market one.

The essays in this book by Wladimir Andreff and Dominique Redor cite successful experiments in privatization undertaken by EEC countries with capitalist economies (henceforth CE) - the United Kingdom and especially France - as extremely instructive examples for the ET to follow. I, however, take the view that these experiences can only provide limited guidelines for the ex-socialist countries as they embark upon their privatization programmes. The privatization of the mid-1980s in the EC came about in a context that was already privatized to a large extent, as can be seen from the following table. In the ET it proceeds in a setting where no activity is private (if one excludes agriculture in Poland).

Table 1
The State Sector as Percentage of Value Added in the mid-1980s

Czechoslovakia	97	France	12
DDR	97	Italy	24
USSR	96	BDR	11
Yugoslavia	87	United Kingdom	11
Hungary	86	Denmark	6
Poland	82	United States	1

Source: D. Milanovic, *Liberalization and Entrepreneurship: Dynamics of Reform in Socialism and Capitalism*, New York: M. E. Sharpe, 1989.

The differences between the two kinds of privatization are of major importance if one considers the following factors.

1. State-owned enterprises in the ET operate in a context where they must compete with private firms. Enterprises in the ET, all of which are state-owned, have strong bonds of reciprocal, sometimes exclusive, dependence.

2. In the EC, most managers of state-owned enterprises have business training and an entrepreneurial mentality which makes them interchangeable with those in the private sector.[10] In the ET managers often behave like bureaucrats, passively implementing the orders handed down by the hierarchy.

3. In the EC, state-owned enterprises in difficulties can, as happened in France, be restored to profitability before being privatized, so that assets yielding revenues higher than costs calculated at market prices are on offer. In the ET these costs and revenues are of little significance because they are at prices which do not reflect production costs and an assessment of demand elasticity. It is exceedingly difficult in the ET to assess the prospective incomes or the goodwill of enterprises on the basis of results achieved in previous years, when profit was not an objective and in any case could not be calculated.

4. In the EC, the public sale of large-scale state enterprises takes place via their transformation into limited companies (if they do not already have this legal form) followed by the sale to the public of the desired amount of shares - just like any private firm which wishes to be listed on the stock exchange. There is as yet no stock exchange in the ET, and it will take decades before one large enough to function as an efficient place of transaction comes into being.[11] Moreover, while the securities market of an EC can be expanded by privatizing the state-owned enterprises[12], this is impossible in an ET, for the following reason.

5. In the EC, private saving (by the public and by firms) is many times higher than the value of the enterprises to be privatized. In the ET the opposite holds: private saving is a tiny fraction of the (present) value of the capital to privatize (rough calculations given in the essays in this book by Ruben Yevstigneyev and by Roman Frydman and Andrzej Rapaczynski put this fraction at 7 per cent for the USSR and at between 2.4 and 3.6 per cent for Poland). This not to imply that this route to privatization is impracticable, only that, should it be taken, decades will pass before the process is complete.

In the following pages I shall concentrate on privatization in the ET, referring to the EC only for the purposes of comparison. One should not forget, moreover, that in the ET the final target is the building of a market economy. This target is certainly not obtained through price liberalization and privatization. It can be achieved, as Siro Lombardini forcefully argues in his contribution to this book, only by fruitful interaction between the agents' behaviour and a state strategy which is geared to economic development. To accomplish this task, the state has to rely on economic instruments which act on aggregate demand and on the supply side, instruments which are not yet available to the ET. However, the issues dealt with below only concern the privatization process.

4. Privatization not only of what is new but also of what already exists

The privatization process in the ET can come about both through the creation of new activities and by privatizing those that formerly belonged to the state.

The scale of the first of these processes depends on the opportunities created for private entrepreneurs by the state-owned enterprises' inability to stay in the market, and above all on the expansion of national and international markets. Since such expansion is slow, privatization through the birth of new enterprises certainly cannot be considered to be a process of rapid and diffused privatization of an ET.

Indeed, even if we assume that new private enterprises account for the entire increase in national production, in economies that grow at 2 per cent annually, after ten years only 19 per cent of the economy will have been privatized. The views of those who maintain that managing large-scale private enterprises first requires the development of managerial skills through the spontaneous creation and management of small enterprises are not to be undervalued.[13] Nevertheless, given the protracted nature of this process, one understands why all the principal ET of Central and Eastern Europe are privatizing by selling off state-owned enterprises, and not only those of small size.

The forms of transfer and the problems connected with privatization obviously vary greatly according to the size and sector of activity of the enterprise to be privatized.

The following discussion will concern neither the creation of new private enterprises, nor the privatization of small agricultural, commercial or service units (restaurants, guest-houses, etc.) which previously belonged to the state, nor reprivatization - that is, the restitution of property (generally real estate) to its owners prior to the statization of the economy. I shall restrict my treatment to the privatization of large and medium-sized state enterprises.

In all the ex-socialist countries, political institutions have been appointed or created to handle privatization: the Parliament and the State Property Agency in Hungary, the government in Bulgaria and Romania, the Ministry of Finance (or, in exceptional circumstances, the Parliament) in Czechoslovakia, a special Ministry for Ownership Transfer in Poland.

5. The privatization in progress

In the principal ET of central Europe - Poland, Czechoslovakia and Hungary - there have been a number of rapid privatizations in non-industrial sectors. In Czechoslovakia, the law of 2 October 1990 passed by the General Assembly sanctioned the restitution of real estate expropriated by the Communist government between 1955 and 1961 to the original owners or their heirs. Since industrial enterprises had been expropriated in the period 1948-55, this law reprivatized dwellings, hotels, restaurants, shops and crafts workshops. A similar law was passed in Hungary, in April 1991, which stipulated the restitution (or compensation in lieu) to their owners of goods and activities nationalized after 1949: land, apartments, shops and crafts workshops. In Poland 76 per cent of the land was already private under the Communist regime, and before 1990 it was calculated that 70 per cent of wholesale trade and 50 per cent of retail trade was in private hands.

The situation of industry is different, however. As Table 2 shows, in 1989 between 80 and 90 per cent of industrial employment was still in the state sector.

Table 2
Structure of Employment by Private/State Sector, 1989

	Total	private sector	coop. sector	state sector	% state sector
	(000)	(000)	(000)	(000)	
Hungary (total economy)	2215	168	248	1799	81
Poland (industry)	4753	717		4036	85

Source: Official statistics of the countries concerned.

Some changes, however, have been made or are now under way. Of these, of notable importance is the transformation of enterprises which were previously legally ownerless but effectively state-owned, and whose management depended on various ministries, into limited companies belonging to the Treasury. This was the first step towards privatization (the so-called 'commercialization' stage); a preliminary step necessary for all subsequent measures. Such has been the pattern of the 'Western-style' privatization of certain enterprises in Poland. Some of the enterprises selected were valued by foreign investment banks and sold to private individuals for cash in what was called 'an initial public offering'. However, the very high price paid to the foreign banks (around 25 per cent of the value of the enterprises), the extremely small number of enterprises privatized (between January 1990 to mid-1991 they amounted to no more than ten) compared with the overall number of enterprises to privatize (7 to 8 thousand), and frequent errors in assessment of their worth (not a few privatized enterprises are now close to liquidation) have made this a slow and inefficient process.

The pattern has been repeated in Czechoslovakia, where the process has involved a few but significant cases: the purchase by Volkswagen of 30 per cent - which will become 70 per cent in 1995 - of Škoda; the takeover by the Belgian company Glaverbel, controlled by Asahi of Japan, of 70 per cent of Sklounion, the principal Czechoslovak glassworks; and other purchases in the cement and detergents sectors. The advantage of the system is that it creates an inflow of foreign currency into the country, and it is for this reason that all three of these countries have resorted to it.

In Poland the privatization process has been flanked by another (since July 1990): the so-called 'liquidation' of some hundreds of small to medium-sized enterprises (with fewer than 500 employees). These enterprises may submit a privatization plan to the Ministry of Ownership Transfer which, if accepted, allows the employees themselves to purchase their enterprise through a form of 'management buy-out'. As one reads in the essay by Marie Bohatá in this book, a similar process is now under way in Czechoslovakia. The Hungarian case is examined by Eva Voszka's essay, which I discuss in Section 7 below.

6. Enterprise management: ownership, managers and workers

In the ET of the countries of Central Europe, centralized planning has given way to a system of decentralized enterprise decision-making. Nevertheless, as we saw in the previous section, almost all medium and large-sized enterprises are still state-owned. What is to prevent these countries' governments from leaving things as they are and putting their trust in a slow process of 'spontaneous privatization'? The answer changes according to the institutional and macroeconomic conditions of the country concerned.

In Poland the ousting of the old regime was principally the achievement of *Solidarnosc*, a workers' trade union movement. It is therefore understandable that today 'workers' councils' should have a great deal of influence on the running of Polish enterprises. In Hungary, since 1984-85 (as one reads in Eva Voszka's contribution to this book) enterprise councils have been set up. These are bodies consisting of managers and workers which elect the chief executive and are empowered to undertake mergers, demergers and joint ventures. In Czechoslovakia, by contrast, 'workers' councils' have no influence whatsoever.

Moreover, these countries find themselves in very different situations as regards their macroeconomic equilibria. One of the principal instruments of stabilization policy in Poland is the wage control imposed on workers in state enterprises. An alliance between workers and management has therefore grown up in the country which is strongly in favour of 'spontaneous privatization'. This collusion is in the interest of both parties concerned. It suits the workers because a private enterprise is not subject to wage control, and because thoroughgoing privatization might mean a restructuring of enterprises with a consequent loss of jobs. For managers, alliance with the workers means an absence of control over their capacity to maximize the value of the enterprise, in terms of assets and goodwill.

It might be objected at this point that these enterprises have only to be placed in a competitive market setting to impose a hard budget constraint that will induce them to operate according to efficiency criteria. Nevertheless, if the managers-workers alliance is cemented by the interests outlined above, it is extremely likely that the budget constraint will not induce the restructuring of the enterprise immediately, but only when there is no other option but the enterprise's liquidation.

Sixty years ago, Berle and Means[14] demonstrated how important the separation between ownership and control was for enterprise management. Later, in the 1960s, Baumol, Marris, Galbraith, Williamson and Chandler[15] wrote the standard texts on 'managerial capitalism' - the theoretical foundation of which was that large enterprises have objectives other than the maximization of their profits. This thesis was called into question by the consideration that if an enterprise does not maximize its market worth represented by its share quotation, it may be taken over by those in a position to do so. From the 1970s onwards, however, awareness grew that outsiders (shareholders) do not possess the information about the firm available to insiders (managers), and that information is costly. This explanation of the poor functioning of the shareholder vote and of takeovers[16] laid a new basis for the theory of managerial capitalism[17] and identified the existence of another control mechanism in which the banks play a central role.[18]

Today the literature on this subject (known as 'principal-agent' theory) abounds, and it would make little sense to embark on a review of it here. I shall merely single out three possible forms that control over management may take. The first is what, for simplicity's sake, I shall call 'Anglo-Saxon'. Here the control mechanism takes the form of the takeover of the enterprise whose management has failed to enhance its share prices by achieving high profits. The second form of control is the German and Japanese system where managers receive support, but are also subjected to control, from a complex banking and financial system. The third method is control over management exerted by the workers.

There may then be numerous sub-cases. The two most emblematic examples of the third method of control are the following: Yugoslavian-style self-management, where workers are owners of capital shares which cannot be transferred, not even when they leave the enterprise; and Western cooperatives, where worker-members own parcels of shares of varying value which, although they give entitlement to only one vote ('One man, one vote'), generate a flow of income proportionate to their value.

On superficial comparison among the results of these methods of exerting control over management, one may state that the first control system tends to maximize the short-term rate of profit and the second gives better results in terms of the long-term rate of growth of output, whereas the third method (self-management) leads to the maximization of the employees' incomes but reduces the employment of outsiders and is detrimental to the maximization of the firm's asset value.[19] In an initial situation of full employment, one might be led to believe that self-management was a means to perpetuate this social target. In reality, however, this is not the case, because the inflationary tendency of a system of this kind (a tendency to increase the price of the flow of output from firms and to reduce the net worth of their financial and real assets) provokes macroeconomic stabilization policies with long-term negative effects on employment itself. This, of course, is not to imply that workers' rights should not be guaranteed: the problem is that the guarantee should be provided, not by the enterprise's property rights, but by the trade unions' rights, the legal system, public works, and more in general by macroeconomic policies for full employment.

Rather similar is the case of ownership of the cooperative enterprise by its worker-members. This is perhaps why several observers have suggested that the privatization process in the ET should consist of the transfer of enterprise ownership to the workers themselves; a thesis sustained by economists[20] and, especially in Poland, by politicians with a trade union background.[21] In fact, because of political pressure, Poland's legislation on privatization now includes the obligatory sale of 20 per cent of the shares of privatized enterprises to their employees, at prices much lower than their market value.

Some factors militate in favour and others against this solution of the free transfer of an enterprise to its employees. The main argument against rests on a principle of distributive justice: should privatization take this particular form, some workers will own shares in profitable companies, others will own shares in loss-making companies, and others (for example, state employees or workers in private firms) will own nothing. It should also be pointed out that if enterprises were sold to their workers in exchange for wage cuts, the workers themselves would strongly object to this type of privatization.

Another factor militating against the creation of self-managed cooperative enterprises is managerial efficiency. If the worker-members have the right to appoint the cooperative's directors on the 'one man, one vote' principle (although this opinion is not shared by Branko Horvat in his contribution to this book), it is extremely likely that, although they own shares and are therefore interested in their profitability, the worker-members' overriding concern will be to maximize their labour incomes and to safeguard their jobs, even if this entails the reduced profitability of their shares. It is therefore probable that the cooperative directors will be selected with this objective in mind.

The situation is aggravated by excess employment, a problem affecting the economy of the socialist countries, and which still today persists in the ET.[22] Accordingly, one of the objectives behind the transformation of the economic structure of these countries is to achieve greater flexibility of employment and greater labour mobility. Systems of self-management and cooperation applied to large and medium-sized enterprises would retard rather than accelerate this process.

This is not to say that a system of 'profit-sharing' may not be a viable solution should the workers relinquish their powers of veto and control over the management.[23] It may also be true, as Branko Horvat argues, that a social corporation is a more democratic organization than a private one and that, moreover, participation by workers in management of the cooperative enterprise can enhance their sense of loyalty and commitment to it, with stimulating effects on labour productivity.

The balance of the pros and cons of self-managed cooperative enterprise has a sign which depends on the size of the firm and on the sectors in which it operates. When there is greater technical homogeneity among workers, as in the service sector, there are fewer cases of 'free riders', and reciprocal control yields better results. Also, social supervision in a cooperative is very weak if the enterprise is large in size, while it is more effective in small-to-medium sized ones. Moreover, as Branko Horvat argues below, a better system is one where cooperative enterprises are not part of a totally self-managed system but must compete with capitalist firms. Another important argument in favour of the creation of cooperatives is advanced by Siro Lombardini and Branko Horvat in their essays. The cooperative cannot be a definite organization model (Lombardini shows why it is an intrinsically unstable system) but the diffusion of cooperatives could usefully contribute to the process of transition, because it could enable workers with entrepeneurial capacity to emerge. These would probably go on to transform the cooperative into a personal enterprise.

One concludes, therefore, that although a cooperative enterprise sector cannot be entirely ruled out, a privatization process consisting of the transfer of share-holding ownership to the work force can only concern a small part of the economy, not the entirety of the medium-large sized enterprises of the ET.

7. Privatization: a spontaneous or governed process?

There are two major areas of debate on privatization in the ET. The first centres on the question of whether privatization should be spontaneous or whether it should be the outcome of a conscious political choice made from among various kinds of social engineering. The second area of debate concerns the form that such social engineering should take; an issue which is examined in the next section.

First of all, there is a terminological confusion to deal with. In the countries of Central Europe, the expression 'spontaneous privatization' is often used for a process allowed by legislative norms and by means of which management (on agreement by the workers) transforms a state enterprise on two levels. Legally, the enterprise is transformed into a limited company ('commercialization'); managerially, its transformation must come about organizationally and financially so that the enterprise is able to pass from a 'soft' to a'hard budget constraint'.[24]

This is the kind of privatization that has been under way in Hungary. The Hungarians were the first to undertake transformation into company form and privatization. As Eva Voszka points out in her essay, a law was passed in Hungary as early as the 1970s which gave equal status to non-state and state ownership. Discussion on the transformation of state enterprises into company form had already begun with the reform of 1968 without, however, any practical outcome until the first effective transformations of 1985. In that year Hungarian enterprises were divided between enterprises dependent on a ministry and those that were self-managed (around two-thirds of the total) and in which, as we saw in Section 5, top management was under the supervision of an 'enterprise council'. The first case of transformation into a limited company (the state enterprise Medicor) came two years later, followed by the transformation of a further fifty large-scale state enterprises, which were wound up and re-formed into joint stock companies and limited liability enterprises. This gave rise to 300 firms with majority shareholding in the hands of holdings consisting of banks or state-owned firms, and thus with greater managerial autonomy. Finally, in 1988, the stage of real and proper privatization began with the sale of shares to the public.

This process was 'spontaneous' in the sense that it was not preceded by the law but followed by it. In fact, only in July 1989 was the transformation of state property into company form legally sanctioned. In March 1990 the 'State Property Agency' was set up under direct government control with the purpose of re-examining the spontaneous privatizations of 1988-89, either to ratify or to reject them. These privatizations had, in fact, provoked not a few criticisms from those who saw them as enabling the *nomenklatura* of the previous regime to preserve its control over enterprises - to the detriment of both state revenues and the productive reorganization of enterprises.

Beyond this historically specific meaning of the term, however, the 'spontaneous' (or 'gradual', as some authors call it, e.g. Brigita Schmögnerová) privatization process essentially involves the following:

a. ample recourse to management buy-out and/or the transformation of a state-owned firm into a cooperative enterprise;
b. large sales of national enterprises to foreign investors, who alone possess the capital with which to buy medium-large enterprises;
c. the maximum possible number of sales to national citizens with sufficient money capital or credit, following Western selling procedures;
d. the prolonged presence of many medium-large enterprises in the state sphere.

The principal advantage of this process is that it is 'non-traumatic'. It is a slow process which allows errors to be corrected as and when they are committed, and which identifies the core shareholders without difficulty. In his essay in this book, Dominique Redor refers to the 'evolutionary theory' of Nelson and Winter[25] and argues that enterprises should be given enough time to adapt their nature and their ownership structure to external environmental conditions. It is towards changing these external conditions that the proponents of the spontaneous approach direct their proposals for the structural reform of the ET; proposals which include deregulation, demonopolization, and destatization without denationalization (that is, management independent of ministerial decisions). Siro Lombardini is in favour of a synchronized process, and in his essay he suggests that 'privatization must go hand in hand with the building of a market economy: in particular with the new industrial structure'. Similarly, Alistair McAuley maintains that in the ET the creation of contestable markets is more important than ownership *per se*. Other authors are even more radical advocates of a slow, spontaneous process as opposed to wholesale privatization: Wladimir Andreff and Branko Horvat argue this case in their contributions to this book, and a similar view is held by Mario Nuti.[26]

Nevertheless, the spontaneous approach is not without its shortcomings. The defects of self-management with or without worker ownership were described in the previous section. The drawback to the foreign sale of the best enterprises is that these enterprises have to be sold cheaply, given the systemic risk faced by an investor in these countries; and in some countries the political reaction to this 'clearance sale' abroad of the national wealth may turn into hostility against privatization as such (this attitude seems not to have taken root in Hungary, although in Poland it has indeed given rise to a political party). Selling enterprises to national citizens who possess ample personal capital in the aftermath of the collapse of a socialist regime (and therefore also ample credit potential) raises problems of equity and efficiency. Problems of equity because large amounts of capital accumulated under a socialist regime are certainly not the fruit of thrift and entrepreneurship. Problems of efficiency because there is no guarantee that those who have been adept in accumulating wealth by means of favouritism, corruption and the black market will be competent managers of medium-large enterprises. Lastly, the persistence of a broad sector of enterprises in the state sphere signifies that the problems listed in the second section have not been resolved.

This is not the place to discuss the problem of whether institutions are born by historical accident or whether they are created 'rationally'[27] by economic agents unable to specify ex-ante optimal solutions to their problems of choice. What is certain is that the institutions of capitalism were not generated by natural processes but by deliberate political action. I quote Polanyi's paradoxical proposition: 'There is nothing natural about laissez-faire. Free markets could never have existed had things been left to take their course ... laissez-faire itself was created by the state'.[28] Market economies today are highly diversified: in particular as regards the present discussion, in the governance and control of medium and large-sized enterprises. I referred to this aspect when I briefly compared the Anglo-Saxon model, where firms depend on control by the stock exchange, with the German and Japanese models where, in the first, firms are governed by banks and, in the second, groups are governed by financial holdings.

As regards the ET, the alternative to the spontaneous process is legislative action aimed to establish a new privatist system, a sort of 'big bang' of mass privatization by decree; one which has been called, with critical intent, a process of social engineering. (This process would involve between 7 and 8 thousand enterprises in Poland and around 4 thousand in Czechoslovakia. Of these, according to Marie Bohatá's essay printed below, only 50 per cent would be able to withstand the process of transformation). Among the advocates of this view, there are those who propound a sort of paradox which runs: 'the most important aspect of the transition to a spontaneously functioning market economy cannot be initiated by the market forces themselves'.[29]

8. Techniques of privatization: a scheme

To simplify my treatment, I shall use the following double entry table in illustration of the features of the main 'families' of techniques suggested for the privatization of medium-large enterprises in the ET.[30]

Table 3
Methods of privatization

| | | Method of price determination | |
		predetermined price	auction
Means of payment	Money	A	B
	Vouchers	C	D

The cases in the first row are those in which privatization involves the sale of enterprise shares on the market in exchange for money: by means of an offer for sale at a predetermined price or by means of one of the many mechanisms of competitive auction.

Selling shares in exchange for money raises a series of problems which have already been mentioned on previous pages, and which I summarize under the following points:

a. Citizens possess modest amounts of monetary savings; hence privatization in exchange for money would risk turning into an extremely lengthy process.
b. Given the aggregate money supply, the use of money for the purchase of shares has deflationary effects on the economy.
c. These two difficulties can be resolved if the government provides credit for those purchasing shares (a sort of equity debt swap); but this requires the creation of a state agency capable of assessing credit worthiness, which is very unlikely.
d. The high risk country undervalues the shares if they are sold on foreign markets.
e. The proliferation of purchasers would make it difficult to identify the core shareholders exerting control over management.
f. The takeover as a market mechanism used to control management, irrespective of the shortcomings of the mechanism itself which tends to privilege the maximization of short-term profit rather than long-term performance, is difficult to apply and inefficient because these economies lack a stock exchange.

I now consider the methods by which sales prices are determined. The two columns of Table 3 represent extreme cases of the determination of enterprise sale price: the first based on valuation of the enterprise by 'experts', the second on an auction system. As the essay by Wladimir Andreff in this book shows, there are numerous intermediate cases. One of these is the technique used by the Thatcher Government for the privatization of its first five enterprises, namely the 'tender price offer'. This technique involves offering a market-clearing price, provided it is above a minimum price fixed by a Privatization Agency on the basis of assessments by investment banks, chartered accountants and auditors. In an ET, a method which attributes a predetermined value to shares would encounter the major problem of assessing the net worth and goodwill of an enterprise. This difficulty is principally due to the fact that, regardless of the accounting method used, the enterprise's books are worthless - because there are no markets to refer to, neither of output nor of net capital. Even less is it possible to refer to future markets to assess the enterprise's value in terms of its discounted stream of earnings. Then there is the added problem that enterprises in all the ET of Central Europe are tied together in a network of mutual credit linkages. This renders estimation of their worth even more difficult, because valuing an enterprise depends closely on the solvency of its debtor enterprises. Furthermore, the industrial structure is such that many enterprises are closely dependent on - in fact, almost 'imprisoned' by - suppliers who are often monopsonists. Other enterprises are difficult to evaluate because they are structured almost exclusively for the Soviet market, which, as they say, is a 'riddle wrapped in an enigma'. To this we must add the fact that the instabilities of the economies, and macroeconomic stabilization policies themselves, in many of these countries - Poland most of all - provoke sudden changes in short-term and even long-term rates of interest and in the exchange rate. And when, moreover, we consider that (as Marie Bohatá reminds us) profitability cannot be assessed if we do not know what a country's tariff and anti-monopolistic policies are - and they have yet to be defined in Czechoslovakia - then it is evident that the method of the public offer for sale of shares at predetermined prices is impracticable.

Having analysed the first row and the first column of Table 3 from a critical perspective, we may conclude that case A and the privatization methods mainly used in the West[31] are ill-suited to mass privatization in the ET.

I now turn to the case of the free transfer of industrial assets to the general population by means of a voucher system (second row). The idea of privatizing through the free distribution of vouchers to the population has aroused a great deal of argument among the political forces of the Central European countries. At the time of writing, Poland's Minister for Ownership Transfer must submit a plan along these lines to the Polish Parliament by September.

In February/April 1991 the Federal Assembly and the Czech Parliament approved the so-called 'great privatization' law, which envisages from January 1992 onwards the free distribution of the shares of between 40 and 80 per cent of enterprises submitting a privatization plan for ministerial approval.

The Czechoslovaks are the most determined to undertake a process of rapid mass privatization, which is scheduled to take place in two stages: 1,400 enterprises should be privatized by autumn 1992, with the second stage starting in 1993. The distribution of vouchers to Czechoslovakian citizens should get under way on 30 March. Citizens will be allowed to exchange their vouchers directly for shares in enterprises to be privatized or for shares in investment funds, which at present number about three hundred. The financial intermediaries will, in turn, exchange the vouchers for shares in privatizing enterprises. Citizens are not allowed, at this stage of the process, to buy and sell vouchers among themselves. However, as soon as the vouchers-share auction has been held, they will be allowed to sell their shares for cash.

The Romanian Minister for Privatization, Theodor Stolojan, has also drawn up a plan based on the principle of the free voucher transfer of a proportion of enterprise shares to the population.

Without going into details concerning the differences among these various plans, I would merely point out that the Polish plan stipulates compulsory financial intermediaries between the public and enterprises (see Section 9 below), while the Czechoslovakian plan envisages, as I said above, the direct purchase by citizens (in exchange for vouchers) of enterprise shares or, if they wish, shares of investment funds which are in turn constituted by shares of the enterprises to be privatized.

Among economists, too, there is intense debate between those against the voucher system, like Mario Nuti[32], Wladimir Andreff and Ruben Yevstigneyev who argue their positions in the essays printed in this volume, and those in favour, for instance D. Lipton and Jeffry Sachs[33], who advocate that the system should be combined with the fixed-price evaluation of enterprises (case B in the above table) and others who suggest it should be linked with an auction (case D), like Roman Frydman and Andrzej Rapaczynski[34] (Lombardini also shares this view).

The voucher system has been criticised on three main grounds. First, it would hinder the formation of a genuine stock market. To which the counter-argument is that the free distribution of shares to the population would eliminate not only the problem of the fair distribution of industrial wealth, but also that of the shortage of household savings, which is the principal reason why a stock market is impossible to create.

The second criticism maintains that if the state resorts to the free transfer of its wealth, it will be unable to reduce the public debt. However, this proposition neglects the fact that a clearing transaction of this kind can also be undertaken if the debt is reduced by the revenues that will accrue in the future from the taxes levied on the income and property of the privatized activities.[35]

However, there still remains the problem that very diffuse shareholding would enable owners to control the actions of management. As Stiglitz has recently written: '(T)he theoretical "possibility" that management may run the corporation in their interests rather than in the interests of their share holders has been borne out, all too dramatically, during the last decade'.[36] This raises the problem of control which is not exercised through the simple risk of takeover, bearing in mind that in the EC during the eighties most takeovers were more in the interests of managers than in the interests of the shareholders. However, since gathering the information necessary for control is a costly process, it cannot be undertaken by the small shareholder. Control can be exercised in various ways in capitalist systems: by the core shareholder (which is often, especially in Italy[37] the family nucleus that founded the enterprise), by financial institutions like banks (Germany)[38], by parent holding companies (Japan)[39], or by institutional investors (the UK).[40]

The free distribution of shares to millions of citizens would create the problem of the wide diffusion of ownership and the consequent absence of control. A solution to this problem exists; it takes the form of the creation of a system of financial intermediaries (FI) acting as intermediaries between the public (the final owner) and the enterprise to privatize.

The idea here is that citizens (I shall not go into details of how these are defined by age and by residence) each receive an equal number of vouchers, either for free or, under the Czechoslavakian plan, on payment of a small fixed contribution towards the expenses of managing the voucher system. Citizens can exchange their vouchers for FI shares or for shares of the investments funds created by the FIs. The FIs, for their part, use these vouchers to purchase shares in the enterprises being privatized from the state. (This system therefore gives rise to a market in which the values of the FI shares are expressed in vouchers and which is parallel with, but entirely distinct from, the market in which asset values are expressed in money).

The transfer may come about with the attribution (by auction or administratively) of blocks of shares to the FI which represent a percentage of the total share capital of the enterprise and which can vary according to the objectives to be pursued. A large percentage enables an FI to act as a core investor and to exercise an efficient and legitimate monitoring function over the enterprise. However, the FI may not be the only shareholder, and part of the share capital may be assigned to other receivers - which may be foreign investors, the enterprise's own employees, the state (one can envisage the state holding an English-style 'golden share'), or Pension Funds collecting contributions and paying out pensions to the country's workers.

Citizens possessing shares in the FI will enjoy the income that accrues from them and/or their increase in value. In order to ensure that the national wealth is diffused and not concentrated into a few hands, it is to be recommended that as long as the enormous shortage of consumption goods in the ET continues, these shares should not be exchangeable for money. Above all, this measure would ensure that their share quotation does not drop to a drastic extent. This is the road that Poland seems to have chosen, while the Czechoslovakian privatization plan envisages that citizens will be able to purchase shares in the enterprises to be privatized and transform themselves into small investors in competition with the IF, contributing in this way to the formation of a genuine stock market. If instead the Polish approach is adopted, and if one still wishes to encourage the creation of a stock market in the proper sense, and to provide citizens with an institution that allows them to liquidate their savings invested in shares, shortly after massive privatization one may envisage the sale for money of the shares which the state initially kept for itself.

The Polish approach, where certificates obtained from the IF for vouchers cannot be exchanged for money for a certain number of years, is preferable. It avoids a situation where a large number of citizens sell their shares to purchase consumer goods, behaviour which has a doubly negative effect: it fuels demand-inflation and leads to an uneven distribution of wealth among citizens. Nevertheless the creation of a market where the FI certificates can be exchanged should be allowed from the very beginning, since this would enable citizens to choose the FI that they believe best able to manage its wealth.

As we have seen, the allocation of the shares of privatized firms in FI portfolios may take place either through the exchange of vouchers for shares of predetermined value (case C in Table 3) or by auction (case D). The first of these methods is much more rapid, and this is why it has been widely advocated. However, it suffers from the serious drawback I described when discussing the first column in the table, namely the impossibility of 'objectively' valuing an enterprise in an ET.

When the auction method is used, however, assessment is no longer by subjects who have nothing to lose if their calculations are wrong, but by those who must invest in the shares that they are evaluating. As Frydman and Rapaczynski argue in their contribution to this book, this method brings out the 'subjective' preferences of a particular investor vis-à-vis an enterprise; preferences which derive from entrepreneurial assessment of its future prospects. It is very probable that the managers of the FI will make sure that they invest in those enterprises that they believe have the best chances of success. These managers will also take into account the financial and commercial support that they can bring to the enterprises they have bought and which they 'protect'. On the other hand, in criticism of this view, one must also accept that investor preference in purchasing a.block of shares in an enterprise may be a gamble on the future price of such shares, and not necessarily the outcome of specific managerial expertise in that particular sector or enterprise.

It should be borne in mind that, should the auction method be adopted, it is extremely likely that not all the enterprises to privatize will be purchased, and that a certain number (not definable *a priori*) of them will be judged by the FIs as having no prospects of profitability. On the one hand this is a drawback, because the state would be left with the 'no-hoper' enterprises; on the other, it is an advantage because those responsible for running the economy will know which part of the national productive system is unprofitable, and therefore to be restructured, and which part of it is profitable (even though such knowledge would only be approximate, since privatized enterprises can also fail). In this case, the country would be less susceptible to the shock of mass failure of the kind that has occurred in the ex-DDR. And the authorities would be better able to draw up industrial policies based on a specific strategy rather than merely doling out indiscriminate subsidies, and less inclined to postpone the necessary task of industrial conversion.[41]

The auction method can be implemented in a variety of ways. The difficulty consists in defining a method that secures a core investor for each enterprise (this can be done by selling blocks of shares that represent a large percentage of the enterprise), which excludes collusion among the participants, which 'clears the market' (that is, leaves no residual vouchers), and which leads to successive rounds of privatization so that the FIs can correct their mistakes.[42]

9. On financial intermediaries

The core of mass, free privatization is therefore the FI. Obviously, if these organizations are state-owned, the same problems as those described in the second section will arise within enterprise management (risk aversion, reluctance to take decisions, pursuit of clientary favours not of economic targets, etc.).

The problem is that the ex-socialist countries of Central Europe do not possess the financial institutions capable of performing this function. The motive for creating the FIs is not only to find controllers of management, but also to use smaller numbers of qualified personnel. The qualified personnel would be the managers of some dozens of FI, instead of the thousands of managers of the enterprises to be privatized. When the search for qualified personnel is shifted from the enterprises to be privatized to the FI the problem diminishes, but it does not disappear. One solution to personnel formation would be to resort to foreign FI or, better, to foreign managers of national FI. In this case the foreign contribution would be mainly imported know-how and not the transfer abroad of the country's industrial assets. This does not rule out - indeed it makes more likely - the development of activities involving international collaboration among enterprises like joint ventures.

However, the difficulty with this solution lies in the provision of sufficient incentives to persuade international FI or international managers to become involved in the ET. This raises the problem of fixing the pay rates for FI managers, a process which cannot be left to the managers themselves or to the FI owners (the citizens), who would be too numerous to decide on the matter. The only alternative is for the state itself to establish FI managerial pay scales. At the same time the state must also decide how many FI to create. This is a crucial problem: on the one hand, the higher the number of FI, the less they will be tempted to collude; on the other, the higher the number of FI, the more difficult it will be to find an adequate number of foreign managers who are not simple adventurers but people with the expertise to fulfil the delicate and vital task required of them.

A decisive factor in the effectiveness of the system based on FI is whether or not an efficient mechanism for controlling the controllers can be found. One imperfect but basic control mechanism is exerted by the competitive context in which the controllers operate. If the controllers are numerous, and if citizens can immediately exchange FI shares (or shares of the FI funds) at relative prices that tend to reflect relative profitability, and if managerial salaries depend on the profitability of these assets, then the system acts as a sort of ex-post control on FI operations.

The essay by Roman Frydman and Andrzej Rapaczynski in this book examines the rules that should govern the 'boards of directors' of the FI and their remuneration. Apart from examining FI relations with enterprises, the state, foreigners and the public, Frydman and Rapaczynski also analyse the relationship between the FI and other credit institutions; a relationship which can be based on either the Anglo-Saxon or the German model.

Under Anglo-Saxon law, bank and FI (investment funds, the financial holding companies of industrial groups, institutional investors, etc.) must be kept separate, and this ensures that there is no conflict of interest between the two. In this case, however, the FI would have no role to play in developing another very backward sector of the ET: the banking system. In the socialist countries, the only function of banks has been to collect household monetary savings: they have never fulfilled the function of evaluating the creditworthiness of enterprises which some commentators, from a neo-Schumpeterian perspective, have described as an indispensable engine in a growing capitalist economy.[43]

If instead the FI adhered more closely to the German model they could become banks in their own right. Thus, apart from supervising and controlling 'their' enterprises (also through their representatives on the boards of directors) and helping them to place their shares on the market (rather like the Anglo-Saxon investment houses), they would supply them with short and medium-term credit. In this way the FI would both exert control over enterprises and provide a training ground for operators with new banking expertise.

In this case, though, the countries in question would have to establish a set of norms which protect shareholders against conflicts of interest resulting from this bank-industry symbiosis - no easy matter. And the central bank would also have to devise a system of vigilance consisting of rules (ratios) and discretionary inspections and sanctions, otherwise the privatization process would risk being compromised by financial crisis and by grave financial scandals.

This, however, as we shall see in the next section, is not the only risk attendant on the process of privatization.

10. The risks and difficulties of privatization

So far we have considered the questions of 'Why privatize?' and 'How to privatize?'. What we have not yet dealt with are the political conditions for privatization and the risks and difficulties that privatization may generate in weak systems like the ET.

The forces hostile to rapid and extensive privatization are many. Hostile to it are the employees of efficient enterprises who would prefer such enterprises to be sold to themselves. Hostile are those employees and managers who feel more protected, in terms of their own job security, under a state-owner. Hostile are those political and government forces which, as in the USSR, have not yet resigned themselves to surrendering the power they enjoyed as managers of the economy. Hostile are those social forces (especially in the USSR) which, although they reject the old, are afraid of the new.

But such fears are not only aroused by vested interests and risk aversion; dispassionate analysis of the risks that an ET is exposed to as it undergoes the privatization process also plays a part.

A first difficulty, contingent in nature but nevertheless of major significance, concerns public finance. In some countries, Poland for example, stabilization policy has reduced tax revenues because of the fall in the level of income, and it has also drastically curtailed essential public spending (on health and education, for example). The tax revenues of all the socialist regimes were based on taxes levied on enterprise earnings. The privatization of enterprises imposes a preventive fiscal reform which shifts the main burden of taxation onto households and reduces those on enterprises to 'Western' levels. But until the tax system has had time to come into effective operation, this structural transformation may further reduce the overall amount of tax revenue.

In addition to this, privatization - especially if it comes about not through the auction system but via a method which also privatizes enterprises in trouble - will certainly lead to widespread bankruptcies. It is difficult to predict the numbers of these bankruptcies[44] - as sadly confirmed by the example of the ex-GDR. In this country the privatization process is much more advanced than in the other ex-socialist countries. In fact, at the time of writing (September 1991) 2,986 of the 8,000 state-owned enterprises which existed when the *Treuhandanstalt* was set up in 1990 have already been privatized. However, immediately before unification, only 20 per cent of enterprises were judged unable to cope with the free market, and an unemployment rate of 12 per cent was predicted. Today, the rate forecast for the end of 1991 is around 50 per cent!

Therefore, to ensure that privatization is not judged (rightly so) socially intolerable, in the countries undertaking radical privatization 'safety nets' will have to be provided for those who suffer its harmful effects. These measures, though, will inevitably lead to increased expenditure by the public administration, and here again the German example is premonitory.

Thus, before the positive effects on the supply side of privatization become visible, the process may be interrupted because of a crisis in public finance, or it may go into sudden reverse, or, as the essay in this book by Ivo Bićanić and Marko Škreb's essay illustrates, there may be an increase rather than a decline in state intervention in the economy because of the aid and subsidies paid out to enterprises in trouble.

A second difficulty concerns price rises and income distribution. The liberalization of the market will engender two kinds of price increase: the first is a market-clearing price rise, which does not induce a drop in sales volume; the second is an increase in prices induced by the exploitation of monopoly positions, which *does* induce a drop in quantities sold and exploitation of the consumer. As pointed out by Siro Lombardini, privatization implemented without demonopolization may aggravate this latter outcome. The problem of demonopolization in the ETs is therefore of prime importance, because it is very often the case that a single enterprise, sometimes a single plant, is responsible for an extremely high share of the national production of a particular industry. Marie Bohatá gives numerous indicators of the very high degree of concentration and monopolization in the Czechoslovakian economy. For example, in 40 per cent of industrial sectors 100 per cent of production is accounted for by only four enterprises. The various ways of dealing with this problem - the splitting up of enterprises, the passing of anti-monopolization laws, and the introduction of international competition by abolishing barriers - take time, however. If, on the one hand, privatization cannot be delayed until the economy becomes competitive, on the other, the share value of a monopolistic enterprise is greater than those of the same enterprise de-monopolized: which suggests demonopolization first and then privatization. The issue of which kind of action should be taken first and which should come later is addressed by Brigita Schmögnerová's essay.

Another problem arises from the links that tie enterprises together. These links are of two kinds. First there are reciprocal input-output relations in industry or commerce, which in the ET are made more complex by the particular form of market in which many enterprises operate; a market in which they are dependent - sometimes wholly dependent - on monopsonist suppliers. Here, if the supplier fails the customer is deprived of its supply markets; if the customer fails then the supplier is deprived of its outlet markets.

A second 'pathological' link is interfirm credit. The enterprises of the ET depend much less (compared with their counterparts in capitalist economies) on bank credit, and much more on the credit that they grant to each other. In capitalist economies, credit selection is undertaken by the banks; in the ET, however, (where the central planner has disappeared) no institution capable of performing this function exists. The present situation is therefore one in which although an enterprise X has a net credit vis-à-vis Y, and although it has good prospects for future profit, it may be liquidated once it has been privatized only because enterprise Y cannot meet its commitments since it, or its creditor enterprises Z, have been liquidated because they show no prospects of future profitability. This so-called 'domino effect' is the reason why, in the credit sector of the EC, the central bank acts as 'the creditor of last resort' for the commercial banks. And it may also explain why (apart from reasons of a social nature) enterprises in the ET are kept alive even though they have no economic viability and even when all the countries concerned by now have bankruptcy laws.

The two types of connection that 'pathologically' tie enterprises together require specific economic policy measures which sever them before or during the privatization process. This is necessary above all as regards the credit link, which should be dissolved by transforming debt and credit relationships among enterprises into debt and credit relationships between enterprises and banks. During transition, one can envisage a bank which manages a government fund used to dampen the 'domino effect' by which the failure of non-viable enterprises provokes the failure of ones with good economic prospects.

Last but not least, there is a problem more political than economic in nature, and which in some countries, especially Poland, is a source of disquiet for certain forces on the trade-union left: the concentration into a few hands of 'economic power' and of the political power that derives from it. If privatization is implemented through the sale of enterprises in exchange for money, the concentrated power that this creates will accrue to those private individuals in possession of large sums of money which have often been acquired illegally or because of privileges enjoyed under the previous regime. If privatization comes about by means of the free distribution to the population in the manner described above, considerable political power will be in the hands of the FI management. (The problem could become even worse in the case envisaged by Siro Lombardini in his essay below, where non-professional agents enter the FI sector, or even adventurers masquerading as financial experts). Concern about a finance capital/big business complex replacing state monopoly over the economy has been expressed by Kornai[45], and by Wladimir Andreff in his essay in this book. The phenomenon of concentrated economic-political power is present everywhere, but it is even more pernicious when it arises in societies which are experiencing democracy for the first time and which are poorly articulated in terms of the multiplicity and rootedness in the system of the various forms of economic ownership (one thinks of the political appeal of Stan Tominski as a candidate in the Polish presidential election merely because he was a dollar millionaire in Canada).

11. A diversified 'portfolio' of ownership arrangements

The discussion of the previous section, although cautious, should not be taken to be over-pessimistic as regards a relatively rapid process of privatization. The arguments in favour are numerous, and several of them are set out in the essays by Ivo Bićanić and Marco Škreb and by Eva Voszka. First of all, gradual transition would require personnel in the public administration with skills in managing a mixed economy that are unobtainable in the ET. Secondly, slow transition would increase the political weight of those who demand increased intervention by the state in the economy, not in order to act as a regulator but as a dispenser of indiscriminate or, even worse, clientelistic subsidies. Thirdly, if the vested interests created by the present situation are given time to consolidate, they will be much more difficult to eradicate. The mature democratic systems are more susceptible to the pressure of lobbies and interest groups than are young democracies like those of the ex-socialist countries of Central Europe. To date, traditional-type political parties have not formed in any of these countries. But should they do so *before* most of the enterprises have been privatized, all these countries will run the risk (as described under the second thesis of Section 2) of the party feudalization of their enterprises, which will make any sort of future privatization policy very difficult.

The privatization process in the ET should not be too slow, therefore. But we should also bear in mind the considerations of the previous section and the difficulties that lie in the path of the ET. And we should also remember that caution is required when creating an institution: as political and economic history shows, once created and once it has become rooted in society, an institution will persist for a long period of time even though it has outlived its usefulness. Accordingly, the wisest solution would be a diversified 'portfolio' of ownership arrangements in the ET.

Inevitably, the state will continue to predominate in several sectors, notably services. Indeed, in her contribution to this book, Marie Bohatá assesses publicly provided services in Czechoslovakia as giving the state a 30 per cent weight in the overall economy.

The two methods of enterprise privatization – sale for money and the voucher system – should be used jointly. In the case of small enterprises, the first of the two methods should be applied so that these enterprises are sold to employees and private individuals in a cooperative form which develops a spirit of enterprise. The method should also be used with a certain number of large-scale enterprises in order to lay the basis for an equity market and to breathe life into the stunted stock exchanges created in Hungary and Poland in the last two years. Nevertheless, the privatization of large and medium-sized enterprises should not be pursued only using this method. It should be accompanied by the large-scale, free privatization to the population of most of the ETs' medium-large enterprises, through the intermediation of private FI. This process should not take place at once, so that the errors committed in a social process of so radical a nature can be corrected. The method must be one of trial and error: a trial and error system involving several kinds of privatization is preferable both because it helps to accomplish the economic target of efficient enterprises, and because different forms of ownership will produce diversified centres of powers and hence a more pluralistic society.

Even though all these privatization processes will eventually come about, one may envisage that, for a certain number of years, not a few enterprises will continue to be state-owned; a prospect taken for granted in Hungary and feared in Poland and Czechoslovakia. It is to be recommended, therefore, that privatization should be combined with a training programme which teaches the state management how to operate efficiently and profitably in a competitive context, and political-institutional measures should be devised which induce state managers to pursue these objectives and not others. This is more likely to happen, however, if the state-owned enterprises operate in a context where large numbers of private enterprises are present.

Finally, it should be pointed out that privatization programmes should be implemented in harness with programmes for de-monopolization and with others designed to transfer the majority of enterprise credit and debt relations to the banking sector.

It goes without saying, therefore, that this programme will be extremely difficult to bring into effect, bearing in mind the large number of vested interests either in favour of it or against it.

Notes

1 Certain sections of Italy's left-wing opposition are increasingly in favour of the privatization of part of the public economy, although one cannot say that this is the predominant opinion of the Italian Left. See the draft law on privatization proposed by Filippo Cavazzuti, a senator on the independent left (A.S. no. 2320 of 19.6.1990).

2 In the essay by Robin Marris in this book, the social welfare function is more highly articulated and also includes equitable ends. Marris uses it, however, to draw comparisons among overall economic systems, not comparisons among enterprises.

3 Concluding remarks to the Third International Economics Seminar on Privatization, Villa Mondragone, Rome 25-27 June, 1991.

4 One explanation advanced for hyper-accumulation in excess of the maximization of growth is that individual economic (or non-economic) ministers seek to obtain more resources than other ministers in order to extend their sphere of economic-political power. See Targetti and Kinda, 1984.

5 Hlávaček, 1991.

6 A second example can be found in a recent study by John Kay of the London Business School which examines enterprises with turnovers of less than 1 million ECU and classified according to the value added/turnover efficiency parameter. Only one Italian enterprise, SIRTI, a state-owned enterprise belonging to the IRI group, appears among the top thirty enterprises worldwide.

7 See Milgron and Roberts, 1990.

8 Italy in the fifties perhaps provides an example of this, as also mentioned by Siro Lombardini in his essay in this book. The private steel industry relied on the scrap steel production technique, while the state steel enterprises implemented the 'Sinigaglia Plan' by developing the then innovative technique of continuous cycle. This latter was a risky method because of the major 'sunk costs' involved, but it was a decisive factor in Italy's ensuing economic 'miracle'.

9 Kaldor, 1980.

10 See Section 1.3 of the essay by Redor in this volume, and the research data contained therein.

11 It is perhaps superfluous to point out that many observers judge the Milan *Borsa*, the principal stock exchange of the sixth or seventh industrialized country of the world, to be so small as to be considered a 'thin market', with all the contradictions this entails. See IRS, 1988.

12 See Cavazzuti, 1991.

13 Witzman, 1992.

14 Berle and Means, 1932.

15 Baumol, 1959; Marris, 1964; Galbraith, 1969; Williamson, 1966; Chandler, 1977.

16 Stiglitz, 1972.

17 According to a recent theory, the more large corporations behave like managerial firms (not, that is, like neoclassical firms where the management is the passive instrument of ownership interests), the greater the economy's rate of growth. See Odagiri, 1981.

18 Stiglitz, 1985.

19 As is well known, this is the result of the so-called Ward-Domar-Vanek model. See Ward, 1958; Domar, 1966; Vanek, 1970.
20 See Witzman, 1991.
21 One of the best known is the deputy Andrzej Stanistaw Mitowski, a leading member of the parliamentary club *Solidarnosc Pracy*.
22 Associazione Italiana degli Economisti del Lavoro, *La ristrutturazione del mercato del lavoro nei paesi dell'Europa dell'Est*, Milan, 13-14 June, 1991.
23 Witzman, 1984. On the risk that a model *à la* Witzman will degenerate into one *à la* Ward-Domar-Vanek, see Nuti, 1986.
24 This expression has been introduced into economic usage by J. Kornai. Among his most recent publications, see Kornai, 1990a.
25 Nelson and Winter, 1982.
26 Nuti, 1992.
27 This seems to be the view taken by O. Williamson, 1975.
28 Polanyi, 1944.
29 Frydman and Rapaczynski, 1991.
30 For a review of methods of privatization in Western economies see Vickers and Yarrow, 1988.
31 French privatization between 1968 and 1988 steered a middle course between tender price offers and direct sale (not through the market) to individual private firms. The sale in Italy of Alfa Romeo to Fiat followed the same pattern.
32 Nuti, 1991.
33 Lipton and Sachs, 1990.
34 Frydman and Rapaczynski, 1992.
35 Blanchard et al., 1991.
36 Stiglitz, 1992.
37 Brioschi et al., 1990.
38 Nardozzi, 1983.
39 Goto, 1982.
40 Nyman and Silberstone, 1978.
41 The following defects of the ETs' industrial structure are well known: a) their specialization in products with low growth of demand; b) product quality standards suited for Comecon, not for international markets; c) poor production flexibility; d) high internalization of production of productive inputs and therefore low specialization; e) enterprises that are either very large or very small; f) a high degree of monopolization.
42 For details of an auction mechanism of this kind, see R. Frydman, A. Rapaczynski, 1991, Appendix.
43 Ciocca, 1982.
44 Estimates can, however, be made using multiple criteria of foreign competitiveness. See Marie Bohatá's contribution to this book.
45 Kornai, 1990b.

Bibliography

Baumol, W. J. (1959), *Business Behavior, Value and Growth*, New York: Macmillan.

Berle, A., Means, G. (1932), *The Modern Corporation and Private Property*, London: Macmillan.

Blanchard, O., Dornbush, R., Krugman, P., Layard, R., Summer, L. (1991), *Reform in Eastern Europe* (1990 Report of the WIDER World Economic Group), Cambridge (Mass.): The MIT Press.

Brioschi, F., Buzzacchi, L., Colombo, M. G. (1990), *Gruppi di imprese e mercato finanziario: la struttura di potere nell' industria italiana*, Rome: NIS.

Cavazzuti, F. (1991), 'Privatizzazioni: "laboratorio" per lo sviluppo di un mercato dei capitali', *Economia Italiana*, no. 1.

Chandler, A. D. (1977), *The Visible Hand*, Cambridge (Mass.): Harvard University Press.

Ciocca, P. L. (1982), *Interesse e Profitto*, Bologna: Il Mulino.

Domar, E. D. (1966), 'The Soviet Collective Farm as a Producer Cooperative', *American Economic Review*, LVI, no. 4.

Frydman, R., Rapaczynski, A. (1991), 'Evolution and Design in the East European Transition', in Paganetto, L., Phelps, E.S. (eds.), *Privatization Processes in Eastern Europe: Theoretical Foundations and Empirical Results*, London: Macmillan.

Frydman, R., Rapaczynski, A., 'Markets and Institutions in Large Scale Privatization: An Approach to Economic and Social Transformations in Eastern Europe', in V. Corbo and F. Coricelli (eds.), *Adjustment and Growth: Lessons for Eastern Europe* (forthcoming).

Galbraith, J. K. (1969), *The New Industrial State*, Harmondsworth: Penguin Books.

Goto, A. (1982), 'Business Groups in a Market Economy', *European Economic Review*, 19, pp. 53-70, 1982.

Hlávaček, J. (1991), 'Preconditions for Privatization in Czechoslovakia in 1991', Central European University Seminar on Privatization, Prague, 26-30 July, 1991.

IRS (1988), *Rapporto sul mercato azionario*, Milan: Edizioni del Sole-24 Ore.

Kaldor, N. (1980), 'Public or Private Enterprise: The Issue to be Considered', in Baumol, W. (ed.), *Private and Public Firm Management*, London: Macmillan.

Kornai, J. (1990a), *Vision and Reality, Market and State, Contradictions and Dilemmas Revisited*, New York: Harvester Wheatsheaf.

Kornai, J. (1990b), *The Road to a Free Economy. Shifting from a Socialist System. The Example of Hungary*, W.W. Norton & Company.

Lipton, D., Sachs, J. (1990), 'Privatization in Eastern Europe: The Case of Poland', *Brookings Papers of Economic Activity*.

Marris, R. (1964), *The Economic Theory of Managerial Capitalism*, London: Macmillan.

Milanović, D. (1989), *Liberalization and Enterpreneurship: Dynamics of Reform in Socialism and Capitalism*, New York: M.E. Sharpe.

Milgron, P., Roberts, J. (1990), 'Bargaining Costs, Influence Costs and the Organization of Economic Activity', in Alt, J. E., Shepzle, K. A. (eds.), *Perspectives in Positive Political Economy*, Cambridge: Cambridge University Press.

Nardozzi, G. (1983), *Tre sistemi creditizi*, Bologna: Il Mulino.

Nelson, R., Winter, S. (1982), *An Evolutionary Theory of the Firm*, Cambridge: Cambridge University Press.

Nuti, D. M. (1986), 'L'economia della compartecipazione: critiche al modello di Witzman', *Politica ed Economia*, January.

Nuti, D. M. (1992), 'Property Restitution and Voucher Privatization', in

Paganetto, L., Phelps, E.S. (eds.), *Privatization Processes in Eastern Europe: Theoretical Foundations and Empirical Results*, London: Macmillan.

Nyman, S., Silberstone, A. (1978), 'The Ownership and Control of Industry', *Oxford Economic Papers*, 78, pp. 74-101.

Odagiri, H. (1981), *The Theory of Growth in a Corporate Economy*, Cambridge: Cambridge University Press.

Polanyi, K. (1944), *The Great Transformation*, New York: Holt, Rinehart & Winston Inc.

Stiglitz, J. (1972), 'Some Aspects of the Pure Theory of Corporate Finance: Bankruptcies and Takeovers', *Bell Journal of Economics and Management Science*, 3 (2), pp. 58-82.

Stiglitz, J. (1985), 'Credit Markets and the Control of Capital', *Journal of Money Banking and Credit*, vol. 17, no. 1, pp. 133-52.

Stiglitz, J. (1992), 'Some Theoretical Aspects of the Privatization: Applications to Eastern Europe', in Paganetto, L., Phelps, E.S. (eds.), *Privatization Processes in Eastern Europe: Theoretical Foundations and Empirical Results*, London: Macmillan.

Targetti, F., Kinda, B. (1984), 'Problemi di accumulazione nei paesi socialisti: il caso polacco', *Note Economiche*, no. 1.

Vanek, J. (1970), *The General Theory of Labour-Managed Market Economies*, Cornell University Press.

Vickers, J., Yarrow, G. (1988), *Privatization. An Economic Analysis*, Cambridge (Mass.): The MIT Press.

Ward, B. (1958), 'The Firm in Illyria. Market Syndicalism', *American Economic Review*, pp. 566-89.

Williamson, J. H. (1966), 'Profit, Growth and Sales Maximization', *Economica*, 33 (129).

Williamson, E. O. (1975), *Markets and Hierarchies: Analysis and Antitrust Implications*, New York: Free Press.

Witzman, M. (1984), *The Share Economy*, Cambridge (Mass.): Harvard University Press.

Witzman, M. (1992), 'How Not to Privatize', in Paganetto, L., Phelps, E.S. (eds.), *Privatization Processes in Eastern Europe: Theoretical Foundations and Empirical Results*, London: Macmillan.

PART I

GENERAL ISSUES

Privatization, markets and managers

Robin Marris

1. Research objectives

I believe that current research has twin objectives, namely 1) to consider the most desirable type of economic system to replace the system recently dismantled in Eastern Europe and expected soon to be dismantled in the Soviet Union; 2) to consider the significance for 1) of the 'wave' of denationalizations of publicly-owned conventional industries or enterprises that is said to have occurred in Western Europe in the 1980s.[1]

Objective 1) implies discussion of general forms of ownership in some kind of post-communist society, while 2) implies discussion of the transfer of ownership of specific means of production from 'public' to 'private'.

At the risk of being boring, I suggest this programme needs some preliminary definitions. It needs, in my opinion, clarification of descriptive terminology and stylized characterizations of alternative economic systems.

2. Definitions

The problems of definition can be posed as questions, namely:

1. What are the criteria?
2. What is meant by ownership?
3. What is meant by 'private' or 'public' ownership?

Economists tend to think that the answers to such questions are obvious and that they use the obvious answers consistently in debates. In reality, when two people disagree about something in this field, it is often because they are implicitly using different definitions. For the present paper, we must insist on standard answers. In fact, only the following will be admitted:

1. *Criteria*

Criteria of desirability imply criteria of social performance and for the latter, as far as the present writer is concerned, there is only one, namely the performance of the society in question in promoting the long-term economic welfare of the least advantaged socio-economic groups.[2]

2. *Ownership*

A. **Personal/family**. The adult human being (or small group of close relatives) who is the 'owner' has all residual rights of use and disposal of the thing owned, subject only to specific legal restraints - for example, if it is an animal I may kill it, but in many countries explicit laws deny me the right to torture it; disposal includes the right to transfer ownership, for a consideration, for example, money; the owner also has responsibilities, she or he can be held civilly or criminally responsible for some specific actions of, for example, a personally-owned business or a personally-owned animal.

B. **Collective**. A specific group of human beings has collective rights apparently similar to personal ownership but in reality, owing to potential conflicts of interest, much constrained. In consequence, individuals within a collective receive the same protection from one another as from non-members; if I commit arson against the property of a capitalist corporation, I shall be treated at law in the same way whether or not I am also one of its shareholders; similarly, if, as a citizen, I commit arson against public property (see below), I shall be punished at least as severely as if I commit the same crime against private property. Collective ownership raises a number of severe questions:

  (i) **Control**: How are decisions taken and in whose interest? For example,
  a. Under Stalinist socialism, in what sense do the people, who supposedly collectively 'own' the means of production, actually control them? (a rhetorical question, of course)
  b. In the modern capitalist limited-liability shareholder corporation (hereafter called the capitalist corporation), how significant is the well-known divorce of power between small shareholders and management?
  (ii) **Disposal**: In the event of a proposed sale, what happens if this will benefit some of the owners and not others; or if it will benefit the owners (e.g. shareholders) but not the controllers (e.g. managers), let alone the public? This question is crucial, for example, to the whole problem of capitalist mergers.
  (iii) **Responsibility**: If the collective, e.g. a capitalist corporation, commits criminal acts, who should be punished and how?

  C. **'Public/private'**. 'Public' ownership is a particular form of collective ownership where the 'owner' is a political entity representing the citizens of a region of nation. 'Private' ownership is then defined as any other form. Thus 'private' ownership includes non-'public' collective ownership such as the capitalist corporation. (In England, but less in Scotland and not in the USA, this way of making the distinction has produced rich semantic confusion: see box below.)

Hence 'Private Sector' = that part of the economic system which is not in public ownership as thus defined.

---

1. How the English Confuse Public and Private

'Public School' (in England)
A not-for-profit educational trust, exempt from taxation, to sell the service of education for full-cost fees. Another name is 'independent' school. In practice, the term 'public school' is restricted to a smaller group of socially-superior old-established schools belonging to an Association which may reject applications for membership from excellent schools on various, apparently arbitrary, grounds, for example if it is a girls' school.

'State School' (in England)
A publicly-owned and controlled school in the sense defined in the accompanying text.

'Private School' (in the USA)
What in England would be called a Public School.

'Public School' (in the USA)
What in England would be called a State School.

'Public Company' (in England)
A limited-liability corporation with a relatively large number of shareholders which has the right to offer shares for sale on an open market and the duty to publish detailed accounts at regular intervals.

'Private Company' (in England)
A limited-liability company with a relatively small number of shareholders whose shares may be traded only privately and which is not required to publish accounts; in law the company must, however, submit some accounts to the government at regular intervals.

'Company/Corporation' (in the USA and other countries)
Terminology is affected by varying laws. In the USA, company law is a State affair, but the Constitution requires every State to recognize companies registered in other States. Consequently, a person or persons planning to found a company may choose in which State they wish to be registered. In practice, a very large part of US private-sector economic activity is accounted for by companies registered in the smallest State, Delaware. The reason is not that the company law of Delaware is especially benign or favourable to shareholders or consumers, rather it is because the Delaware laws are especially favourable to managers against shareholders! (The explanation being that the State is so small it can significantly benefit from registration fees.)

---

3. Economic systems

I identify five stereotypes (the sociological term 'ideal type' would be better).

1. *Nineteenth Century Capitalism*

    i. The default system for economic activity is private ownership; any citizen has the inherent right to privately own economic assets (means of production) subject only to specific constraints; no general permission or charter is required to initiate.

    ii. The typical private mode of economic organization is personal ownership rather than collective (corporate) ownership.[3]

    iii. The average size of industrial firms is small.

    iv. A market economy, with the typical market being an imperfect polipoly.

    v. Some, but limited, economic activity by the method of public ownership, e.g. public administration, defence, postal services.

    vi. Zero or very limited public services.

    vii. Zero or very limited income or profit tax.

    viii. The legal suppression of trade unions and collective bargaining.

    ix. Zero or very limited anti-monopoly legislation.

    x. A partial majority-voting democracy with limited franchise (women, black people, poor people varyingly disenfranchised), free speech and other civil liberties.

2. *Twentieth Century ('Managerial') Capitalism*

    i. As i. above.

    ii. A major difference from ii. above - a radical increase in the role of the collective mode of private ownership in the form of increasingly large, eventually often gigantic, capitalist corporations, with a sharp separation of ownership from management; shareholdings widely dispersed, although, especially towards the end of the period, increasing importance of large 'institutional' shareholders such as insurance companies and pension funds; also, in the event of a take-over raid, shareholding becomes concentrated in the hands of the raider.

    iii. A sharp increase in 'natural' economic concentration.

    a. industrial concentration:

    - by the end of the first quarter of the century, in a typical private-sector industry, the largest four firms held over 50 per cent of the sales;

    - in US manufacturing industries, after 1950, the median four-firm concentration ratio stabilized, i.e. industrial concentration appears to have ceased to increase.

2. Concentration Overview: Organizational Structure
of Typical OECD Economy circa 1970

Type of Organization	Probable Number	Employment Range	Employment Share (%)	Asset Share (%)
one-person	$EMP^{0.83}$	1	5	negligible
small	$EMP^{0.82}$	2-100	20	small
medium	$EMP^{0.63}$	100-1,000	30	10
large	$EMP^{0.51}$	1,000-25,000	30	35
giant	$EMP^{0.30}$	25th-750th	15	55

N.B. EMP = private, non-farm civil employment.

In a country with EMP = 50 million,

$$EMP^{0.83} = 2.46 \text{ million}$$
$$EMP^{0.30} = 204$$

In a country with EMP = 10 million,

$$EMP^{0.83} = 646\text{th}$$
$$EMP^{0.30} = 126$$

b. organizational concentration (also known as 'business concentration'):
- during the first half of the century, in a typical OECD country, the share of the largest 100 private corporations in private-sector industrial GDP increased dramatically (e.g. measured by assets, from 5 per cent to 60 per cent);
- by the end of the first third of the century, there was intensive merger activity, including involuntary mergers (for example, on Wall Street, in a typical year in the mid-1930s, weighted by assets 3 per cent of listed companies were taken over by other listed companies);
- in the USA but not in other countries, the net force of organizational concentration may have weakened after 1965; concentration may have ceased increasing;
- for further discussion, see boxes.
iv. The typical market becomes a heterogeneous oligopoly.
v. In the second half of the century, public provisions for health, education, public administration and defence take an increasing share of GDP (stabilized towards the century's end). A similar tendency in social services and other features of the Welfare State.
vi. Varied experience in the field of natural monopolies (electricity, railways, etc.) as between public corporations and regulated utilities. In France, Italy and the UK, but little elsewhere, some conventional industries were

taken into public ownership in the second half of the century; this was partly reversed towards the end of the century. (It is, however, even to this day, illegal in the UK for a private body to undertake underground coal mining unless it employs fewer than 125 miners).

---

3. The 'Natural' Process of Capitalist Concentration

The process of organizational concentration in capitalism occurs within the legal framework as a result of the operation of natural economic phenomena and mechanisms, as follows:

Industrial concentration
1. Constant or increasing returns to scale in production
2. Oligopolistic competition

Organizational concentration
1. Constant or increasing returns to scale in administration
2. Gibrat's Law
3. Mergers
4. New entry (a crucial de-concentrating force)

Gibrat's Law (modified by present author)
1. The proportionate growth of a firm, measured by assets, in period t is correlated with profits (normalized by assets) in previous periods.
2. Let normalized profits be a stochastic phenomenon normally distributed between firms in any given period - and without serial correlation through successive periods.
3. Then proportional growth rates will be like profits.
4. If a population of firms more or less equal and small in size is subjected to the process implied in 3, then
   a. it will gradually become log-normally distributed with log variance $\sqcup$, say, o_L; a large number of small firms will co-exist with a small number of large firms;
   b. the 100-firm concentration ratio is directly mathematically related to o_L;
   c. merely through the mathematics of the stochastic process, o_L will inexorably increase through time;
   d. but the identity of the top 100 is never constant, there are always some firms rising, others falling back.
   e. Hence, in the absence of new entry, organizational concentration will inevitably increase through time.

Mergers
If, as is in fact the case, there is a substantial proportion of mergers where the acquired firm is larger than a third of the size of the acquiring firm, arithmetical simulations will show that mergers increase organizational concentration.

Entry
New firms are typically small. If the number of new entrants significantly exceeds the losses due to mergers, the effect is de-concentrating.

  vii. A sharp increase in income and profits tax.

  viii. The suppression of trade unions replaced by legal protection and support.

   ix. Increasing, varyingly vigorous (strongest in the USA) anti-monopoly legislation.

    x. A more complete political democracy with the gradual enfranchisement of previously disenfranchised groups (in Switzerland, women only recently); the strengthening of civil liberties.

3. *Neo-Classical Capitalism*

An abstract system in which Twentieth Century Capitalism is modelled as if it were organizationally structured like Nineteenth Century Capitalism with the additional constraint that markets are assumed to be perfect, rather than imperfect polipolies.

4. *Communism ('Totalitarian Socialism')*

    i. Public ownership the default mode; only small-scale deviations legal.

   ii. Production and distribution carried on by networks of centrally controlled administrative entities.

  iii. Price-controlled markets.

   iv. The suppression of trade unions and collective bargaining.

    v. A one-party state ('totalitarian democracy'); no genuine majority voting, free speech or civil liberties; a police state.

5. *Democratic Socialism (not 'Social Democracy')*

An ideal system combining the economic system of Communism with the political freedoms of Twentieth Century Capitalism, with a major question as to whether the 'freedoms' would include privileged trade unions and collective bargaining.

4. Feasibility

Only two of the above systems, namely Communism and Twentieth Century 'managerial' Capitalism (hereafter 20thCMC) have actually existed in the twentieth century. Communism, for all that has been said against it, proved a viable economic system for three-quarters of a century, and at the end of the day, if allowance is made as a value judgement for the burden of defence of expenditure, it performed against the Rawls Criterion perhaps no less than half as well as 20thCMC. It is my personal opinion that inferior economic performance on this scale would not have been itself sufficient to bring the system down had it not been for the very much more severe political horror. I also hold the unfashionable view that the political crisis was brought to a head by the moral contradictions of the Afghanistan war.

    The reasons why Democratic Socialism, on the one hand, and Neo-Classical Capitalism on the other have had such a vigorous life on paper and no life at all in practice have been the subject of some debate and could be debated further at length. The absence of practical examples of Democratic Socialism is a particular mystery. We cannot say that it does not work because it has never been tried. But there is no space in the present paper for the discussion of these mysteries. We shall simply assume that the only alternatives are Communism and 20thCMC. Since Communism is on the way out, in reality for Eastern Europe and the Soviet Union only one future road exists, namely 20thCMC. Anyone who clings to other ideas, such as some kind of 'reformed' Communism, Neo-Classical Capitalism or Democratic Socialism, is wasting their own and everyone else's time. I accept that this is harsh towards sensitive people who search for an economic system that retains the benefits of 20thCMC but does not employ some of its key institutions, for example, shareholders.[4] Having thought and published along those lines in the past, I am deeply sympathetic, but in my old age I have come to see that in practice, for whatever reason, no such systems will ever actually be operated. At the present time, a substantial number of distinguished American Professors of Economics are intensively researching and advising on institutional development in Eastern Europe. Some, but by no means all, are ostensibly trying to recreate 19th Century Capitalism. It makes no difference. In the long run what will inevitably emerge will be 20thCMC.

5. The social performance of 20thCMC

1. *Credits*
    i.   A high level of production per capita.
    ii. Sufficient political democracy to devote a significant (not necessarily morally adequate) proportion of total production to least advantaged groups.
    iii. Imperfect/oligopolistic market competition better than no competition.
    iv. Organizational competition (competition for growth among giants) by financially and administratively autonomous organizations which may appropriate their own profits to promote their own growth.
    a.   Managerial motivation.
    b.   Flexibility/fluidity in the organizational-economic structure of the society.

2. *Debits*
    i.   The distortions of oligopoly.
    ii. Concentration of private property.
    iii. Manipulation of the consumer.
    iv. Environmental pollution (but see also Communism).
    v.   Bias to military expenditure (*pace* Baran and Sweezy but see also Communism).
    vi. Marcuse, Galbraith, etc.

6. The transition

Because political developments were so uniquely rapid, so also are the dynamics of the transition. As a problem in economic development, it is a case without precedent. But economic development is like the herb parsley in its Northern European varieties; one man or woman sows the seeds, but they do not germinate. Another sows, the seeds germinate, but the plants do not flourish. Yet another has the experience that not only do the plants flourish, they grow profusely. Everyone has a theory about the right conditions. No one's theory tests out reliably. The human race is amazingly resourceful. But, like parsley or the weather, we are also amazingly unpredictable. A problem of chaos?

Notes

1   In the special case of the UK, there are also currently in train (in my opinion rather successful) experiments where specific activities (the sales counters but not the deliveries of the post office; this or that branch of social-service administration) have been given some, but not all, of the features of independent enterprise. In the UK, now, if you need a particular type of benefit your enquiry is steered to a semi-autonomous specialized unit, which may be located anywhere in the country. The superficial impression is that the morale of the bureaucrats concerned is good and that they have become more polite and responsive to the public. Similarly, the post-Thatcher government is vigorously pursuing the idea of converting the state schools into independent educational trusts. They receive all their finance from the government, charge no fees, but are otherwise independent as regards administration, budget holding, staff appointments, and so on, and may also compete with other schools for students.

In the present paper, however, we are not, repeat, not concerned with social services, education, health, public administration, defence, telecommunications, broadcasting, gas, water or electricity - these all being activities which to a varying extent come under public ownership and management in capitalist countries; and where they do not, in creating 'private' natural monopolies, they must be strongly regulated ('regulated' utilities). In other words, I have nothing to contribute to the debate on the relative merits, for a given task (such as electricity distribution), of the public corporation and the regulated utility, although I increasingly subjectively favour the latter. It seems one should be able to get as good or better performance from a public corporation in principle, but not in practice.

2   The so-called Rawls Criterion. In the present writer's interpretation, economic welfare is defined as personal consumption per capita modified for the economic effects of explicit public goods and bads, in the Samuelsonian sense, e.g. pollution. 'Advantage' (in the writer's interpretation) refers to inherited human and material endowment or to subsequent exogenous shocks, such as illness on the one hand or a huge success in the national lottery, on the other. Being poor is not sufficient proof of disadvantage. Being born into a poor family is.

In the writer's opinion, the Rawls Criterion is the only rationally viable criterion for judging the economic performance of societies. If one is considering entering one of two alternative societies without knowing how advantaged or disadvantaged one will be in either case, and if one is risk-averse, one can only prefer the society whose structure best protects the least advantaged. Similarly, if two people are arguing about society, and insist they are impartial, they must mean that their judgements are free of self interest, i.e. free from the effects of knowing who they actually are. Of course, one protagonist may prefer the society which favours a particular religion or particular ideology, but these are not criteria of economic performance.

3   Laws creating ground rules for limited-liability incorporation were passed in different countries progressively through the century from 1837 (State of New York), through

the fifties and onwards (England and Western Europe); but at the end of the century only a small proportion of private-sector GNP of what is now the OECD world was accounted for by genuinely collective-ownership corporate forms. The limited-liability company was often employed, however, in its more restricted form by family businesses which could be seen, in effect, as essentially 'personal' in our system of definitions.

4   At the end of the day, seen from the viewpoint of the least advantaged groups, who tend not to be shareholders, what harm do shareholders do? Answer: supposedly, they exert pressure for short-term profits. Unfortunately, however horrible this motive may be, we have seen that other types of motive, such as that of the Commissar, do worse.

Human fallibility, economic enterprises and organizations

Roberto Tamborini

1. Introduction

Market theory was born under the pervasive infatuation with naturalism of the eighteenth and nineteenth-century social sciences, the climax of which was perhaps Marginalism. The key feature of the economic thinking of the time was that economic activity, in particular the establishment of private ownership and free market relationships, were as strong and irresistible as natural laws; phenomena independent of human intentionality and design. Sensational accounts of the 'collapse of communism' and of the 'will of capitalism' in Eastern Europe still convey the idea that something 'unnatural' has eventually, indeed necessarily, come to an end. Likewise, transitional difficulties towards a market economy are largely ascribed to political factors (for example, the design and timing of the reform of economic legislation), as if market relationships in the social sphere tended to develop by themselves quite naturally.

However, in retrospect, twentieth-century economic thought has turned out to be a slow, painful, but inexorable divorce from naturalism. The seeds of change were planted by the great social scientists working at the time of the 'marginalistic revolution' - Weber and Pareto - who recast economic theory in the mould of the sciences of human behaviour. Today, the Nobel laureate Herbert Simon views economics as a branch of 'the sciences of artificial'.[1]

At present, the key issues in fundamental economic research and in debates among different schools largely concern the characterization of human economic behaviour. The Arrow-Debreu axiomatic theory of choice which underpins modern market theory has had the merit of clarifying the assumptions on economic behaviour that underlie the Two Fundamental Welfare Theorems of market general equilibrium. In brief, these assumptions are cognitive in nature: they require that the economic agent should possess an unlimited amount of knowledge, information and computation capability so that he is able to trade optimally on all markets for current as well as for all possible future needs. The 1980s saw active research along three lines which led beyond the Walrasian core of market theory: (i) the intrinsic limits of the human mind in terms of its capacity for computation and prediction, (ii) imperfections and limits in information endowment, dissemination and acquisition, (iii) the irreducibility of uncertainty to complete and stable probability distributions.[2] Each of these cognitive limits is in itself sufficient to prevent the market economy from achieving socially optimal results in resource allocation - the most critical cases being unemployment, output fluctuations and financial instability. However, here I wish to stress some further, perhaps more radical, consequences, namely the consequences which may hinder *the establishment* of market relationships.

In so doing, I shall first review the basic issues discussed by the literature on knowledge and information, with special reference to the debate on alternative system organizations (Section 2). Then I shall concentrate on recent developments in the analysis of a well-known characteristic of market economic activity: risk-taking (Section 3), which is another field where the cognitive approach has brought substantial modifications to previous traditional views based on given (or missing) individual (or social) attitudes towards risk. Finally, I wish to draw attention to a particularly interesting point where the cognitive approach departs from traditional wisdom: the attitude towards risk-taking in economic enterprises cannot be taken to exist independently of the means whereby 'entrepreneurs' can cope with the intrinsic fallibility of risky human decisions (Section 4). From this point of view, the strength of 'entrepreneurship' and the width of market-oriented activity in society, far from being natural manifestations of individuals, are closely related to the development of *non-market* devices designed to reduce risk and fallibility.

2. Knowledge, information and system organizations

2.1. Modern market theory seeks to dispense with naturalistic metaphors and armchair anthropology and to root itself in some theory of individual action, and possibly social interaction, restricted to the class of *intentional and rational choices aimed at economic ends*.[3] I begin with a very broad justification for this claim.

First of all, rationality can be introduced as a corollary to intentionality, where intentionality is defined as the aiming of an action at a desired end. Secondly, rationality may be invoked as a prerequisite of, or perhaps as entirely synonymous with, the so-called 'intersubjective intelligibility' of action which is necessary for agents to understand each other and interact. At this level of generality,

> rationality denotes a style of behaviour (A) that is appropriate to the achievement of given goals, (B) within the limits imposed by given conditions and constraints.[4]

The above is Simon's definition of *procedural rationality*, where he stresses the 'appropriate' connection between action and end. As is well known, whereas Simon maintains that economic theory neither need nor can assume a higher standard of rationality, *substantive rationality* - i.e. the actual achievement of globally optimal goals - is the standard traditionally assumed in economic theory.[5]

The debate over the standard of rationality of economic agents has made it clear that cognitive assumptions often implicitly play a role in economic theory. In fact, individuals who choose intentionally and rationally must have some *knowledge of the consequences of their actions*; in particular with reference to (i) the material environment in which they live (including their own needs and preferences), and (ii) other individuals' economic behaviour. Thus different views and theories on the width and depth of human knowledge have provoked major revolutions and conflicts in contemporary economic thought.

2.2. The issue of the extension of individual knowledge can be addressed with the help of a highly simplified representation of economic activity, i.e. a transaction between two individuals. Any transaction (Θ) between two agents (i = 1, 2) contingent on the state of nature (present or future, s) will generally depend on the decision variable $V_{\Theta s}$ (or a vector of such variables), on the state information I_{is} and on the decision technology K_i available to each agent. Note that K_i (say a matrix) associates an outcome (e.g. the utility of umbrella x) to an action (buying umbrella x) given a state of nature (rain, here, today), whereas I_{is} (say a vector) tells the agent what state actually occurs. Each agent is thus defined by the set 'preferences-knowledge-information'. If the transaction is feasible,

(1) $$\Theta_{s1} (V_{\Theta s} , I_{1s}, K_1) + \Theta_{s2} (V_{\Theta s}, I_{2s}, K_2) = 0$$

The (K, I) arguments of the transaction function can be characterized in three major forms:

(i) Agents have complete knowledge of 'the economy' (i.e. they know the consequences of any possible action, for any possible state, within the given economy) and full information about all possible states ($I_{is} = I_s$, $K_i = K$, i = 1, 2).[6]

(ii) Agents have incomplete knowledge and information ($I_{is} = I^{\wedge}_s$, $K_i = K^{\wedge}$, i = 1, 2) where ($\wedge$) denotes incompleteness with respect to (I_s, K).[7]

(iii) Agents' knowledge and information is, at least a priori, subjective and heterogeneous ($I_{1s} \neq I_{2s}$, $K_1 \neq K_2$).[8]

Assumption (i) is necessary for agents to be able to pursue and to achieve global optimization; in fact, global optimization occurs when each agent chooses the action associated with the best possible outcome in any possible state.[9] If Simon's principle of incompleteness (ii) holds, agents will make decisions which are locally 'satisficing', but not globally optimal. On the other hand, if agents move from heterogeneous K&I *à la* Hayek (iii), equilibrium transactions will yield results different from those obtained in case (i); in particular, individual optimality may not lead to social optimality.

The controversy over the standard of rationality - which is a controversy over cognitive assumptions in economic theory - can be decided on either empirical or theoretical grounds. Empirically, the recent cross-fertilization between economics and cognitive sciences has produced overwhelming evidence against the hypotheses of perfect K&I and global optimization, even if it has not come up with a single well-defined alternative.[10] By and large, if empirical relevance were the choice criterion of economic hypotheses, variations on the theme of heterogeneous and/or incomplete K&I would become normal practice. On the other hand, while no-one doubts that Walrasian theory is internally coherent, serious doubts have been raised as to the correspondence between deductions and observations, and even between its fundamental hypotheses on economic behaviour and the market paradigm. The claim that heterogeneous and incomplete K&I alone are the most powerful inducements for individuals to make decentralized decisions and transactions has proved to be much more effective than claims against the empirical irrelevance of hypotheses.[11]

A good point to start with is the famous Hayek-Lange interchange, which showed that if all the K&I necessary to achieve optimal resource allocation on all markets and states were in fact freely available, at least one individual could be elected as the almighty social planner and the planned economy would be undistinguishable from the market economy. Put very simply, the market-type transaction 1 $\{\Theta_{1s}, \Theta_{2s}\}$ may be superior to the planned allocation $\{\Theta_{\sim 1s}, \Theta_{\sim 2s}\}$ only if its determinants $\{I_{1s}, K_1, I_{2s}, K_2\}$ cannot freely become common knowledge.

> The economic problem which society faces [...] is not merely a problem of how to allocate "given" resources - if given is taken to mean a single mind which deliberately solves the problem set by these "data". It is rather a problem [...] of the utilization of knowledge which is not given to anyone in its totality.[12]

In modern organizational parlance, *markets are a means to reduce complexity*. In fact, we can go further than heterogeneous and incomplete K&I taken as a matter of fact. These characteristics of K&I are due to the particular way that the human mind works, namely by *selecting and elaborating* external inputs and then *constructing* a 'model of the world'. These 'models' are the result of the heuristic activity of the human mind *and* of its interactive feedback with subjective experience. Both these factors operate in such a way that improvements of knowledge are more in depth than in width, a process which enhances both individual K&I specificity in the decision process and the need for cooperation in dealing with problems whose complexity exceeds individual competence.[13] Hence markets are viewed in relation to the fact that human rationality operates using active procedures to reduce the complexity of the environment.[14] Markets are an effective means to achieve this, as compared, for example, with systems of centralized K&I, in so far as they allow individual K&I *not* to exceed the boundaries of subjective experience and skill (and perhaps of self-interest with little or no concern for the *systemic* consequences of individual actions).

The serious threat to the Walrasian market paradigm posed by imperfect

K&I has prompted a new line of enquiry in economic theory: the economics of learning. In point of fact, the basic intuition is not a new one. Advocates of the perfect K&I hypothesis and of global optimization have long argued that markets themselves diffuse and equalize K&I, and that if there are agents who fail to attain the standard of global optimization they will simply be wiped out by natural selection. Hence the Walrasian market paradigm is often thought of as the culmination of an alleged learning-adaptation process by which the fittest survive.[15] It is only in this last decade or so that this argument has been given rigorous examination, and the results of this examination, though mixed, cast serious doubt on its solidity.[16]

To give a very rough idea of the difficulties that the alleged learning process may face, one can begin with the so-called 'reduced form' of the market relationship created by the transaction 1:

(2) $V_{\Theta_s} (I_{1s}, I_{2s}, K_1, K_2)$

The reduced form is a functional expression of the market relationship that agents can use in order to learn how to relate the observed decision variable (e.g. a price) to the determinants of the transaction (e.g. the demand and supply functions). Let us start with agent 1, which only knows or observes $\{\Theta_s, V_{\Theta_s}, I_{1s}, K_1\}$ while agent 2 only knows or observes $\{\Theta_s, V_{\Theta_s}, I_{2s}, K_{1s}\}$. Note from 2 that perfect K&I would require each agent to discover and acquire the K&I possessed by the other. A basic precondition for a viable learning process (say a Bayesian one) is the stationarity of the market relationship 1 under repeated transactions. Yet, at the same time, any learning process entails errors and revisions of the decision model currently being used by the agent. Therefore, whenever each agent cleverly revises its own K_i it also compromises the stationarity of the market relationship, and hence undermines its own learning process as well as that of other agents: convergence of the collective learning process towards the unique 'true' knowledge of 2 is far from certain. Secondly, even more problematic, if not hopeless, is the case that, if convergence does take place, the market relationship will still be the same as it is under conditions of perfect K&I. To quote Bray and Kreps, the conditions of successful learning process according to the Walrasian standard 'set a benchmark of extreme rationality, [while] the best work to be done on this subject will be in models where learning is a bit more realistic and a bit (or even a lot) less rational'.[17]

2.3. The K&I approach to the market economy raises a number of new and crucial questions on how market relationships are established and on how they work. I shall only touch on some of these very briefly.

First, it is interesting to note that in Smith's *Wealth of Nations* the *enlargement* of market is a factor of social progress because markets engender labour division and hence greater social productivity. The K&I approach starts with individual preferences and knowledge as a highly subjective and specialized endowment, and then explains the *establishment* of market relationships as a response to the problem of achieving the orderly satisfaction of disparate skills and needs.[18] Market relationships become a serious organizational issue only when the complexity of final needs, and hence of production, exceeds the competence of the single individual or of small self-organized groups of individuals.[19]

Secondly, if on the one hand the rationale for market relationships lies in the need to reduce the complexity of the economic problems of large numbers of individuals, on the other, (i) market relationships will not take the form they do in the Walrasian paradigm (i.e. auction meeting points of large random numbers of individuals), and (ii) markets will hardly solve the economic problem optimally (where optimality is defined as in the Walrasian paradigm).

Indeed, the actual form and evolution of market relationships is an extremely complex and entirely open problem. It is all too easy to observe that the ideal auction market of the Walrasian paradigm does not exist in reality; even those markets which are usually regarded as the closest approximation to the ideal - financial markets, for example - differ from it in at least one important respect: they are costly to open and manage; and typically auction markets are worth opening only beyond a certain operational scale. Only a few centres in a country and in the world as a whole reach this critical operational scale. And where size matters, perfect competition breaks down. Hence even a very orthodox element of economic analysis - running costs - may interfere with the ideal market paradigm.[20]

More serious obstacles are raised by imperfect K&I, since these may also hinder an individual's ability or willingness to enter a market transaction. A perfect market transaction should consist of a contract which specifies *with certainty* the nature of the object, the date and the conditions of delivery; only rarely do the parties concerned have all the knowledge and information about all three of these items in the contract. For instance, time is a crucial element which blurs what one wishes, when one wishes it, and under what external conditions; and this may explain why insurance and future delivery markets are so poorly developed relative to the prediction (or the prescription) of the Walrasian model.[21] It has also been pointed out that market transactors are generally bound to accept contracts covered by a veil of uncertainty which exposes each party to the risk of being fooled by the other; market transactions can only survive within a protective belt of non-market means of incentive and defence of goodwill[22], but there may be cases in which market relationships break down anyway.[23] It might be argued that these aspects of market relationships give incentives for the improvement of knowledge and information, which is in fact one of the most celebrated achievements of market economies. Again, countervailing forces operate here. The crucial point is that in contrast to what happens in the Walrasian world, improving K&I is hard, slow and costly; the really valuable K&I is not the amount that is publicly available, but the private further bit that one can secure for oneself.[24] If markets were channels of free dissemination of private K&I - that is, if the use of private K&I gave no extra profit to the owner, as in the case of Walrasian markets - no-one would ever bear the cost of acquiring K&I.[25] If there is a persistent economic incentive for individuals to improve their own and social K&I, such improvements (from inventions to inside stock-market information) are to be protected against becoming 'public goods' through 'too perfect' market transaction, whether by means of legal restriction (e.g. patents) or self-limitation of the extent of market relationships.

Far from being the spontaneous result of a natural attitude of individuals, the establishment of market relationships requires a good deal of design, learning and institutional support - which brings us back to Simon's view quoted at the outset of economics as a science of the artificial. Even then, market relationships are not necessarily bound to dominate economic life. As Coase remarked as early as 1937, the core of the market economy - the firm - appears in reality to be a cluster of hierarchic relations embedded in outer market relations. This extremely fruitful intuition suggests that in a number of circumstances the above-mentioned obstacles to market-type transactions are such that the economic problem of coordinating different preferences, needs and skills has to be solved by non-market organizational devices - namely those based on personal· ties and/or hierarchical relations.[26] Nowadays, successful Western economies could hardly be defined as 'market economies' according to the Walrasian paradigm. The joint output of the public sector and of the top ten large corporations exceeds half of the GDP of almost all OECD countries, and most medium to small-size businesses are vertically integrated with large corporations. The way businessmen compete does not suggest an extension of the law of large numbers of impersonal auction markets; rather, they restrict it by growing in size and by personalizing their ties with suppliers, workers and customers.[27] We spend most of our life receiving or giving 'orders' within our families, schools, universities, factories, offices, clubs, political organizations and churches, all of which play a role in the way society solves our vital economic problem.

3. Risk-taking and economic enterprise

3.1. I stressed in the previous section that the K&I approach to the market sheds light on an aspect which may be of some relevance to the *transition* towards the market: difficulties may also arise from 'below', not just from 'above'. In this section I shall pursue this issue further in a rather classical direction: the willingness in society to undertake economic activities and the surge of private economic enterprises as an attitude to risk-taking.

The rise of the capitalistic firm is still mostly approached from two competing standpoints[28]: the Marxian standpoint based on material factors (initial capital accumulation and the disruption of self-organized production) versus the Weberian one based on cultural factors (entrepreneurship as a result of pre-market attitudes towards calculation, self-interest and risk). Only those blinded by ideology would deny that both factors have had a major impact on the historical evolution of capitalism. Indeed, both views have made dramatic strides forward with respect to the old, naive claim of man's natural tendency to exchange which was criticized at the outset. Yet, even when these two broad *explanations* are integrated, one feels that they may lead to the mechanical and unwarranted *prediction* that economic enterprises will spring from capital plus risk.[29]

The three great economists who made the most innovative contribution to this issue - Knight, Schumpeter and Keynes - focused, in fact, on capital and risk. Knight[30] made the first serious attempt to give a theoretical basis to the popular notion that the entrepreneur's profit is his reward for risk. Schumpeter[31] and Keynes[32] viewed the entrepreneur's particular attitude towards the future as the key to innovation and growth - although they also pointed out that capital (that is, idle capital) was a powerful constraint. The subsequent systematization of risk-taking in the axiomatic decision theory recalled in Section 2 has long been regarded as the best way to save the baby while throwing out the bathwater of those earlier intuitions.[33] Risk arises from the existence of more than one possible state of nature under which the agent's decision will fall; from the fact that the agent does not know in advance what state will in fact occur; and from the assumption that the agent is able to represent all the possible states by a coherent probability distribution. This definition of risk is necessary for the agent to take the optimal decision, which is equivalent to the maximization of expected utility (see Section 2 and note 3). The attitude towards risk is also given an extremely rigorous meaning: it is the subjective utility-based rate of exchange of certain for actuarial outcomes (geometrically, the curvature degree of the utility function). Risk and different degrees of risk aversion across agents have thus become the dominant rationalization of most market activities and transactions. One may thus straightforwardly explain entrepreneurship as relatively lower risk aversion and profit as a risk premium, or extend expected utility theory to the individual firm's decisions.[34]

It now seems that both the bathwater and Knight's, Keynes's and Schumpeter's baby have been thrown away. The main point of the K&I approach in this vast debate is again that the axiomatic theory of risk-taking is totally subordinate to the cognitive assumptions of perfect K&I discussed above. The firm as an *organized* decisional body can hardly descend from such axioms, whereas even in the neoclassical tradition the service performed by the entrepreneur is organizational in nature. Is it the case that the whole corporate edifice is solidly based on the 'fact' that n individual suppliers of production services need n+1st individual who combines their services to deliver the list of goods sent by the market only because this n+1st individual is less risk averse? Further, given that as a consequence of these assumptions market demand for all goods and states exists and is common knowledge (all present and future markets are open), and that the 'blueprint' of all possible factor combinations also exists and is common knowledge, is there really any entrepreneurial risk? What can we do to promote entrepreneurship in society if it is a matter of subjective preferences?

3.2. The above are only a few examples of the quite radical questions that have oriented researchers in their examination of entrepreneurial risk-taking outside the axiomatic individual choice paradigm. When choice and risk-taking analysis trespasses the axiomatic protective belt and moves into the cognitive field, it changes dramatically, and one finds the organizational and entrepreneurial issue in a prominent place from the outset.

As already explained in Section 2, a major discovery was that decision-making always takes place within a 'model' or 'frame' *actively predefined* by the agent (the agent *acts* not only as he chooses but also, indeed primarily, as he *constructs* the decision frame). Such decision frames reflect individual K&I specificity and at the same time call for cooperation among different specific K&I inputs in order to deal with complex problems beyond individual competences. In this view, entrepreneurship is the interface between the framing of the 'external' environment and the 'internal' coordination of individual competences which are necessary *prerequisites* of rational decision making.[35]

This view departs radically from the traditional theory at various points.[36] In the first place, risk evaluation is hardly represented by given parameters of a probability distribution (such as mean and variance of payoffs) at one point in time: in fact the configuration of outcomes is the *result* of both the 'external' framing activity and the 'internal' organizational design (the feasibility of a project is very similar to Machlup's pudding test). As a consequence, entrepreneurship is very loosely related to ex-ante risk evaluation of given alternatives; in fact, risk evaluation cannot be made ex-ante, that is, independently of the implementation of specific individual K&I in the specific decision problem.

Secondly, this vindicates Knight's and Keynes' idea that entrepreneurship has to do, not with actuarial risk (i.e. reducible to probability calculus), but with a different cognitive phenomenon that Knight called *uncertainty*.[37] Nevertheless, Knight was certainly right to relate entrepreneurship and profit to decision situations in which K&I are heterogeneous and incomplete, and hence liable to reward individual K&I specific to the decision process. To put it intuitively, two different individuals may find a project feasible and not feasible respectively, not because they know all and the same things but have different preferences, but because they know different things about the project and/or how to realize it.[38]

Finally, entrepreneurship is not merely given, or not given once and for all, as a subjective attitude towards taking risks. Of course, there is still room for individual specificity as mentioned above, but this is largely present in form of K&I as a 'producible' asset which can be created, acquired, and improved by policy interventions. Moreover, socially relevant economic enterprises are seldom undertaken individually, while this is generally not the case of production; developed market economies suggest that if any social benefit is to be derived from private risk-taking, it largely comes about in the form of *organized risk-taking*. This conclusion is in fact similar to the one drawn about the establishment of market relationships in the previous section: very little is 'natural'; a great deal comes about by social design; not everything can be done by law.

4. Organized risk-taking: economic devices and institutions to cope with human fallibility

4.1. The foregoing conclusions are enhanced by consideration of an aspect of risk-taking and entrepreneurship largely ignored by standard economic theory precisely because it is one of the (unpleasant) implications of imperfect K&I. We have already seen in Section 2 that imperfect K&I may lead to market failures in resource allocations. One reason why this happens may be that uncertainty (e.g. agents' inability to define desired transactions contingent on future states due to incomplete information) prevents the existence of sufficient future markets. These kinds of market failure react back at the level of individual decisions. Whereas the existence of future markets allows the Walrasian expected utility maximizer to deal with risk optimally by trading for his most preferred position in any possible future contingency (which is also called 'full insurance'), the uncertain individual *has to cope with the consequences of unforeseen (or uninsurable) contingencies*. Hence *human fallibility* in forward-looking activities is binding, whereas it plays little or no role in economic theory.

This idea can be traced back to Knight's[39] early emphasis on human fallibility as a consequence of uncertainty and as a cause of departure from the perfect market paradigm. As Sah and Stiglitz have recently written,

> In the conventional paradigm mistakes are never made, either in gathering or transmitting information, or in making decisions, and indeed, there are no costs associated with these activities. By contrast, the view we take here is that "to err is human", and that different organizational systems differ not only in what kinds of errors individuals make in them, but also in how the systems "aggregate" errors.[40]

Below I shall develop two simple examples to show how considerations of fallibility in decision-making affect economic organizational structures on the one hand, and market transactions on the other.

4.2. As Sah and Stiglitz have argued, organizations should also be examined according to the way they cope with the fact that the decisions made by their members may be wrong. By means of a simple model based on the well-known technique of comparison between Type I errors (the probability of rejecting a good project) and Type II errors (the probability of accepting a bad project), the authors show that 'polyarchical organizations accept more bad projects, while hierarchical organizations reject more good projects'.[41] Evaluation of the comparative advantages of the two organizations is difficult, however. Note that the performance of the hierarchy (H) is conservative because it reduces Type II errors, while the polyarchy (P) behave innovatively because it reduces Type I errors. As a consequence, there may be situations in which P performs better than H as well as situations in which the opposite is true. The comparative advantage of H emerges when there is a high ratio of bad to good projects in the pipeline or when bad projects incur greater losses than the gains from good projects. Clearly, this comparative advantage would not be appreciated if fallibility considerations did not matter.

Sah and Stiglitz produce another interesting result which sheds some light on the market economy. Let us consider a 'polyarchy of hierarchies' (P-H).[42] This is a P of m decision units which are hierarchical, and each H has n layers. By choosing n and m appropriately, one obtains an organization which accepts more good projects and rejects more bad projects than does a single decision maker. Moreover, this kind of organization accepts fewer bad projects than a single P and rejects fewer good projects than a single H.

P-H may be a fairly realistic representation of what Western market economies are like. Notably, there are no atomistic individuals, and the optimal number of H units, namely firms, is not infinitely large; though one should say that it is left unclear as to how the m H units communicate with each other (whether through prices or non-price signals). Indeed, *inter-unit* communication is crucial to obtaining the nice properties of this organization.[43] In fact, such properties result from the fact that, while the single H tends to sacrifice good projects, there is a positive probability that these good projects will be picked up by other H with no need for approval from the former. Remarkably, the pursuit of self-interest in each single economic unit does not lead to the maximization of good projects, and yet both the unit and society gain from minimizing bad ones; the aggregate social benefit, however, arises from the P-type organization of the economy as a whole, which is designed to attenuate on average the consequences of the precautionary attitude of fallible decision makers.

4.3. In market economies, inter-unit communication is supposed to take place through price signals collected and channelled by markets. The conveying of information occurs in principle as transactions reveal agents' preferences; however, in actual market economies transactions are mediated by a peculiar instrument, money, and contracts are typically struck in money terms (for instance, workers do not exchange labour for goods directly). One of the most entrenched views of money is that it is a 'good like all the others' whose price reflects the marginal value of its 'liquidity service', namely the circulation of all other goods. However, as is well known, the Walrasian market paradigm, which portrays a perfect communication system, gives no justification for the use of money at all.[44]

Fundamental research in monetary theory following Keynes's *General Theory*, led especially by Hicks[45] and then by Hahn[46], has progressively removed money from its former place among all other goods and has bound it up with uncertainty.[47] Uncertainty, as defined above, arises from a lack of K&I, and hence of feasible contracts, on future states; this interrupts inter-unit communication. Nonetheless, just as economic activity takes time, so purchasing power has to be transferred through time. In fact there are many wealth carriers which are also marketable goods or which have markets like goods: gold, buildings, land, bonds and the whole array of financial securities. Compared with these 'time machines', money turns out to be, not a good like all the others, but rather *a contract*. Money is a very peculiar contract which guarantees the purchase of all other marketable items at a fixed face value, or one which enforces the liquidity rule that 'money buys goods, but goods do not buy goods'.[48] This kind of contract is accepted by fallible decision makers (i.e. they display 'liquidity preference') because it enables them to maintain their purchasing power through time until uncertainty is resolved.[49] Altern-atively, to use Sah and Stiglitz's terminology, one may say that holding money minimizes Type II error (the probability of nominal capital loss) in the problem of transferring purchasing power through time.[50]

It should be strongly emphasized that there is nothing 'natural' in the money contract, and nothing mysteriously hidden in its material support: in fact, (i) this contract resolves transactions between two parties immediately and definitively on behalf of a third party - the money issuer - and (ii) it excludes equivalent contracts other than the constituted monetary unit.[51] The 'third party' is an essential element in the contract. In fact, since the working of money is essentially intertemporal, those who accept it in exchange for goods now should expect anyone else to accept it in exchange for goods in the future. Theoretical experiments and historical experience suggests that this expectation can hardly be based on individual rationality, and consequently that the money contract should be vouchsafed by an instituted 'third party'.[52]

The importance of the *quality* of the money contract for the market economy to work properly is testified by those economies which suffer from hyper-inflation and/or shortage.[53] In both cases - though for opposite reasons of policy mismanagement - one observes unusual money hoarding face-to-face with a clogged circulation of goods; at the same time, the black market for parallel 'strong' currencies (viz. the dollar or the mark) acquires a speculative nature which worsens rather than relieves the goods shortage. As Leijonhufvud has aptly remarked, these experiences show that the presumption in the traditional market paradigm that large-scale free trades tend to self-organization in form of barter, or are able to self-generate 'the' sound means of payment with no need for a monetary constitution, is groundless.

5. Concluding remarks

This paper offers a very 'external' and preliminary contribution to the issue of the transition from planned to market economies. A negative target lies in the background: the popular idea - popular, I am afraid, in both West and East - that establishing market relationships reflects a 'natural' attitude of individuals that can only fail if the authorities intervene. I do not wish at all to defend planning against market, simply to draw attention to a few important aspects of the market economy, and hopefully to give a modest contribution towards helping the East not to repeat the errors of the West.

The cognitive, communicative and organizational aspects of the market economy entail that the rise of large-scale private entrepreneurship and market relations in societies, far from being 'natural', requires a good deal of social design and policy support, and even then the result can only come at the end of complex processes of learning and adaptation. This, which is the main message of this paper, is only seemingly pessimistic compared with the promises of 'a free market at once': it instead means that successful transition is possible, provided that the market economy is correctly understood and wisely pursued.

Notes

1 Simon, 1981.
2 See Egidi et al., 1990.
3 As is well known, in its initial stage of development economics was defined as the science of allocation of scarce resources among alternative uses (See Robbins, 1935). This definition turned out to be simultaneously too wide and too narrow. It was too wide because it denoted, in fact, a choice problem which may be extended to virtually all aspects of human life, and it was too narrow because it reduced an economic problem to an abstract choice with no specific reference as to the objects of that choice. For instance, Neo-Walrasian theory clearly states that the task of economic theory is to show how infinitely many individuals can best satisfy their own preferred needs: scarcity of resources, individualistic self-interest, atomistic behaviour, and so forth, are all subsequent and ancillary characterizations of the economic problem (See e.g. Hahn and Hollis, 1979).

4 Simon, 1964.
5 See Simon, 1979.
6 See e.g. Dreze, 1987.
7 Simon, 1981.
8 See Von Hayek, 1942. By implication, in case (iii) (K, I) should also be incomplete for each agent. A further complication, which I do not consider here, is that the decision variable Vs may also be included in the information set and hence be unobservable, or observable with 'noise', to some agents (see Stiglitz, 1985).
9 The optimal choice is then shown to be equivalent to the maximization of a function (the expected utility function) which is given by the linear (or integral) combination of the utility of each possible outcome with its probability.
10 I only cite a few extremely interesting collections of studies: Khaneman et al., 1982; Hogarth and Reder (eds.), 1986; Arkes and Hammond (eds.), 1987.
11 Admittedly, as Hahn has remarked, provocatively as usual, "if it is the case that today General Equilibrium Theory is in some disarray, this is largely due to the work of General Equilibrium theorists, and not to any successful assault from outside" (Hahn, 1981, p. 12). Even more persuasive is his remark that "the theory itself has often suffered a good deal from its friends. Some friends [...] have taken the theory in practical applications a good deal more seriously than at present there is any justification for doing" (Hahn, 1981, p. 126).
12 Von Hayek, 1945, pp. 77-8.
13 From this point of view, learning is also largely redefined with respect to the abstract idea of passive discovery and accumulation of knowledge about the "whole and true" structure of the environment. Learning always takes place within a predefined frame giving a simplified representation of the environment. For a detailed treatment of these issues see Tamborini, 1990a.
14 Simon, 1981.
15 Alchian, 1950.
16 See the important contributions by Frydman and Phelps (eds.), 1983; Bray and Kreps, 1986; Pesaran, 1987; Hahn (ed.), 1989.
17 Bray and Kreps, 1986, p. 603.
18 See Leijonhufvud, 1986, 1987.
19 See Heiner 1983.
20 Okun, 1981.
21 See, for example, Hahn, 1982a.
22 Williamson, 1985.
23 See Akerlof, 1970.
24 Arrow, 1951, 1970, 1973.
25 Arrow, 1951, 1970, 1973; Stiglitz, 1985.
26 Marris and Mueller, 1980, sec. II; Egidi, 1989.
27 Robinson, 1953; Okun, 1981; Marris, 1989.
28 Morishima, 1988
29 It is often the case that the misuse of history feeds two opposite and equally pernicious attitudes: one an enthusiastic faith in replications, the other a hopeless unicity of experiences.
30 Knight, 1921.
31 Schumpeter, 1934.
32 Keynes, 1936.
33 Arrow, 1951.
34 See, for example, Sandmo, 1971; Leland, 1972.
35 See March (ed.), 1989.
36 For obvious reasons I shall not considere here the ample experimental literature that has put the axiomatic theory of decision to the test and found that individuals, even in very simple choice problems, fail to conform to the axioms of expected utility theory; for

example, because they do not follow probability theory in risk assessment. Very good surveys have been produced by Schoemaker (1982) and March-Shapira (1987).

37   Today one may view the axiomatic choice theory as a particular (perhaps prescriptive) representation of decision processes under uncertainty where the framing activity is reduced to probabilities (whether these are frequencies or degrees of rational beliefs) and the organizational design is collapsed onto the single individual. (See Simon, 1981; March-Shapira, 1987).

38   That this has also to be the environment of the innovative Schumpeterian entrepreneur has been shown in detail by Egidi, 1981.

39   Knight, 1921, ch. III, VII.

40   Sah and Stiglitz, 1985, p. 292.

41   Sah and Stiglitz, 1995, p. 293. In a polyarchy each individual has decision power on a project, and rejected projects are evaluated by another individual. In a hierarchy only projects approved by at least one individual in each layer are undertaken.

42   Sah and Stiglitz, 1985, pp. 294-ff.

43   One should bear in mind that the debate over firms' size, increasing returns to scale, and market efficiency has mostly focused on *intra-unit* communication, on the premise that efficient communication is inversely related to the length of the chain of top-down commands and down-top responses. See Marris and Mueller, 1980, sec. IIB.

44   Hahn, 1982b, ch. II.

45   See Hicks, 1967, 1979.

46   See Hahn, 1982b, 1988.

47   The reader can find an extended treatment in my 1990b paper.

48   Clower, 1967.

49   Or until more is learnt about the decision to make: Hicks, 1979.

50   See again Tamborini, 1990b.

51   As Graziani reports, Keynes wrote that "a Rupee is a note printed on silver": Graziani, 1988, p. xiv.

52   Hahn, 1982b, ch. 1. In developed market economies, this role is usually played by a state agency under parliamentary control (Central Bank), though this is only a relatively stable stage in a long evolutionary process of waves of inventions of private means of payments followed by their statization, while financial innovation is still actively practised: Kaldor, 1982; De Cecco (ed.), 1987.

53   Leijonhufvud, 1990.

Bibliography

Akerlof, G. (1970), 'The Market for Lemons', *Quarterly Journal of Economics*, no. 2.

Alchian, A. (1950), 'Uncertainty, Evolution and Economic Theory', *Journal of Political Economy*, vol. LVIII, June.

Arkes, H. R., Hammond, K. R. (eds.) (1987), *Judgement and Decision Making. An Interdisciplinary Reader*, Cambridge: Cambridge University Press.

Arrow, K. J. (1951), 'Alternative Approaches to the Theory of Choice in Risk-Taking Situations', in *Essays in the Theory of Risk-Bearing*, Amsterdam: North Holland, 1970.

Arrow, K. J. (1962), 'Economic Welfare and the Allocation of Resources to Invention', in *Essays in the Theory of Risk-Bearing*, Amsterdam: North Holland, 1970.

Arrow, K. J. (1970), 'The Value of and Demand for Information', in *Essays in the Theory of Risk-Bearing*, Amsterdam: North Holland, 1970.

Arrow, K. J. (1973), 'Information and Economic Behavior', in *The Economics of Information*, The Collected Papers of Kenneth J. Arrow, vol. IV, Oxford: Oxford University Press, 1984.

Bray, M., Kreps, D. M. (1986), 'Rational Learning and Rational Expectations', in Heller, W., Starret, D., Starr, R. (eds.), *Essays in Honour of K. J. Arrow*, Cambridge: Cambridge University Press.

Clower, R. W. (1967), 'A Reconsideration of the Microfoundations of Monetary Theory', *Western Economic Journal*, vol. VI, December.

Coase, R. (1937), 'The Nature of the Firm', *Economica*, no. 4.

De Cecco, M. (ed.) (1987), *Changing Money. Financial Innovation in Developed Countries*, Oxford: Blackwell.

Dreze, J. (1987), *Essays on Economic Decisions Under Uncertainty*, Cambridge: Cambridge University Press.

Egidi, M. (1981), *Schumpeter. Lo sviluppo come trasformazione morfologica*, Milan: Etas.

Egidi, M. (1989), 'L'impresa come organizzazione e la funzione di produzione: un binomio impossibile', in Zamagni, S. (ed.), *Le teorie economiche della produzione*, Bologna: Il Mulino.

Egidi, M., Lombardi, M., Tamborini R. (eds.) (1991), *Conoscenza, incertezza e decisioni economiche*, Milan: Franco Angeli.

Frydman, R., Phelps, E. (eds.) (1983), *Individuals Forecasting and Aggregate Outcomes. Rational Expectations Examined*, Cambridge: Cambridge University Press.

Graziani, A. (1988), 'Introduzione', in *Moneta e produzione*, Torino, Einaudi.

Hahn, F. (1981), 'General Equilibrium Theory', in Bell, D., Kristol, I. (eds.), *The Crisis in Economic Theory*, New York: Northon.

Hahn, F. (1982a), 'Reflections on the Invisible Hand', *Lloyds Bank Review*, April.

Hahn, F. (1982b), *Money and Inflation*, Oxford: Blackwell.

Hahn, F. (1988), 'On Monetary Theory', *Economic Journal*, vol. XCVIII, December.

Hahn, F. (ed.) (1989), *The Economics of Missing Markets, Information and Games*, Oxford: Oxford University Press.

Hahn, F., Hollis, M. (1979), 'Introduction', in *Philosophy and Economic Theory*, Oxford: Oxford University Press.

Heiner, R. (1983), 'The Origin of Predictable Behaviour', *American Economic Review*, September.

Hicks, J. R. (1967), *Critical Essays in Monetary Theory*, Oxford: Clarendon.

Hicks, J. R. (1979), *Causality in Economics*, Oxford: Blackwell.

Hogarth, R. M., Reder, M. W. (eds.), (1986), *Rational Choice. The Contracts between Psychology and Economics*, Chicago: Chicago University Press.

Kaldor, N. (1982), *The Scourge of Monetarism*, Oxford: Oxford University Press.

Keynes, J. M. (1936), *The General Theory of Employment, Interest and Money*, in *The Collected Writings of John Maynard Keynes*, edited by D. Moggridge, vol. XIII, London: Macmillan, 1973.

Khaneman, D., Slovic, P., Tversky, A. (1982), *Judgment under Uncertainty:*

Heuristics and Biases, New York: Cambridge University Press.

Knight, F. (1921), *Risk, Uncertainty and Profit*, Chicago: Chicago University Press, 1971.

Leijonhufvud, A. (1986), 'Capitalism and Factory System', in Langlois, R. W. (ed.), *Economics as a Process*, Cambridge: Cambridge University Press.

Leijonhufvud, A. (1987), 'Costi dell'informazione e divisione del lavoro', in Yamey, B., Tamburini, G. (eds.), *Aspetti dell'economia dell'informazione*, Bologna: Il Mulino.

Leijonhufvud, A. (1990), 'Economic Behaviour Under Extreme Monetary Instability', International School of Economic Research Workshop: 'Expectations and Learning', mimeo, University of Siena and C.N.R.

Leland, H. (1972), 'Theory of the Firm Facing Uncertain Demand', *American Economic Review*, vol. LXII, June.

March, J. G. (ed.) (1989), *Decisions and Organizations*, Oxford: Blackwell.

March, J. G., Shapira, Z. (1987), 'Managerial Perspectives on Risk and Risk-Taking', in March, J. G. (ed.) (1989), *Decisions and Organizations*, Oxford: Blackwell.

Marris, R. (1989), 'Managerialism, Macroeconomics, Efficiency and Equity. An Anti-Neoclassical Critique', *Annali Scientifici del Dipartimento di Economia*, Università di Trento, vol. II.

Marris, R., Mueller, D. C. (1980), 'The Corporation, Competition and the Invisible Hand', *Journal of Economic Literature*, vol. XVIII, March.

Okun, A. (1981), *Prices and Quantities: A Macroeconomic Analysis*, Oxford: Blackwell.

Pesaran, H. M. (1987), *The Limits to Rational Expectations*, Oxford: Blackwell.

Robbins, L. (1935), *An Essay on the Nature of Economic Science*, London: Macmillan.

Robinson, J. (1953), 'The Economics of Imperfect Competition Reconsidered', in *Contribution to Modern Economics*, Oxford: Blackwell, 1980.

Sah, R. K., Stiglitz, J. E. (1985), 'Human Fallibility and Economic Organization', *American Economic Review*, vol. LXXV, May.

Sandmo, R. (1971), 'Theory of Firm under Uncertainty', *American Economic Review*, vol. LXI, March.

Schoemaker, P. J. (1982), 'The Expected Utility Model: Its Variants, Purposes, Evidence and Limitations', *Journal of Economic Literature*, no. 2.

Schumpeter, J.A. (1934), *The Theory of Economic Development*, Cambridge, Mass.: The MIT Press.

Simon, H. (1964), 'Rationality', in *A Dictionary of the Social Sciences*, Glencoe, Ill.: The Free Press.

Simon, H. (1979), 'Rational Decision Making in Business Organizations', *American Economic Review*, vol. LXIX.

Simon, H. (1981), *The Sciences of the Artificial*, Cambridge, Mass.: The MIT Press.

Stiglitz, H. (1985), 'Information and Economic Analysis: A Perspective', *Economic Journal*, Supplement.

Tamborini, R. (1990a), 'Knowledge and Prediction of Economic Behaviour. Towards a Constructivist Approach', *Discussion Papers*, Dipartimento di Economia dell'Università di Trento, no. 4, Trento; 'Conoscenza e previsione del comportamento economico. Per un approccio costruttivista', in Egidi, M., Lombardi, M., Tamborini, R. (eds.) (1991), *Conoscenza, incertezza e decisioni economiche*, Milano: Franco Angeli.

Tamborini, R. (1990b), 'Towards a Consistent Characterization of the Financial Economy', *Discussion Papers*, Dipartimento di Economia dell'Università di Trento, no. 2, Trento; *'Errare Humanum Est.* Comportamento precauzionale, economia finanziaria e usi della moneta', *Economia Politica*, forthcoming.

Von Hayek, F. A. (1942), 'Scientism and The Study of Society', in *Individualism and Economic Order*, London: Routledge and Kegan Paul, 1949.

Von Hayek, F. A. (1945), 'The Use of Knowledge in Society', in *Individualism and Economic Order*, London: Routledge and Kegan Paul, 1949.

Williamson, O. (1985), *The Economic Institutions of Capitalism*, New York: Free Press.

Market failure versus state failure: the scope for privatization in a planned economy

Alastair McAuley

1. Introduction

One objective of economic organization is to secure the efficient use of available resources. And much of the current preoccupation with privatization, in the East and West, is based on the belief that present forms of organization fail to guarantee that efficiency. Advocates of privatization often claim that the market possesses an almost magical power to ensure efficiency; sometimes, they also suggest that the state is incapable of using resources effectively. Orthodox economists, surprising as this may seem, do not share this faith in the market. Indeed, neoclassical theory has expressed a naive faith in the ability of the state to cope with those allocative problems that the market cannot solve efficiently. In the past thirty years, however, this assumption has been challenged - for example in the theory of public choice.

In this paper, I look at recent contributions to the debate over efficiency. I attempt to do two things: to suggest to ardent privatizers that there are some situations in which markets will not work. I also suggest that, sometimes, the solutions to the problem of market failure proposed by orthodox theorists involve greater welfare losses than the failure itself. Society would be better off living with the imperfection.

This paper, then, is concerned with the efficient use of resources. I start with a brief definition of the concept and of the analytical context in which I will use it. The focus of neoclassical theory is allocative efficiency: resources are allocated efficiently when a reallocation of inputs between enterprises or industries will not increase the output of any one good without at the same time reducing the output of a second good. In terms of conventional diagrams, allocative efficiency ensures that an economy is located on its production possibility curve; or, what amounts to the same thing in factor space, it implies that the economy is located on the so-called contract-curve in an Edgeworth-Bowley Box diagram.[1]

In this paper, I adopt a partial equilibrium approach: that is, I shall be concerned with the efficient production of commodities taken one at a time. Individual goods confer benefits but their production incurs cost. In such circumstances, efficiency implies the maximization of net social benefit; that is, it entails setting marginal social cost (msc) equal to marginal social benefit (msb).

(1)   msc=msb

This is the standard efficiency condition. It is the single-market equivalent to the general equilibrium criteria referred to above.[2]

There are other concepts of efficiency that have been used by economists. At certain points in the argument, I refer to some of them. But the basic purpose of the paper is to explore the implications of these allocative efficiency conditions on the organization of economic activity. It is wholly concerned with analytical issues; I do not discuss empirical studies of efficiency in various sectors or countries. In Section 2, I consider the question of resource allocation in a Soviet-type economy; I discuss some of the reasons why traditional forms of central planning have led to inefficiency. Section 3 deals with the market economy; it explores the reasons why markets fail to achieve efficient outcomes. Section 4 contains a critique of the orthodox responses to the problem of market failure. The final section contains a brief summary of the argument.

2. Socialist planning and resource allocation

It is generally agreed that resources are allocated inefficiently in the Soviet-type economy (henceforth STE). Indeed, the desire to overcome this problem has been a major motive for reform in the USSR and Eastern Europe since 1956. I will not, therefore, spend a great deal of time describing the system's shortcomings. Rather, I will attempt to show how characteristic features of the planned economy relate to the concept of efficiency set out above.

In the STE, prices are not set to clear markets; this means that consumers cannot use price-income calculations as to how much of what to acquire. Access to goods may also depend upon status or privilege, upon luck or upon the expenditure of real resources (for example in queueing or through the employment of *tolkachi*). In such circumstances, it is difficult to know what might be meant by the marginal social benefit to be derived from an increase in the output of a commodity: it would depend upon who received it. Furthermore, prices in an STE do not reflect the marginal social (opportunity) cost of producing specific commodities. So, even if a particular 'market' clears, one cannot assume that the efficient level of output has been attained. Prices cannot be used to determine a rational pattern of production.

In theory, this need not matter. It is the plan, rather than enterprise responses to pseudo-market pressures that determines the structure of output.

In the past, Soviet economists have often implied that planners can determine efficient levels of output independently of financial information. Engineering data and reports submitted by enterprises provide them with a detailed knowledge of production possibilities; contact with the political leadership (and other sources of information about popular preferences) allow them to formulate social objectives. Together, this material allows the determination of efficient output plans formulated in physical terms.

Unfortunately, this whole argument is misconceived. First, the degree of complexity involved in the production possibility set of a modern industrial economy is such that it cannot be specified; or at least not in formal physical terms. Too much depends upon 'know-how' and so forth. More important, the whole 'success-indicator' issue shows that enterprise managers seek to conceal information about production possibilities from planners. As a result, the central authorities have an incomplete and inaccurate idea of what can be produced. They have even less idea of what consumers would like to purchase. Centrally specified output plans, conceived largely in physical terms, cannot claim to involve an efficient allocation of resources.

Resource allocation in STEs is inefficient in a wider sense. Economic welfare involves not only static efficiency, it is also concerned with growth over time. A major source of such growth is technological innovation: the discovery of new, improved ways of doing things - and their rapid dissemination through the economy. In the postwar period at least, STEs have been characterized by sluggish innovation. Various explanations have been suggested for this shortcoming. I have argued that it is a consequence of the incentives facing enterprise managers. It is not so much the absence of rewards accruing to the successful innovator that is important: it is the absence of penalties for those who do nothing. This is a consequence of the fact that plans inevitably assign consumers to suppliers, thus creating the conditions for a sort of sellers' market.[3]

Central planning and the pseudo-markets to be found in STEs result in the inefficient allocation of resources. Economists should therefore ask: can the introduction of market elements into an STE improve its efficiency?

This question is not new. It even formed a starting point for Oskar Lange's development of the theory of market socialism in the 1930s. The debates over *perestroika*, moreover, have conferred a new relevance on this idea of market socialism. Having identified the system of central planning as the major source of inefficiency, early proponents of reform sought to replace it with a so-called socialist market. Here, the bulk of enterprises would continue to be state-owned, but they would be required to interact through markets; the state would limit its participation in the economy to the issue of state orders, *goszakasy*.[4] Elements of this system were adopted in 1988. The subsequent history of the Soviet economy shows that the socialist market system driven by *goszakasy* failed to improve the efficiency of resource allocation. But it is still worth asking: was this inevitable on theoretical grounds, as Shatalin and others who favour the reintroduction of private property appear to argue? Or was the recent failure of the economy a consequence of other factors, primarily an irresponsible approach to macroeconomic policy?

As I point out below, the focus of neoclassical theory is market structure and not the identity of the owners of capital. Provided that the rules of the market-game are adhered to, whether enterprises are state-owned or private is irrelevant. But it is difficult for the state to impose market discipline on elements of itself; it may even be meaningless.

Inter alia, market discipline means that enterprises should face hard budget constraints; those which cannot cover costs at market determined prices should go bankrupt. This has the effect of converting (some of) the social losses which result from bad investment decisions into private losses. It thus acts as a spur to improved decision-making. If the enterprise is owned by the state, its losses are shared by all members of society; they remain social. "...[B]ankruptcy offers little in the way of incentives for better investment decisions." [5]

The STE is inefficient because it is unable to identify marginal social benefits; it is also incapable of identifying - and minimizing - marginal social costs. As I argue in the next section, marginal social benefit is normally equated with marginal social cost on a competitive market. This is the justification for advocating the introduction of the market. But the socialist market does not go far enough.

3. Resource allocation in a market economy

I now turn to the neoclassical view of market and efficiency. First I restate briefly two relevant properties of market equilibrium. I then go on to explore the ways in which markets can be said to fail. I will focus upon the case of a consumer good; the analysis can be extended to the behaviour of intermediate-good markets without too much difficulty.

The theory of consumer behaviour postulates utility maximization. It is relatively straightforward to show that this entails setting private marginal benefit, (mpb) the utility an individual derives from an additional unit of consumption, equal to price. If all consumers face the same price, there is a sense in which marginal private benefit is equated across individuals as well. Similarly, the theory of the firm assumes profit maximization. This implies that firms set private marginal cost, (mpc) the cost they incur in increasing output by one unit, equal to marginal revenue. If there is a sufficient number of firms in the industry or market, marginal revenue approximates to price; such markets are defined as competitive. Of course, where all firms face the same price, marginal cost is equated across producers. Thus, traditional economic theory claims that competitive markets ensure that

(2)   mpc=p=mpb.

This is the standard market equilibrium condition.

The preconditions for a competitive market are quite restrictive; it is doubtful whether any of the markets in a modern industrial economy satisfy them. It is therefore not clear how much assurance about the efficiency of a market economy can be derived from the above result. An argument due to Baumol suggests, however, that the result can be strengthened considerably. He has developed the concept of a contestable market: this need not contain a large number of firms; so long as there are no sunk costs and no legal barriers to entry, potential competition will ensure that price does not diverge from marginal cost. Thus, one can claim that not only competitive markets ensure that mpc=p=mpb; contestable markets do so as well.

We now have two results relating to allocative efficiency: from the Introduction there is the efficiency condition

(1)   msc=msb

and from the above discussion, there is the market equilibrium condition

(2)   mpc=p=mpb.

Now, it should be clear that if one can combine the two relations

(3)   msc=mpc=p=mpb=msb

one can demonstrate that markets are efficient. On the other hand, if one or more of the equalities in (3) do not hold, one can say that the market has failed. There are three basic types of market failure: monopoly, externality, and public goods. Each is associated with the failure of one of the equalities in (3). They are described in more detail below.

The simplest case in which the market can be said to fail is that in which there is monopoly or monopsony. Here, profit maximizers will set marginal private cost equal to marginal revenue (mpr) which will be less than price. Thus, we have

(4a)   msc=mpc=mpr<p=mpb=msb

in the case of monopoly. In such circumstances, the marginal social cost of producing the commodity falls short of the marginal social benefit derived from its consumption. Net social benefit cannot be at a maximum; the market has not produced an efficient allocation of resources.

Implicit in the discussion so far has been the assumption that the decision-maker alone derives the benefit from consumption, or bears the costs of production that follow from his decisions. If that is the case, then, other things being equal, the market allocation is efficient. In certain circumstances, however, the decisions of producers or consumers affect the well-being of third parties. Then

(5)   msc≠mpc or mpb≠msb

and one says that the market is distorted by externalities. In the presence of significant externalities, a market allocation is not efficient.

The classic example of an externality is that of the shoe-factory which emits smoke; the smoke soils the laundry that households living near the factory have hung out to dry. In deciding how many shoes to produce, the profit-maximizing factory owner ignores the additional laundry costs incurred by householders since he does not bear them. In equilibrium,

(5a)   msc>mpc=p=mpb

and the market allocation is inefficient. Not all externalities are detrimental. James Meade introduced the example of the beekeeper whose bees pollinate a fruitgrower's apple trees while collecting nectar from his orchards. There are also examples of external benefits (and disbenefits) that accrue to consumers.

Welfare economists suggest that externalities of one sort or another are widespread. It is often possible to see ecological damage as a form of externality. And externalities are particularly prevalent in activities that have traditionally been undertaken in the public sector. Thus, for example, mass innoculation against disease confers a social benefit since it reduces the risk that others will be infected. Similarly, as well as increasing productivity, literacy is supposed to encourage social integration; the greater social stability that this produces is seen as an external benefit. Recognition of the importance of such external effects indeed helps to explain why activities like education or health care are often undertaken by the state in a market economy.

There are some goods whose consumption by one individual does not affect their availability to other potential consumers. Such goods are defined as public goods. An example of a public good is street lighting. If such lighting is supplied, the same quantity is available to all; also, the fact that one individual derives benefit does not reduce the benefit that others might derive. One can show that, technically, the market equilibrium condition p=mpb does not hold for public goods. This is another example of market failure. There are certain other circumstances, for example involving uncertainty and asymmetric information, where the efficiency of markets can be questioned. But they will not be discussed at any length in this paper.

Market failure creates a *prima facie* case for intervention, and much of applied welfare economics is concerned with analyses of how this might be achieved. In the next few paragraphs I provide a brief summary of approaches that have been most favoured by neoclassical economists - and frequently adopted by governments in market economies.

The first type of market failure to be discussed is monopoly. Here one should distinguish between so-called natural and other monopolies. A natural monopoly exists if the technology implies that average costs are still falling at the level of output demanded by the market. This means that there is room for only one firm in the industry. It also means that if the firm charged the efficient price (=mpc) it would make a loss. This follows since, if average costs are falling, marginal cost is less than average cost. The most common form of natural monopoly involves the distribution of a good or a service through a dedicated network: electricity supply, for example or, traditionally, the telephone system. Other monopolies exist if firms have managed to erect legal or other barriers to entry.

The most common approach to non-natural monopolies has been legislative control. Anti-trust law has attempted to prevent the formation of monopolies, and the courts have sometimes forced the break-up or disvestment of conglomerate firms. Anti-trust policy has been pursued more vigorously in America than in Japan or Europe; and in the USA, it has been pursued more vigorously at some times than at others. As far as natural monopolies are concerned, in America the tendency has been to leave them in private hands, but to set up a regulatory body to ensure that they do not exploit their monopoly power excessively. In Europe, or at least in Britain, natural monopolies were more likely to be nationalized - and instructed to price in the public interest.

Pigou's analysis of externalities suggested that governments could use taxes and subsidies to bring private costs or benefits into line with their social equivalent. This may be done in some instances. More usually, the state attempts to limit the impact of external effects through regulation; for example, using planning controls or zoning laws to separate industrial and residential land use. There is no reason to assume that such an approach improves allocative efficiency.

Alternatively, attempts can be made to 'internalize' the externality, that is, to make decision-takers take account of the 'external' consequences of their decisions. One way to do this is to create new property rights, for example to clean air, and allow these rights to be traded. Or, externalities can be internalized by expanding the boundaries of the decision-making unit; for instance, in Meade's example, there would be no externality if the beekeeper owned (or managed) the orchard. It is sometimes claimed that nationalization allows the internalization of externalities.

For most public goods, there is no alternative to public provision. The major exception to this is broadcasting. Broadcasting is a public good because, once a signal is provided, the marginal cost of its reception by another listener/viewer is zero. Hence, (3) implies

(6) $$msc=mpc=p=0.$$

This is *one* justification for public service broadcasting organizations like the BBC. In the USA, however, broadcasting is a by-product of commercial advertising. This is increasingly true in other countries, including Britain. There is no guarantee that the amount (and variety) of programmes produced in this way is efficient. Where cable and satellite distribution are concerned, (6) asserts that they are inefficient.

The discussion of the last few paragraphs has shown that when faced with market failure, neoclassical economists have often suggested that the state should assume responsibility for the provision of particular goods and services. Or at least, the state should regulate the behaviour of private producers. In many cases, this advice has been followed. These analyses assume, however, that the state (and its agencies) can work costlessly - and unproblematically - in the public interest. This assumption has been challenged in recent years and this challenge has provided part of the impetus for the wave of privatization that the world has witnessed in the past decade or so. The nature of the arguments that have been put forward are discussed in the next section.

Before turning to the problem of state failure, however, there is one other comment that I would like to make about the industrial policy proposals I have been discussing. The focus of analysis in this paper is the individual market, but it is worth making one comment about the general equilibrium implications of market failure. It is implicit in the definition of efficiency that (3) should hold for each good. If, due to monopoly or the presence of an externality, (3) does not hold in any one market, there is no reason to assert that net social benefit will be maximized by satisfying (3) in remaining markets. This is known as the general theorem of the second best.[6] It undermines claims for the effectiveness of piecemeal industrial policy.

4. The state as economic agent

The conception of the state that emerges from neoclassical economic theory is somewhat contradictory. On the one hand, theorists are clear that socialism will not achieve an efficient allocation of resources; on the other, they assume that the state or its agencies will operate efficiently when private enterprise fails. Until the 1950s or 1960s, however, this belief in the efficacy of the state was not accompanied by the development of a positive theory of state enterprise. Instead, economists concentrated on the articulation of such things as pricing rules. There has been a change in the last thirty years or so; some analysts have recognised that public enterprises and the state itself are economic agents. They have attempted to produce a positive theory to describe how they function, how they interact with each other and with private enterprises. As a result, it is possible to formulate - and even to answer - questions about the efficiency of resource allocation in the state sector. It is possible to talk about state failure as a parallel concept to market failure.[7]

I cannot hope to summarize all of this literature in a short paper; but a convenient discussion can be found in McLean.[8] What follows in this section are no more than comments on some of these topics. They are organized around nationalization and regulation - the two alternative forms proposed for response to market failure.

Nationalization has been proposed in the first instance as a solution to the problem of natural monopoly. The word can also be used to describe the public supply of services like education or medical care. The remarks which follow do not really apply to this second usage.

In most countries, nationalized firms are set up with a requirement to operate in the public interest. It is usually assumed that it is obvious what that is: it involves efficiency; it will also often include some element of equity in the distribution of benefits. As I pointed out above, one requirement for the efficient allocation of resources is mpc=p. In much of the neoclassical literature on market failure, it is assumed that all that is required is for public enterprises to be instructed to adopt the above criterion as a pricing rule and the problem is solved.

Unfortunately, things are not so simple; the difficulties associated with this 'solution' can be discussed under the three headings used in the analysis of the shortcomings of Soviet-style planning: information, incentives, and ideology. In economic theory, the concept of marginal cost is straightforward. In practice, undertakings like British Rail (the nationalized railway undertaking in Britain) have had a great deal of difficulty in determining the relevant time-period - and hence which elements of cost should be included - for its calculation. Similar problems have arisen in other cases. It has not been possible to agree on and implement appropriate behavioural rules to guide managerial behaviour.

The question of managerial information is tied up with that of incentives.

Economists have come to recognize that managers of public enterprises may have personal objectives that conflict with the public interest as defined above. If so, one is faced with a so-called principal-agent problem. It has proved difficult to structure incentives and to maintain supervision so as to ensure that the government's objectives are pursued. It is for this reason that some politicians argue in favour of privatization: they believe that private shareholders can and will exercise much closer supervision over management than civil servants; as a result, enterprises are more likely to be operated efficiently.

There is some confusion in this argument. For most of those who propound it, efficiency appears to be understood as technical efficiency. This can be thought of as the factors which determine the location of the isoquants of the production function or the cost curves that are derived from it. And it may be true that shareholders are better than civil servants or politicians at restricting management's discretion, at limiting their ability to convert monopoly power into on-the-job consumption or a quiet life. But it is not the case that managers supervised by shareholders will avoid exploiting their monopoly power. Implicitly, then, the argument contains an empirical assertion: that the losses from technical inefficiency suffered by public enterprises are greater than the gains from improved allocative efficiency. As far as I am aware, there have been no attempts to measure these gains and losses in any actual country, so the assertion remains unproven. But, insofar as technical inefficiency in public enterprises can be equated with what Leibenstein has called X-inefficiency[9], it possesses a certain plausibility.

In fact, the so-called principal-agent problem has been more complex than that suggested above. In Britain at least, it has proved difficult to prevent politicians from interfering in managerial decisions when politically sensitive issues have arisen. There has been a tendency to substitute the *government's* interest for that of the public. In France, the system appears to have worked more successfully in this respect. There has also been a tendency, however, in both countries, to use the public sector for demand management purposes.

As I pointed out above, the American response to natural monopoly has favoured regulation over nationalization. It is possible to argue that this is an improvement over the nationalization solution, since private shareholders ensure that the enterprises operate in a technically efficient manner while the regulators ensure that outcomes are not too far from what is prescribed by allocative efficiency. First, this was not the reason why Americans chose the regulation solution: that choice appears to have been dictated more by ideology than analysis. Further, regulation itself is not without its problems - problems that are scarcely addressed in standard analyses of the issue.

At the risk of some oversimplification, it is possible to argue that American regulators have attempted to restrain firms' attempts to earn monopoly profits by imposing a ceiling on the rate of return they were allowed to earn. From the point of view of allocative efficiency, this has two unfortunate consequences: first, it provides no incentive towards the adoption of public-interest pricing policies; second, it contains a positive incentive towards the adoption of excessively capital-intensive technologies. This is known as the Averch-Johnson effect.[10] To avoid this, regulators of recently privatised monopolies in Britain have adopted an explicit (RPI-x) pricing rule; but as far as I can see, this has little theoretical justification.[11]

A second problem with this approach is known as 'regulatory capture'. The regulation of any industry requires knowledge of the production processes involved. On the one hand, this knowledge is most likely to be found among those who have worked in the industry; on the other, once acquired, it is an asset of value to the industry. There is therefore likely to be a fair amount of mobility between employment in the industry and in the regulatory authority. There is a tendency, consequently, for regulatory agencies to become advocates of industry interests, to develop into pressure groups. There is even the possibility that civil servants may be suborned by the promise of subsequent employment. The US experience suggests that this is a significant problem.

This analysis suggests that there are social costs associated with the operation of the state - either as an economic agent or as a regulator of the economic activity of other agents. It is thus possible that the social cost/welfare loss associated with attempts to correct a market failure may exceed to cost/loss associated with the failure itself. The cure is worse than the disease! Ultimately, whether this is the case or not in any particular instance is an empirical question; but much of the analysis provided by neo-Austrians and others can be seen as an attempt to suggest *prima facie* reasons why this might often be the case.[12]

Neo-Austrians like Hayek or Littlechild argue that neoclassical theory fails to identify the factors that make a market economy successful, that guarantee efficiency as it is commonly understood at any point in time, and that ensure innovation and growth. They suggest that the focus upon equilibrium and market structure is misplaced. Progress, and hence improvements in popular welfare, are achieved as a result of rivalry between suppliers. Such 'competition' can be intense even between two firms; it will lead to the identification of new and better ways of satisfying consumer demand. The insistence on large numbers of firms is an irrelevance. This analysis emphasizes what I have called technical efficiency and the incentive to innovate as the primary objectives of industrial policy. It implies that the welfare losses associated with duopoly or oligopoly are not very large. It thus goes back to Leibenstein's claims. It also contains echoes of Schumpeter's theory of growth.

In this section, I have concentrated on recent thinking about the shortcomings of traditional solutions to the problem of natural monopoly. Doubts have also been expressed about the effectiveness of state intervention as a way of correcting the distortions caused by externalities. Again, one strand in the argument has been that the inefficiencies introduced as a result of public provision often result in greater welfare losses than the original externalities.[13] Unfortunately, there is no space to discuss these issues here.

5. Conclusion

In Section 2 it was argued that the centrally planned economy fails to secure an efficient allocation of resources. It has also failed to ensure a rapid rate of innovation - and the improvements in welfare that this generates. It was suggested that this failure was due primarily to the absence of functioning markets. It is also possible that the absence of private property in the means of production contributed to the failure of Soviet-type economies to perform effectively.

In Section 3, I argued that in general, a market economy will ensure that resources are allocated efficiently - provided markets are competitive or at least contestable. But markets will fail in the presence of monopoly or monopsony, or if there are externalities. It is also impossible to organize markets for public goods. When markets fail, neoclassical economists have tended to assume that the state can correct failures costlessly. This provides the theoretical basis for the so-called mixed economy.

This assumption is most unrealistic and, in the last thirty years or so, it has been challenged. Some of the arguments relating to the state as an economic agent were given in Section 4. It was suggested that nationalized enterprises will not necessarily operate in the public interest. It was also pointed out that *regulation* may introduce separate or additional biases which undermine allocative efficiency; in any case it will involve costs. It is thus possible that the welfare losses associated with policies designed to correct for market failure will exceed those of the initial failure. Whether this is true in particular instances is an empirical matter; no attempt has been made to review existing comparative studies of economic performance to see how often this is the case. Rather, I referred to the arguments of neo-Austrian theorists which suggest that this is likely on a priori grounds.

If this analysis is accepted, what lessons does it hold for the privatization of planned economies? I think that there are three. First, reform in Soviet-type economies should aim at creating contestable markets. Structure is more important than ownership *per se*; little will be gained if public enterprises are replaced by private monopolies. Second, reformers should be aware of the possibility of market failure - and the costs that this may impose. They should be prepared to retain particular enterprises or industries under public control. Third, they should also be aware of the possible social costs of correcting for such market failure. It is always possible that the welfare losses associated with public ownership or intervention exceed those due to the original market failure. A cautious attitude to intervention should be adopted.

Notes

1   Bator, 1957.
2   Legrand and Robinson, 1976, ch. 1.
3   McAuley, 1985.
4   Aganbegyan, 1988.
5   Brada, 1990, p.15.
6   For more details, see Lipsey and Lancaster, 1956.
7   Jänicke, 1990.
8   McLean, 1987.
9   Leibenstein, 1966.
10 Averch and Johnson, 1962.
11 Waterson, 1988, ch. 5.
12 Littlechild, 1986; Tullock, 1988, ch. 7.
13 Barr, 1987, chs 12-13.

Bibliography

Aganbegyan, A. (1988), *The Challenge: The Economics of Perestroika*, London: Hutchinson.

Averch, H., Johnson, L. L. (1962), 'Behaviour of the Firm under Regulatory Constraint', *American Economic Review*, vol. 52, pp. 1053-69.

Bator, F. (1957), 'The Simple Analytics of Welfare Maximization', *American Economic Review*, vol. 47, no. 1, pp. 22-59.

Barr, N. (1987), *The Economics of the Welfare State*, London: Weidenfeld and Nicholson.

Brada, J. (1990), 'The Comparative Economics of Bankruptcy: Dealing with Loss-Making Firms in Socialist and Labor-Managed Economies', mimeo, Arizona State University.

Jänicke, M. (1990), *State Failure: the Impotence of Politics in Industrial Society*, Cambridge: Polity Press.

Legrand, J., Robinson, R. (1976), *The Economics of Social Problems*, Macmillan.

Leibenstein, H. (1966), 'Allocative Efficiency vs "X-Efficiency"', *American Economic Review*, vol. 56, no. 2, pp.393-415.

Lipsey, R., Lancaster, K. (1956), 'The General Theory of the Second Best', *Review of Economic Studies*, vol. 24, no. 63, pp. 11-32.

Littlechild, S. (1986), *Economic Regulation of Privatized Water Authorities*, London: HMSO (for the Department of the Environment).

McAuley, A. (1985), 'Central Planning, Market Socialism and Rapid Innovation', in Schaffer, M. (ed.), *Technology Transfer and East-West Relations*, London: Croom Helm, pp. 32-49.

McLean, I. (1987), *Public Choice: An Introduction*, Oxford: Basil Blackwell.

Tullock, G. (1988), *Wealth, Poverty and Politics*, Oxford: Basil Blackwell.

Waterson, M. (1988), *Regulation of the Firm and Natural Monopoly*, Oxford: Basil Blackwell.

PART II

PRIVATIZATION AND ECONOMIC TRANSITION TO A MARKET ECONOMY

Mass privatization proposals in Eastern Europe: ownership and the structure of control*

Roman Frydman and Andrzej Rapaczynski

1. Introduction

Transition to a market economy in Eastern Europe must accept the challenge of divesting the state of its control over the productive resources of society, instituting a real system of property relations, and setting up the corporate governance structure characteristic of the developed market economies. The linch-pin of these processes is privatization, understood here not as the simple transfer of title from the state to private individuals, but as a complex process of institutional transformation designed to fill the void left by the state's withdrawal from active management of the economy.

1.1. *Reestablishing a regime of ownership and control*

An immediate impediment to the transition process is the absence of a genuine property system governing the productive activities of the socialist economies of Eastern Europe; even the concept of genuine *state* property is missing. A 'command economy' which eschewed market mechanisms replaced most property-related arrangements with an administrative system which relied on the state's direct control over the behaviour of each economic agent. Most decisions were thus made through the political system, with factory personnel playing the role of state functionaries. Consequently, in all East European countries, it is often impossible to answer the simple question of who owns what in the state enterprises: the legal determination of ownership was simply irrelevant under the old order.

Given this absence of an effective property system, privatization cannot be viewed simply as a transfer of title. What Eastern Europe lacks is a system of corporate governance in which property matters. Indeed, without transforming the whole institutional setting of Eastern Europe, and without creating the social and economic regime under which private property operates in the developed countries, any mere transfer of title will remain largely ineffectual.

From a technical point of view, the transformation of the East European economies therefore involves two distinct problems: the mechanics of state withdrawal, and the creation of institutional arrangements (in particular the new corporate governance structure) to replace bureaucratic governance by the state.

1.2. Sales

The obstacle in the way of state withdrawal is the need to find and to empower new owners of hitherto state enterprises. The initial instinct of East European policy-makers and their Western advisers was to follow well-known precedents, such as British-style privatizations involving a sale of shares to the public or to a selected number of private investors. In the highly developed Western European countries, however, privatization has had an entirely different significance from that of the process embarked upon in Eastern Europe: the Western European countries did not restructure their economies, but merely transferred the ownership of a few state-owned enterprises which were operating in a fundamentally market environment dominated by private property. Thus, already prior to their privatization, state enterprises often had to compete with private companies, and their system of governance and management (even if this was often less efficient than its private counterpart) was basically a product of the surrounding capitalist business culture. As a preliminary step, some measure of subsidy and reform could easily restore loss-making state enterprises to profitability. The sale transaction itself was also a relatively easy matter. In a full market economy, in which most of the industry is in private hands, in which there exists a developed stock market, and in which all enterprises use modern accounting methods, the sale of a state enterprise does not differ very much (except perhaps in scope) from the process whereby a closely held corporation is sold privately or 'goes public' by issuing shares to investors at large. Also, a number of investment firms with great experience in such matters are usually at hand to offer the necessary assistance.

This simple description of privatization in the West is enough to demonstrate that it cannot serve as a dominant model for Eastern Europe, where capital markets still do not exist and the structure itself of the market economy has to be introduced precisely through the process of privatization. The very idea that the East European states could rapidly prepare a large number of companies for traditional privatizations is not to be taken seriously: even in the West, the process takes many years for each company, and the East European states are by no means equipped, financially or otherwise, to deal with the complicated process involved.

The first obstacle to sale in Eastern Europe is the problem of valuation. In the West, the approximate price of the shares of the companies to be privatized can be established with some degree of reliability by using standard accounting methods. In the context of Eastern Europe, however, where those few market mechanisms that do exist are very thin and where financial markets simply do not exist at all, the necessity for valuation is a tremendous obstacle to the traditional mode of privatization. Moreover, even in the advanced market economies, valuation is extremely costly and time-consuming, and the Eastern European countries face the task of privatizing thousands of state enterprises within a small number of years.

To complicate matters, the potential domestic market for the shares of privatized companies is extremely small: according to one calculation (which is not out of line with the others), if every person in Poland was prepared to spend 20-30 per cent of all his or her savings to buy the shares of the privatized enterprises, the amount of money available for the purchase of the state companies would come to between 2.4 and 3.6 per cent of their book value! This means that if purchases by foreigners are left aside for the moment, the privatization of a large segment of the Eastern European economies through so-called sales would in fact be simply a form of giveaway which would increase the existing inequalities by a factor of several scores. And given the fact that the wealth differences in Eastern Europe are perceived by society not as a legitimate reward for thrift or for industriousness, but as spoils distributed by the old regime to its loyalists, the giveaway would provoke enormous political difficulties for the new authorities.

Finally, the practical and political problems would be just as serious (if not more so) if the state were to contemplate selling a very large proportion of the economy to foreign investors. To begin with, despite lively Western interest in the transformation of Eastern Europe, the amounts of foreign capital available for investment in the region have so far been rather modest. Furthermore, given the uncertainty about the viability of East European economies and political stability in the area, the discounts applied to the shares of the privatized enterprises might be extremely high, and the prices fetched by most of them very low. Sales at these prices might, in turn, provoke a strongly xenophobic reaction in the nationalistic climate of Eastern Europe. Thus, while foreign entry in some form is a prerequisite for successful transformation, it is unlikely to be accomplished by the wholesale sell-out of the East European economies.

1.3. *Giveaways*

All this is not to imply, however, that traditional privatizations, especially if suitably adapted to East European conditions, have no role to play. Nevertheless, it is clear to most commentators at this stage that, apart from a small number of enterprises, large-scale privatization cannot be accomplished through sales. Instead, in order to extricate the state from the day-to-day running of the East European economies, and to do so before these economies collapse, a very large number of state enterprises must simply be given away in one form or another. Among the giveaway schemes most often mentioned are plans to hand a part of the privatized enterprises over to the workers employed in them, to distribute vouchers to all citizens which entitle them to purchase (directly or indirectly) the shares of privatized enterprises, or to give citizens shares in special investment funds which would in turn be invested in the former state enterprises.

However, finding new owners for the privatized companies is only the first step. After all, a mere transfer of title will not improve the performance of the huge post-communist enterprises: they must be fundamentally restructured. This in turn involves setting up a whole new institutional environment comprising an effective system of corporate governance.

In the few cases where the state is able to find a large (usually foreign) investor willing to buy outright a state enterprise, or to take a very large stake in it and to play the role of an active owner, the control problem is solved together with the transfer of ownership. But, as we have noted, these cases are very rare, and the number of East European enterprises for which a 'core investor' has been found is still extremely small. In all other cases, whether the shares are sold through a public offering or whether they are given away to a large number of beneficiaries, ownership is certain to be very fragmented and the new shareholders extremely unlikely to exert any influence on the way in which the enterprise is run. Thus, if nothing else happens, privatization is unlikely to have a significant effect on the restructuring of the economy.

To remedy this state of affairs, many mass privatization proposals involving free (or largely free) distribution of ownership to a large number of beneficiaries (such as the citizenry at large) also envisage a corporate governance issue which concentrates control over the privatized enterprises in the hands of special intermediary financial institutions. Schemes of this kind are now being prepared in Poland, Czechoslovakia, and Romania. Given the slow progress of conventional privatizations in Hungary, it may be only a matter of time before similar solutions are adopted there as well.

In most privatization proposals of this kind, the intermediary institutions function as holding companies or mutual funds, although some plans foresee a role for pension funds and other institutional investors. The intermediaries are often expected to involve an essential foreign component, commonly under a management contract where the newly created funds are awarded to a foreign financial institution. These proposals usually envisage the conversion of state enterprises into joint-stock companies, with the intermediaries as the legal owners of a large portion of their shares (some plans set aside a block of shares in the privatized enterprises for the state to distribute a portion of the shares directly to the population). Following privatization, the intermediaries would appoint the boards of directors of the privatized companies and exercise a degree of supervision over their management. The shares of the intermediaries themselves will in turn be owned by individuals who will acquire them free of charge or for a nominal fee. The use of vouchers is often contemplated, either to allow the individuals to choose the intermediary of which they want to own a share, or to allow the intermediaries to choose the privatized companies for their portfolio.

Among the advantages of these kinds of privatization proposal (although there are significant differences among them) are the speed with which they can be implemented, the avoidance or lessening of the problems involved in the valuation of the enterprises, the legitimization of the privatization scheme by the distribution of the national wealth among the population - which will ensure a degree of equality - and, above all, the facilitation of the restructuring process by the institution of an effective mechanism for control of management performance. Other advantages are the possibility of the rapid development of a financial infrastructure and a link to outside sources of capital and expertise.

2. The main danger of mass privatization proposals

The intermediaries created during a mass privatization plan of the type considered here could become extremely powerful and influential institutions. Their power - like all power - could be easily abused, and it is important to take great care over the incentives offered to the fund managers in the still largely unknown environment of the future Eastern European economies.

The managers of the intermediaries must make a basic choice of strategy: whether to position their funds as primarily economic or as primarily political agents. The first strategy available to them is to prevail over their competitors in restructuring by enhancing the value of the privatized companies and by profiting from their expansion. The second strategy is to collude with the other funds, to divide the markets by mutual agreements, and to increase revenues by fixing prices, extracting rents from public officials, and entrenching a complex system of state subsidies. This latter alternative is the greatest danger posed by the mass privatization programmes.

All the mass privatization proposals involving intermediaries incur this danger. Competition and restructuring is an arduous process, and fraught with perils and uncertainties for the manager who undertakes it. Genuine restructuring will also mean that the fund will provoke considerable hostility from those who have been dislodged from their positions of influence and control. It is quite likely, therefore, than an alliance of disgruntled special interests will attempt to use whatever channels of political influence they may have at their disposal to produce a new wave of state interventionism in Eastern Europe. The ability of the fund managers to resist these political pressures may then be further limited by their foreign connections and by the xenophobic attitudes present in all East European societies. The charge of 'a sell-out to foreigners' may always destroy an intermediary's truly competitive strategy.

By contrast, becoming a monopolist and a rent-seeker is always an attractive proposition to a fund manager. Eastern Europe has a long tradition of government paternalism, and forty years of communism have only advanced it. In addition, there are innumerable ways in which fund managers can associate the government with their own performance and shift some responsibility for their own failures onto it. The intermediaries will have very considerable resources at their disposal and the quality of the governments supposed to regulate them will be rather low for a while. The funds may thus find it quite easy to capture the governmental agencies responsible for their regulation. Tariffs, subsidies, monopolies, and other evils would then not be long in coming. Once entrenched, a system of this kind may be very difficult to eradicate.

3. The governance of the intermediaries and their environment

There are many ways in which reformers may try to prevent the funds from degenerating into rent-seekers; indeed, most of the programmes address this issue in one way or another. Some of the main problems involved are the following.

3.1. *Internal governance*

The corporate governance structure of the intermediaries will play an important role in determining their behaviour. The intermediaries are likely to be organized as domestic companies in their countries of operation. Since the management of these companies will probably be foreign-dominated, the authorities may try to make the fund's manager responsible to a board of directors representing local interests. Unfortunately, the real owners of the intermediaries - their shareholders - cannot be expected to exercise their powers directly, since each fund might be owned by millions of people who will face insuperable collective action problems in trying to control the funds they own. Indeed, the very inability of the funds' owners to be actively involved in the monitoring their property is the reason for the intermediaries' existence in the first place.

3.1.1. *Boards of directors*. If the shareholders of the intermediaries cannot be expected to monitor their performance, it might be very difficult to find an appropriate substitute for them on the boards of directors of the funds. It would be very tempting for the reformers, for example, to advocate political appointments to the boards of directors of the intermediaries - which would mean a management more responsive to special interests than to the interests of the shareholders. The best corporate governance structure, in our opinion, is one that does not seek to ensure that the directors 'represent' anyone in a strict sense, but which gives them a personal stake in the monitoring of managerial performance. The idea of 'independent directors' used in the United States seems appropriate.

The role of the board of directors is also a matter of a more general concern. If the intermediaries are to be genuinely entrepreneurial, business-oriented institutions, their management - chosen because of its experience and foreign contacts - must be primarily responsible for the policies of the fund. The board of directors should be a reactive body, safeguarding the interests of the shareholders against managerial abuse. If, on the other hand, the board's role becomes more active with respect to policy formulation and interferes with what are essentially business decisions, it may well reduce the fund's effectiveness and inject into its objectives a number of special-interest aims, unrelated to the maximization of returns on investment.

3.1.2. *Compensation*. Designing the compensation structure of the intermediaries is another crucial aspect of the properly competitive character of their activities. While this component of the plan is extremely difficult to devise - especially in the absence of financial markets that would help determine the value of the assets under the intermediaries' managements (and thus also allow for a proper evaluation of their performance) - the tying, however imperfect, of the fund managers' compensation to their performance is, of course, a fundamental feature of every healthy incentive structure.[1] But it is also very important to determine the extent to which the state should regulate the fund managers' compensation. While it is quite clear that the state should regulate the compensation *structure* (so as to ensure a proper set of incentives), the regulation of the *size* of the compensation (say, by fixing it at a certain specific percentage of the funds' assets or at some other benchmark value) should, if possible, be left to the market. Not only will this increase competitive pressures, but it will also avoid significant mistakes. If the state sets the amount (rather than the type) of compensation, it will most probably fail to get the numbers 'right' so that only transfer earnings and no rents are included. But then if the state sets the amount of compensation too low, the appropriate actors will not enter; if the compensation is set too high, the funds will earn unnecessary superprofits (rents).

3.2. *The intermediaries and the state*

One of the surest ways of turning the intermediaries into essentially bureaucratic institutions is to associate their activities with those of the state, and to make them dependent on the state for their existence and functioning. The foreseeable effects of such an arrangement would be a dramatic reduction in the funds' readiness to take decisions on the basis of ordinary business principles, their reluctance to take risks, and above all their certainty that the state, closely identified with the intermediaries in the minds of the public, will be obliged to come to their aid if either they or the companies in which they have heavily invested ever find themselves in danger of going under.

3.2.1. Control of entry. The way that intermediaries are formed is one of the decisive factors in determining their relations with the state. If the funds are essentially the state's creation (as would be the case, for example, if it determined their number and composition), the state will also be associated with their success or failure from the very beginning. Knowing this, the funds may exploit the state's vulnerability and extract various types of concession by threatening to produce economic effects which the authorities would find difficult to defend. If, on the other hand, the entry of the intermediaries is essentially free (as would be the case, for example, if anyone satisfying some minimum conditions could create an intermediary), the degree of the association of the state with the particular funds in existence would be lessened, and so would be its vulnerability to rent-seeking behaviour by them.

3.2.2. Internal governance and portfolio. We have mentioned already that a prominent role played by the state in the internal governance of the intermediaries (in the appointment of their boards of directors, for example) is likely to increase the state's association with the intermediaries to the point that it becomes vulnerable to their opportunistic behaviour. Another way to make the state vulnerable to blackmail is to have it assume an active role in the allocation of the shares of privatized companies to the intermediaries. In this case, the funds may demand that the state subsidize their supervision of those companies that the intermediaries did not want in their portfolios but which they were forced to accept.[2]

3.2.3. Regulatory structure. Some regulatory system must exist to protect the shareholders from managerial overreaching and to control self-dealing, insider trading, and so forth. However, this same system might also place bureaucrats firmly in control and make the funds attend more to capturing the bureaucracy than to the restructuring process itself. An additional danger associated with intrusive regulation stems from the relatively low quality of the civil service in Eastern Europe. Although the new governments have started to replace the old personnel chosen on the basis of political reliability, the process is slow, and the new people are often rather inexperienced (especially when the required expertise involves familiarity with business methods). Consequently, it should come as no surprise that the civil service in Eastern Europe will need as much painstaking and time-consuming rebuilding as does industry and the service sector, and that the viability of the privatization proposals will very much depend on how much they presuppose in terms of the quality of government services. There are basically two ways in which such an 'economy' of government service could be accomplished.

First, to minimize bureaucratic interference, it might be safer to rely more on disclosure requirements than on complex approval procedures and outright prohibitions. Also, it might be better to structure the monitoring agencies as basically prosecutorial, with the courts serving as the ultimate enforcers, rather than creating powerful rule-making bodies, which could be more intrusive and easier to capture.

Second, while there can be no easy substitute for governmental regulation which provides a clear set of the 'rules of the game', the very idea of the intermediaries is to remove the state as much as soon as possible from managerial decisions, including, in the first instance, the management of the privatization process itself. Farming out state services is a rather popular concept these days, but 'privatizing privatization' is particularly important in the context of Eastern Europe.

3.2.4. *State ownership.* Many privatization proposals envisage the state's retention of a substantial portion of shares in privatized companies for budgetary and other reasons. But to the extent that the state continues to be a serious player as part-owner of the companies in the intermediaries' portfolios, political behaviour by the funds remains a dangerously attractive option.

3.3. *Relation to the small investor*

The main question regarding the relation between the intermediaries and small investors is whether the latter will be able to choose the intermediaries in which to invest, or whether they will simply receive a certain number of shares in the intermediaries allocated to them automatically.

3.3.1. *Consumer choice and free entry.* There are some advantages to not giving the beneficiaries, at least initially, the right to choose the intermediaries in which they are to become shareholders. The reasons for these restrictions are always the same: administrative simplicity (which eliminates many of the transaction costs involved in other solutions) and the informal barriers facing small investors, which would limit their ability to avail themselves of the benefits deriving from the choice unavailable to them.

A decision to restrict consumer choice in these matters, however, also incurs very serious costs, since the curtailment of consumer choice restricts the free entry of the intermediaries and an important element in their mutual competitiveness.

The only practical way to ensure the free entry of the intermediaries (subject, of course, to the fulfilment of some minimum qualification requirements) is to distribute privatization vouchers to the population and to have the funds compete for those vouchers (which they would later use to acquire the shares of the privatized enterprises). If the consumer cannot choose which intermediaries to 'invest' in, however, the entry of the intermediaries will have to depend on a decision taken by the state. But this, in turn, will render the state seemingly responsible for allowing some institutions to enter; and such certification might make it very difficult for the state to avoid being blamed if some of the funds fail to perform well in the future. Awareness of this might induce the state to be more intrusive in its regulation of the funds, and fund managers to rely on subsidies rather than on entrepreneurial success.

3.3.2. *Limiting the class of beneficiaries.* Given the importance of the free entry precluded by an administrative allocation of shares in intermediaries to the population, it might be better to look for other ways to cut down on the transaction costs involved in the allocation. The best approach might be to set some sort of restriction on the number of beneficiaries (as is planned in the Czechoslovakian version of this programme) by having the recipients pay a relatively small amount of money for the vouchers to be distributed. (The size of the payment could be adjusted to arrive at the 'right' number of fund shareholders.) As well as cutting down transaction costs, this solution might also lead to a much higher level of interest among shareholders in the performance of the funds, a greater amount of information, and even - at some time in the future - a concentration of holdings sufficient to induce more active shareholder involvement in the governance of the funds. Finally, the smaller number of shareholders (each of whom would invest in a fund of his or her choosing) would enable each fund to develop more extensive relations with its shareholders through, for example, the provision of other financial and banking services (which could help to develop a badly-needed modern banking sector).[3]

3.4. *Relation to privatized companies*

The most important issue under this heading concerns how the intermediaries will acquire shares in the companies to be privatized. There are basically three possibilities. Some proposals envisage a *mechanical* allocation giving each intermediary an equal number of shares in each company to be privatized. Other plans foresee an *administrative* allocation, involving a division of all the privatized companies into several groups of 'roughly equal value'[4] and allocating each group (perhaps at random) to one fund. Yet other proposals envisage a specially designed *auction* as the allocative mechanism, with the intermediaries bidding for shares in the privatized companies using vouchers or investment points.

The choice of the appropriate allocation method is perhaps the decisive factor in this kind of mass privatization scheme; and we believe that only a competitive bidding process like an auction can save the programme from bureaucratic degeneration.

3.4.1. *Matching of skills.* The auction method offers many advantages as an allocative mechanism. First, the potential managers of the intermediaries will probably possess varying skills: some may specialize in certain types of companies, others may have particular foreign business contacts, still others may be good at liquidating businesses and selling their assets. Each manager would thus want to influence the choice of the companies to be included in his fund's portfolio and the extent of the fund's investment in any particular company - which would be impossible if shares were mechanically allocated. By allowing such preferences to be reflected in the ultimate allocation, the auction would match the skills of the individual fund managers to the needs of the economy.

3.4.2. *Informational advantage: valuation.* Unlike the other allocative mechanisms, an auction would force the managers of the intermediaries to invest seriously in research into the companies to be privatized. If a list of these companies is announced a few months before the auction, all the fund managers will know that their future success depends to a large extent on the wisdom of their initial assessments. They will therefore try to discover as much as they can about the enterprises, particularly those which offer some competitive advantage. As a result, as a necessary precondition for genuine restructuring, the preparation of plans with the help of which the privatized enterprises may be turned around will begin in earnest as soon as the auction is announced.

3.4.3. *Governmental use of information.* The results of this competitive process of information-gathering by the private sector will also be available to the government. Unlike the endless valuations commissioned by the East European states in their efforts to sell some of their enterprises, in this case the research will be conducted by businessmen and entrepreneurs who will back their estimates with investment decisions.[5] Although no valuations of post-communist enterprises can be entirely reliable (the level of uncertainty being simply too high), these entrepreneurial estimates are probably the best available.

From the government's point of view, the most important item of information to be gained from the auction will be the number of enterprises that fund managers believe to have no potential for recovery.[6] This will provide the government with a relatively good and rapid estimate of the amount of worthless capital stock in the state sector. This is important information because it enables the government to take appropriate decisions as to the final disposition of non-viable state enterprises, without risking an unexpected shock wave of plant closures and unemployment, and without compromising the restructuring of enterprises with potential.

The perverse evolution of the planned economy blocked the weeding out of non-viable enterprises and contributed to the creation of enterprises that had no *raison d'être* from the very start. The natural temptation of East European policy-makers (and, surprisingly enough, many Western analysts as well) is to ensure that the state does not wind up bereft of all valuable enterprises and with only the worthless scrap of the communist inheritance on its hands. A mechanical or administrative allocation of shares among the intermediaries would prevent this from happening by forcing the intermediaries to accept the weakest enterprises along with the strongest. The effect of this tempting move, however, may turn out to be unexpectedly harmful.

Since a large part of the country's capital stock may be non-viable, the rapid exposure of a large number of enterprises to the rigours of the hard budget constraint and a truly competitive environment may result in a spate of bankruptcies, leading to a sharp fall in production and skyrocketing unemployment. This, in turn, may destabilize the political situation and endanger the whole reform process. One of the main problems with schemes for rapid privatization, therefore, is that the government is ignorant of the real state of the capital stock and hence cannot know in advance whether its very effectiveness in moving the country into a market environment will not induce this devastating avalanche effect.

Suppose, then, that by using an administrative or mechanical allocation scheme, the government forces the intermediaries to take on an unknown number of non-viable enterprises together with the good ones. In this scenario, if the intermediaries are free to behave as ordinary owners of capital, they will simply allow the non-viable companies to fail. If, on the other hand, the government wants to avoid mass failures, it will have to impose a regulatory regime that will most probably destroy the effectiveness of the intermediaries as agents of genuine restructuring. By providing subsidies, for instance, the state will signal to the intermediaries that the safest source of income lies, not in the strenuous task of restructuring, but in extracting ever greater amounts of money from the state coffers. The state will thus be open to the opportunism of the financial institutions.

This outcome may be avoided, however, if the privatized enterprises are allocated to the intermediaries by auction, since a competitive bidding procedure will reveal the extent of capital stock problems in advance of irrevocable decisions, and allow the state to determine how it can control the resulting dislocations.[7]

3.5. *The relation to other financial institutions*

The future of the intermediaries will depend largely on the regulatory environment in which they are to operate. An important element in this framework is the relation between the intermediaries and other financial institutions, especially banks and investment banks. On the one hand, the American and British models can be followed so that fiduciary institutions, like mutual funds, are restricted by law from engaging in the provision of other financial services, presumably on the hypothesis that the resulting conflicts of interest would lead to abuses of the fiduciary duties due to their shareholders. At the other end of the spectrum is the possibility of adopting the German model where banks supervise companies on their own behalf and also for their trust account clients, in the process also lending money to the companies under their control and providing a range of other services, such as merchant and investment banking or insurance.

An important component in the regulation of financial intermediaries in Eastern Europe will be the determination of their degree of separation from other types of financial institutions. It is clear that the less separation is imposed, the greater the potential for conflicts of interest and political abuses of power by the intermediaries. On the other hand, one of the greatest short-comings of the Eastern European economies is their lack of a modern banking system, as well as other types of modern financial institutions. Moreover, setting up the infrastructure of an intermediary - involving, as it does, the establishment of local branches, the opening of accounts for individual beneficiaries, and so on - is not unlike setting up the infrastructure for a standard bank. And the absence of restrictions on the provision of banking services by the intermediaries may greatly facilitate the establishment of a modern banking system. It may also help the privatized enterprises to obtain finance for their operations. Similarly, the absence of stringent restrictions on combining the fiduciary services of the intermediaries with merchant and investment banking services may turn the intermediaries into very flexible sources of funds for privatized enterprises - by making the excess funds from some companies available to the others in the same intermediaries' portfolio, channelling available domestic savings into investments, or arranging financing from abroad. These services may be particularly important if the intermediaries are linked to Western financial institutions, since they could then provide a transmission belt for foreign banking expertise, and open a window to Western sources of financing.

3.6. *Relation to foreign financial institutions*

Most commentators stress that it is crucially important to induce the inflow of foreign capital and expertise into Eastern Europe. For a number of reasons, however, the entry of foreigners in their capacity as investors raises serious political problems, while their entry as advisers is of very little use.

We believe that the entry of foreign financial institutions in order to set up and run the intermediaries in the privatization programme is particularly appropriate. First, foreign expertise is most needed for the establishment of the infrastructure of a modern capitalist economy, an area where the East Europeans have practically no experience at all. Second, this infrastructure is especially important because its presence liberates market forces and sets off a chain reaction of growth and development. Third, most foreigners will enter, not as buyers of East European industry (although some part of their compensation may, and should, include stock options), but as managers of the funds working on behalf of the local owners of the underlying assets. Since their success would directly contribute to an increase in the value of equity in local hands, their presence might be more easily acceptable than in other contexts. Moreover, if the relations between the funds and their shareholders are structured in such a way that the capital under the intermediaries' management is directly proportional to the number of local citizens who have chosen that fund over others, the degree of foreign influence on the running of the local economy could be also seen as exactly proportional to its welcome by the local population.

4. Conclusions

The idea that markets arise spontaneously, in the absence of government intervention, is dear to many liberals. Our analysis is predicated on the argument that irrespective of one's views on the emergence and functioning of the market economy, a rational structure of corporate governance will not arise 'spontaneously' in Eastern Europe. Thus, the failure to implement institutional reforms designed to impose a new structure of corporate governance on the state enterprises in Eastern Europe is likely to lead to their demise and to undermine the sustainability of market-oriented and democratic reforms. Although institutional reforms are fraught with significant dangers and uncertainties, there are a number of ways in which these dangers may be mitigated. The design of new institutions is the most challenging task faced by Eastern European reformers.

Notes

* We would like to thank Professor Targetti for his helpful comments and encouragement in the writing of this paper.
1 Having compensation in part depend on the value of the intermediaries' own shares may introduce a dose of competition for the clients on whose behalf the funds manage the privatized companies.
2 For further discussion see below.
3 For further discussion see below.
4 We place this phrase in quotation marks because we believe that the task of assigning (even rough) values to state enterprises before privatization is truly Herculean (or, perhaps, Sisyphean). The idea that anyone could do this for several hundred companies within a span of a few months appears to be entirely unrealistic.
5 Also, valuations will be simpler, since the prospective fund managers looking to purchase the shares of privatized enterprises with otherwise worthless vouchers will try to assess the enterprises' *relative* values (i.e. to rank them with respect to one another), rather than determine their monetary worth (where they have to be compared with all other potential investments).
6 If there is only one bidder for a given enterprise, a well-designed auction might give it to that bidder for free. Thus, if no one bids for an enterprise, this means that everyone thinks it has negative value.
7 Designing an auction to be used in this context is a very complex matter, which goes beyond the scope of the present paper. We have offered some suggestions in Frydman and Rapaczynski, 1992.

Bibliography

Frydman, R., Rapaczynski, A. (1992), 'Evolution and Design in the East European Transition', in Paganetto, L., Phelps, E. S. (eds.), *Privatization Processes in Eastern Europe: Theoretical Foundations and Empirical Results*, London: Macmillan.

Nationalization, privatization or socialization: the emergence of the social corporation

Branko Horvat

The idea of '(re)privatization' has become very fashionable in the former command economies and also in Yugoslavia - equally as fashionable as the idea of 'nationalization' after the Second World War. When fashions replace argument, scholars must become suspicious, and in the case of Yugoslavia the suspicion is doubled. Before the war the economy was privately owned, development was slow, and productivity low: precisely the causes of the social revolution of 1941-1945. After the war, the economy was nationalized, development was accelerated, and productivity raised so that Yugoslavia grew faster than other countries. Compared with the average of the South European countries, Yugoslavian per capita product was around 75 per cent in 1952 and reached 100 per cent in 1980. Since then the economy has been in crisis, and hence the cry has gone up for reprivatization. Let us examine the problem in detail.

1. An institutional analysis of ownership

Legal science has traditionally distinguished between private and public law. Since ownership represents a bundle of legally regulated rights, it will be useful to apply the same distinction to the ownership rights that determine the organization of various types of firms.

Private ownership:
1. Individual ownership - family firm.
2. Collective ownership - cooperative.
3. Split ownership - private corporation.

Public ownership:
4. State ownership.
5. Split ownership.

While the firm types enumerated above are pure types, both organizational forms and ownership types may be mixed. A partnership is a blend between a family firm (where the owner employs workers) and a cooperative (two or more partners). A public corporation is a blend between the state firm and corporate management. The state may own shares in a private corporation and private individuals may own shares in a social corporation. And so forth.

According to the classical definition, ownership rights consist of *ius utendi, fruendi et abutendi* (the right to use, benefit from and dispose of a thing). In family firms, cooperatives and state firms all three rights are undivided. The private and social corporation has a divided ownership where *usus fructus* belongs to the corporation and the right of disposal to the final owner.

In Western legal theory, a corporation is an entity separate from its shareholders. It engages in business contracts on its own behalf, not on behalf of the shareholders. The corporation owns the property (machines, buildings, land) and the shareholders own the corporation. Hence split ownership. The firm is the primary or the active owner, the shareholders are the secondary or passive owners. The shareholders can sell their shares or (in theory) appoint the board of directors, but they cannot interfere with management. The corporation is the representative form of the large firms that constitute the backbone of the modern economy.

The same considerations apply to the social corporation. The difference here is that the social corporation does not have a limited number of shareholders: in the pure ownership form the shareholders are all adult citizens. The second difference consists in the organization of management. The private corporation is hierarchically organized (management directives flow in only one direction, from the top down), the social corporation is a cooperative organization (the sand-glass arrangement of directives). In other words, the former is an undemocratic, barrack-type organization, the latter is a democratic organization. The former belongs to the society which knows only political democracy. The latter belongs to a society which adds economic democracy to political democracy and in this way represents a more developed political arrangement.

From system theory we know that more complex tasks require a differentiation of functions which, in economics, is reflected in the differentiation of institutions. Thus, ownership has been distinguished into two separate functions, primary and secondary, one active and one passive. As a result, the family firm evolved into a private corporation and the state firm into a social corporation. Empirical research in social psychology indicates that democratically organized groups are more effective than hierarchically organized ones.[1] Moreover, the trend in modern technology is towards team work, custom-made products and small establishments, which all foster self-management as a more efficient organizational form.

It may be of some interest to append a historical note. The joint-stock company appeared in Britain two centuries ago and met with public criticism and distrust. Hostility was so great that the necessary legislation was delayed for several decades. But the new business organization survived, thrived and proved to be more efficient that its competitors. It is now dominant in the modern economy. It derives its competitive advantage from three sources.

1. Unlike the family firm, it has no difficulty in delegating management power. When a family firm outgrows the size which allows the owner to manage and supervise the firm personally, it must be organized differently or cease to grow.
2. As a rule, the second generation of owners - occasionally already the first - is tempted to appoint members of the family to management positions regardless of their capabilities. In a joint-stock company, the selection of managers is more objective, and this, as empirical research has found, increases efficiency.
3. The growth of a family firm is limited by its internal accumulation. The corporation may issue shares and so accelerate its growth.

Similarly, the social corporation is more efficient than a state firm. The reasons are the following.

1. The management of a state firm is bound by bureaucratic rules which limit its initiative and adaptability. On the other hand, the social corporation is independent and self-supporting.
2. The state firm is subject to political control and mixes the business and political interests of the party in power. The social corporation is only concerned with the economic welfare of its employees and therefore tries to maximize its economic results.
3. In general, the social corporation can do anything that a private corporation and the state firm can do - and somewhat more.

There is yet another historical similarity. The development of the social corporation (labour-managed enterprise) began in Yugoslavia in 1952. Resistance (by the state) has been so strong that, after four decades, this new business form has yet to take final shape. The first law on the social corporation has only just been drafted, and it is not at all certain whether it will be passed by parliament.

2. The role of entrepreneurship

Modern economy is extremely complex, and efficient management requires a huge amount of firm-specific information. Therefore firms must enjoy independence in their decision-making; an independence which implies the market and the separation of ownership functions.

Economic efficiency also depends on motivations. An autonomous firm, one which can make profits but also suffer losses, provides more incentives than any of the feasible alternatives. Managers are stimulated by high salaries and status, and the same incentives may be provided for its employees: this is why profit (and loss) sharing is becoming increasingly popular. And there is also a clear trend towards involving employees in various managerial functions.

Ever since Schumpeter developed the idea, the role of the entrepreneur has been considered crucial to the efficient operation of a firm. An entrepreneur is a

man of creative ideas who engages in innovations. In conformity with the
system's differentiation of functions, he does not own capital (if he does, he is
also a capitalist). Consequently, entrepreneurship can only work if two
preconditions are fulfilled: opportunities for free economic initiative, and the
availability of capital for productive ideas. Clearly, entrepreneurship can also
be collective.

The fundamental precondition for all three elements of economic efficiency
is the political democracy that makes possible the state of law. A strict legal
framework renders the behaviour of economic agents predictable and
eliminates the arbitrariness so destructive of economic efficiency. Political
democracy also makes the autonomy of firms and free initiative possible.

It is now quite clear why the command economy collapsed and why this
was, in fact, predicted.[2] A lack of political democracy rendered the autonomy
of firms and free initiative impossible. Incentives were eliminated and replaced
by mass irresponsibility. Since the pervasive influence of the state in all social
affairs was also reflected in the state enterprises, these came to be considered
as inherently inefficient. And since the only known alternative was private
enterprises, reprivatization was assumed to be the panacea for all ills.

However, wholesale reprivatization is now as unjustified as wholesale
nationalization was forty-five years ago. What is needed is de-nationalization[3]
in general and the deregulation of economic activities in particular. The most
efficient ownership and organizational forms cannot be decreed; they can only
evolve in a free market in which all agents compete on equal terms. I expect
family-owned firms and partnerships to prove more efficient for small-scale
activities, while large firms will be organized as corporations. Natural
monopolies will continue to be regulated and production will be organized by
state firms.

3. Ownership transformation

There is general agreement that the East European command economies are less
efficient than their West European market counterparts. That this is a not
accidental but predictable fact has been analysed above. Disagreements arise,
however, over the ways and means of transforming the former into the latter.

Most frequently, reprivatization is suggested, only to find that it is
technically impossible to sell off the entire national capital at once. In England,
only two enterprises were denationalized, and even this took a decade to
achieve in an orderly way. In France, a hundred-odd firms were reprivatized,
generating a revenue of 70 billion francs for the Treasury, but also incurring
costs of 43 billion francs. Moreover, it was estimated that the shares sold to the
public were undervalued by 8-20 billion francs[4], the resulting capital gains
being pocketed by speculators. This transformation route is therefore neither
feasible nor very desirable. Clearly some establishments, particularly small
ones, will be sold to the private sector, but this is about all that would make
economic sense; and the government cannot count on any large stream of
revenues.

The next solution considered was to distribute shares to the workers and
thereby turn them into private owners. In this way, it was thought, 'ownership

incentives' would be created. This solution is unjust, however, and the expectations are unwarranted. Because of the extreme differences in capital intensity among different industries, workers would receive very different capital values, and those not employed by commercial establishments would receive none at all. Also, wherever in the world shares have been distributed to workers, after a short while the workers have sold them for cash. Attempts have therefore been made to compel workers by law to purchase shares by deducting their values from wages, a measure provoking a furious reaction from workers, and the threat by the trade unions to go on general strike. Besides, experiments in various parts of the world to turn workers into shareholders have brought no observable improvement in productivity.

Since direct privatization has not proved feasible, the conclusion generally reached is that all firms should be transformed into state enterprises and gradually sold to domestic and foreign private interests. This, however, entails saddling the economy with state management for many years to come - which is exactly the state of affairs that one wishes to avoid. If the state firms are efficient, there is no need for transformation. And if they are inefficient, which seems to be the case in the countries concerned, they will remain so. And for many years, until they are sold, the national economy will be operating at a low level of efficiency.

Thus reprivatization is either unfeasible or inefficient, or both, and a solution must be looked for elsewhere. My analysis in preceding sections indicates where. What must be done is to transform state firms into independent decision-makers, thus creating an environment for entrepreneurship. This implies that many firms already earning profits may be immediately transformed into self-managed corporations and left to regulation by the market. This will be particularly easy in Yugoslavia, where self-management and a market of sorts have been in existence since 1952, but it is also possible in other European countries, where it could be achieved without undue delay. Ownership must be transferred from state to social ownership, which is a formal legal operation involving no costs.

The rest of the economy should be handled as follows. Railways, electricity generation and telecommunications, which are natural monopolies, should be run by state corporations which require no ownership transformation. Communal services will similarly be entrusted to communal corporations. Perhaps a certain number of other enterprises, specific to each country, could also be included in the category of state corporations. This change can be brought about immediately. A great number of small establishments (village shops, restaurants, repair shops, service establishments, apartments), often the unprofitable parts of larger firms, can be sold to individuals and cooperatives, perhaps on the basis of instalment credits. The remaining firms may be controlled by a certain number of holding companies. As soon as a firm becomes viable, it would be granted self-management status; a process which could be be accelerated by appropriate incentives. Finally, a certain number of firms will prove to be hopeless cases, and these will be closed down and their property sold. The entire transformation could be accomplished in about five years (in Yugoslavia, in not more than two years). The end result would be a market economy dominated by autonomous social corporations, with a small number of big state corporations and a fringe of numerous small family firms and cooperatives. Joint ventures and foreign-owned firms would complete the new economic structure.

The financial sector requires separate analysis which would go beyond the scope of this paper. I would, however, point out that in France, for example, 70 per cent of banks are nationalized and that the market functions efficiently.

4. The business corporation in contemporary managerial capitalism

Current legal regulation is rather simple. The law provides for annual meetings of shareholders which elect the board of directors (the supervisory board in continental Europe). This in turn appoints the general manager and other senior executives (the management board). The board of directors is supposed to maximize the profits of shareholders. If the shareholders are dissatisfied, they dismiss the directors and appoint a new executive (subject to the constraints of possible contracts that the executives may have with the firm). Occasionally, the corporation may behave as it is supposed to; in the vast majority of cases it behaves very differently. The dominant group in the corporation comprises those who make daily decisions and who have access to all relevant information: directors-managers and senior executives. The actual practice is well described by Robin Marris:[5]

> It is sometimes supposed that in the corporate sector boards of directors may be regarded as trustees for shareholders, that they are ... akin to watchdog comittees set up to keep management in place. This view ... is not supported by legal authorities and in any case the managers have themselves considerably assimilated the directorial system. Legally, the function of the board is to operate the company. For the purpose it employs the executives who may ... themselves be directors. But board members who are also full-time employees command the power of organization and hence must in general dominate: in the U.S. the majority of directors are in this position. Thus, by combining the functions of employee and employer, the management body is considerably freed from direct external restraints, a condition which is emphasised by the fact that the vast majority of board nominations are proposed by existing directors. In practice, in many firms, the board itself recedes into the background and operations are taken over by committees of senior executives not all of whom are necessarily directors.

In other words, managers manage without asking either the board or the shareholders for clearance. Managers are empowered to take decisions and thus behave like traditional owners. They are not appointed; they practice self-appointment. In the same way they themselves decide on their own salaries, bonuses and stock options.

In principle, all the directors in a corporation can be removed by a simple majority vote at a meeting of shareholders. This legal possibility is almost never used - except in takeover raids - because the shareholders diversify their risks and thus do not own the majority of shares. In 1951, in the largest British and American corporations, the median percentage of votes held by the 20 largest shareholders was 20 to 28 per cent.[6] The management holds 1-3 per cent of votes, but effectively controls the corporation. R. A. Gordon notes:

> Wholesale purges of executive ranks are rare, and top management, usually securely in control of the proxy machinery, seldom has to worry about retaining its position.[7]

In spite of the absence of any direct control over private owners, managers work relatively satisfactorily. Why? Because of the inducements and deterrents provided by the market. The mobility of executives is extremely low. In a survey it was found that senior officers, on average, had had fewer than two employers since the beginning of their careers.[8] Thus they are dependent on their firms and are vitally interested that their firms prosper. The manager tends to identify with his firm, enjoys the approbation of his class if the share price is high, rises faster within his company if vacancies increase because of its expansion; and his power grows with the size of the company. Besides, good share prices make access to financial markets easier and they increase borrowing power.

The market deterrents are equally powerful. The larger institutional shareholders may successfully monitor the corporation by threatening to sell their shares. Such sales may inflict a mortal blow on management. The share price will decline and this incurs the danger of a hostile takeover. In the case of a successful raid, the entire top management is dismissed and they thus lose their jobs, prestige and very substantial material remuneration.

It is administrative independence and market control that make a corporation tick. Clearly, it is not necessary slavishly to imitate private institutions in order to achieve the same or better economic effects. All that is required is to identify the two crucial preconditions mentioned above, and to devise a solution which exploits the full potential of the initial position.

5. The social corporation

The social corporation is a joint-stock company or limited liability company run by its employees, who elect a workers' council and appoint the general manager. Self-management will require both the managers and the members of the workers' councils to undergo an intensive learning process. Courses will have to be organized and consulting agencies set up.[9] The oft-voiced fear that the *nomenklatura* managers may simply remain where they are is unfounded in this setting (although it is very real when the government controls the managerial appointments; even if former personnel are removed, the new appointments will tend to be politically, not economically, motivated). The workers' councils will choose as managers those individuals whom they know from their own experience to be good organizers. Since I have written extensively on self-management elsewhere[10], I shall not discuss this aspect of social corporation any further. I instead turn my attention to how the firm is to be incorporated.

The book value of a firm will usually be only of archaeological interest. Therefore the firm's capital must be evaluated anew by applying the same methodology to all firms. Once the real value of capital is known, it is expressed in shares which remain in the company as an undivided fund of social capital. Henceforth, the social corporation is ready to engage in market operations like any other corporation. It will supplement its working capital with short-term loans from the commercial banks.

The increase in fixed capital will be financed by the issue of bonds and shares and by long-term loans from investment banks.

Shares are internal (social capital) and external (floated on the capital market or sold to employees at a discount). Whether internal or external, shares earn dividends, and dividends determine the market rating of the firm. In this way, market discipline is imposed and any government control becomes super-fluous.

Dividends safeguard minimum profitability and hence solve the problem of the distribution of income between wages and accumulation without any administrative interference. Internal dividends also accrue to an owner, which is a society: they are used for investment and are therefore added to social capital. If there are also undistributed profits, share capital will appreciate. In its business policy, the firm will choose the most convenient combination of a rise in dividends and an appreciation of capital.

Firms may merge and combine their capital and management. One firm may invest in another on a contractual basis. Alternatively, it may invest by buying the shares of another firm. These shares give voting rights. If profitability drops, the value of the shares will drop as well, and this may make a hostile takeover possible. This danger will discipline both workers and managers, since takeover means the suspension of self-management, reorganization, and dismissals.

A social corporation may also go bankrupt. In this case, the law lays down a standard procedure on how the property should be sold in order to compensate creditors. A bankruptcy may be prevented if the Development Bank (a counterpart of the National Bank[11]) declares that it is in the social interest to bail the firm out. In this case, self-management is suspended and a new management is appointed by the Bank, which undertakes to reorganize the firm and to make the necessary dismissals.

In the majority of cases, corporations will have mixed ownership, with a social capital fund representing the controlling package of shares. Nothing changes if mergers and takeovers occur among social corporations. If a social corporation buys a private corporation, the latter becomes social with self-management introduced, and nothing else is required. If a private corporation buys a social corporation, the latter becomes private, self-management is suspended, and the Development Bank, as the custodian of the social capital, becomes the owner of the internal shares. These shares may now be sold on the capital market. Competition on the market will determine these changes, and it would be counterproductive to impose any particular scheme in advance. The government's only concern should be to ensure that the market is not distorted and that everybody enters competition on equal terms. The market will then automatically select the most efficient organizational, financial and ownership forms.

The system described may work efficiently without any private share ownership. It therefore appears that the great emphasis laid on reprivatization is determined by considerations of ideology and not economic efficiency. If only social corporations have access to the capital market, with the rest of the economy unincorporated anyway, the only investors are institutional ones. This would not differ greatly from the situation elsewhere: 75 per cent of the world stock market is already institutional and this percentage is increasing. I have insufficient space for analysis of why this is so: suffice it here to record the fact. Although private shares are not necessary, they may increase the flexibility of the market and for that reason may also be used.

The main institutional investors are insurance companies, pension funds and investment trusts. That means that a sizeable capital market may be put into operation immediately. Thus, the entire transformation from a nationalized to a market economy, if undertaken along the lines suggested, will take no longer that five years (two in Yugoslavia).

Transforming state enterprises into self-managing social corporations means genuine deregulation in the shortest possible time. In this way, a nationalized economy will be transformed into a more efficient market economy.

Notes

1 Lippit and White, 1951.
2 Horvat, 1982.
3 The author uses the word 'de-statization' in his original text, as does W. Andreff in his essay. We have preferred the English word 'de-nationalization' (Editor's Note).
4 Andreff, 1990.
5 Marris, 1964, p.4.
6 Marris, 1964, p.312.
7 Gordon, 1945, p.311
8 Marris, 1964, p.67.
9 Sweden, England and the United States have had valuable experience in this area.
10 Horvat, 1982.
11 See Horvat, 1969.

Bibliography

Andreff, W. (1990), 'Techniques and Experience of Privatization', mimeo, Université des Sciences Sociales de Grenoble.
Gordon, R. A. (1945), *Business Leadership in the Large Corporation*, Washington D.C.
Horvat, B. (1969), 'Development Fund as an Institution for Conducting Fiscal Policy', *Economic Analysis*, pp. 247-54.
Horvat, B. (1982), *The Political Economy of Socialism*, New York: M. Sharpe.
Lippit, R. and White, R. K. (1951), 'An Experimental Study of Leadership and Group Life', in G. E. Swanson et al. (eds.), *Readings in Social Psychology*, New York: H. Holt.
Marris, R. (1964), *The Economic Theory of 'Managerial' Capitalism*, London: Macmillan.

A paradox of the transition to a market economy: how will the role of the state change?*

Ivo Bićanić and Marko Škreb

1. Introduction

Since the first heady days of post-socialist reconstruction when optimism and high expectations reigned, learning-by-doing has brought the majority of politicians and economists in post-socialist East-Central European economies to a mood of sober realism, risk aversion and perhaps even pessimism. One year after transition to a market economy began in these countries, politicians and economists alike, especially the latter, are reassessing the problems, barriers and time horizons of transition.

In the early stages when the political barriers of one-party rule were removed, and a little later when stabilization policies showed their first effects, economists tended to expect a rapid, relatively costless and easy transition. To the more sober-minded minority of the profession, however, their further study of the features of the transition process (and above all of events themselves) revealed that the problems involved are much greater and the barriers, both existing and expected, much higher.

Especially important has been the change in the role of the state and of the administration (bureaucracy) during the period of transition. Simplistic, outmoded and idealized visions of a frictionless, self-regulating market economy (which did not exist even at the laissez-faire beginning of the nineteenth century) initially prevailed. This is understandable, given the above-mentioned initial optimism, and given over forty years of experience with all-embracing centralized economic planning and decision-making dominated by a party apparatus indistinguishable from the state administration. This mentality has now radically changed, and it seems that these visions have been replaced by a more complex approach where, although the state has a new and in many respects redefined role, it is still important. It is a change that may appear paradoxical, given the declared commitment to the development of a decentralized and deregulated private market economy.

The reasons for this change will be the subject of this paper, which discusses the problems that may arise from the redefined role of the state in administering the successful transition of the post-socialist economies into decentralized market ones.

At present, there is no formal theory of transition, and we have therefore been obliged to adopt the pragmatic approach common to all studies of the subject. Moreover, since no country has yet accomplished successful transition to a market economy (and here we include the Yugoslavian experience of the late fifties and sixties), there is only a limited amount of empirical evidence available to support any particular view. The role of the state in the economy is a very complex one, and its many facets are difficult to measure in money terms or to sum up (quality of administration, effectiveness of regulation, and so on). This state of affairs has forced us to resort to speculation and normative analysis, even though we have tried to place the emphasis on those events which may reasonably be expected to occur.

Our paper is divided into three sections. The first deals with the possible factors favouring an important role of the state; that is, it addresses those features of the economic structure which may constitute the causes and incentives for a decision to opt for an increased role of the state during transition. The second section focuses on state failure and the quality of human capital in administration. The third section is partly prescriptive in character, since it attempts briefly to indicate how the pitfalls of the modified role of the state may be avoided and hence unnecessary social costs eliminated - an outcome which we do not see as likely in the short run.

2. Possible reasons for a prominent role of the state

The important (even crucial) role of the state during the transition period can be traced to three different sets of causes. The first pertains to the built-in features of the economic structure, i.e. to the initial structure of the economy. The second set comprises path-specific causes of an increased role of the state, which relate chiefly to the policy options selected, policy sequencing, and the goals chosen. The third and last set of causes stems from the role the state must play in any modern mixed welfare economy that the transition path is undertaken to achieve. Each of these sets of causes will be discussed in turn.

2.1. *Structural underpinnings*

The structural features of the economy figure prominently among the possible reasons for the state to assume an important role during the transition period. By structural features we mean, following Chenery[1], those built-in features of the economic and social system which are relatively stable (those which cannot be changed in the short run) but which, at the same time, are not rigidly determined by resource endowment (which cannot be changed at all). Among these features, the following three seem of especial importance for the role of the state during the transition: (i) the size distribution of firms, (ii) the share of services (infrastructural and knowledge-intensive producer services) and (iii) risk averse behaviour. Each of these will be briefly discussed in turn.

(i) Socialist development showed a 'bias to bigness'. There was a definite tendency towards building large enterprises, regardless of whether the economies were large (as in China or the Soviet Union) or medium-sized (as in most East-Central European countries), whether economies were centrally planned (as most of them were) or self-managed (as in Yugoslavia). This structural characteristic of socialist economies is well known. Nove[2] calls it 'empire building' by an all-powerful administration, Winicki[3] sees it as part of the grand design of socialist development while Bićanić[4] describes it as a rational micro-response to centralized decision-making and administered prices. Consequently, the size distribution of firms has taken a form quite different from that exhibited by capitalist economies. In socialist economies there was a comparatively higher share of large enterprises and, depending on the regulations of the private sector, a higher share of very small ones. What was common to all the economies, however, was a distinct lack of medium-sized enterprises; that is, those employing up to a hundred workers. Vahčić[5] refers to this as a 'black hole' in size distribution. Country studies[6] and comparative analysis[7] alike indicate it as a distinctive feature of socialist economies.

The over-representation of large enterprises can influence the role of the state during transition. Determining the 'synergic' effects of bigness, identifying profitable plants, splitting up overgrown enterprises, solving the social effects of lobbying power, and, perhaps most importantly, introducing anti-monopoly legislation and regulating natural monopolies are some of the tasks which come first to mind. Among these various issues some seem of especial relevance to the issue of the role of the state. Given such a monopolistic industrial structure, the main policy goals become extremely complex: as Killick and Stevens[8] also point out, dealing with monopolies is an essential task.

The simple introduction of 'markets' (i.e. the deregulation of prices and production) would quickly lead to monopolistic behaviour and to quasi-rents, leaving the state with the difficult task of devising and implementing a stringent anti-monopoly policy. Streamlining enterprises by enforced labour-shedding policies, or breaking them up and leaving the unprofitable sections to go bankrupt may have major social effects of a regional nature. There is therefore enormous pressure on the state to continue with its soft budget constraint and to assume responsibility for production under the guise of maintaining production in enterprises of national importance. Finally, the privatization of large enterprises is more difficult because the lump-sum required for purchase is large, business policy less flexible, and valuation even less clear. Replacing a state monopoly with a private one will not solve the problem. The state must therefore take on a prominent role as an organizer, arranger, manager and matchmaker in the 'commercialization', privatization and restructuring of its large enterprises.

(ii) Forty years of socialist development have left the post-socialist economies with their service sectors acting as developmental bottlenecks. Even though services in these countries are generally underdeveloped[9], the backwardness of infrastructural services (transport and communications) and of some producer services (especially knowledge-intensive services like banking, finance, computers, and so on) is more important than in other areas because it may imperil further growth. Not only are these services under-developed, they are also of inferior quality - a fact not adequately shown by the statistics.

The common characteristic of infrastructural services is that they are capital intensive and require large investments (usually sunk costs), long construction periods, and (sometimes) high technology. Infrastructure in general has shown itself to be a more severe constraint on growth than envisaged, and stream-lining it will require not only time but a prominent role of the state as well.

Similar considerations apply to knowledge-intensive producer services, to which we must add their importance for an efficient capital market. The lack of human capital seems to be the greatest obstacle to their faster development.

Private and social consumer services will probably not act as a barrier to growth. While private consumer services (retail shops, restaurants) can be privatized on a large scale, due to their relatively small capital requirements, social consumer services (like education and health) will probably remain under state ownership.

Services are necessary for growth, and in post-socialist countries they are underdeveloped. Since markets alone (even those open to foreign investment) would be unable to ease this bottleneck, state intervention is warranted. And this will entail new activity by the state, whose role may therefore even expand.[10]

(iii) In the context of this paper, risk aversion figures prominently as a cause of state involvement in the economy. It is especially important to two kinds of decision-makers: the state bureaucracy and households. Each of these will be briefly examined in turn.

Discussion of the role of the state during transition often forgets that the inherited state administration has remained and will remain largely intact. Although elections have replaced most elected representatives, those employed in the administration have largely survived.

The administration entrusted with the task of supervising transition has been inherited from the socialist regime. It therefore has a (not unjustified) reputation for favouritism, inefficiency, incompetence, inertia and excessive size. Moreover, it is an administration used to solving economic problems by control and regulation, and it has no experience of market management.

This in turn signifies that policy recommendations (concerning such important areas as privatization schemes and development priorities), budget proposals (in order to streamline the administration and the military, for example) and policy implementation (its toughness and possible loopholes), would depend on a state administration burdened by its notorious past.

Risk-averse behaviour would in this case mean dealing with problems in the 'traditional way', i.e. by increasing the role of the state bureaucracy. The fear of price reform when unregulated markets generate unknown and uncontrol-lable events, the suspicion that privatization can lead to the sell-off and under-pricing of national resources, the protection of national interests so prominent in economies with intra-regional tensions and, above all, the fear of tensions caused by the social costs of the transition: all these provide the excuse for maintaining traditional ways and methods of problem-solving by and in the bureaucracy.

Households also exhibit risk-averse behaviour, as consumer theory has convincingly shown. In the context of post-socialist reconstruction, this may significantly increase pressure towards a more prominent role of the state. The population expects the state to take responsibility for providing many services (education, health, housing, and so forth) and wants job protection to be guaranteed, so that it can be protected from the market and have ample opportunities to engage in unofficial economic activities.[11] Furthermore, the population expects necessary but risky entrepreneurial activity to be undertaken by others, and households are thus insulated against the convergence of business decisions. Markets, with their attendant uncertainty, risk and entrepreneurial behaviour, upset this state of affairs. And when one adds the social costs of transition, which endanger the very existence of many households, it is clear that these factors may stoke pressure for an increased role by the state in this area. Ballot box pressure, fear of social unrest and the 'traditional way' combine.

2.2. Path-specific underpinnings

Apart from the way in which transitional costs can change the role of the state, two other related issues fall under this heading. The first concerns the chosen paths and timing of transition and privatization, while the second (which is no less complex) concerns the maintenance of a coalition which is able to implement economic policy tasks.

In our opinion, the role of the state in relation to the transition path chosen should be examined by comparing between a rapid transition scenario and a prolonged one. The arguments in favour of a rapid transition seem more convincing, since only comprehensive programmes implemented speedily, efficiently, and rigorously stand a reasonable chance of success, and only these would be able to check the expansion of state regulation and control.

The alternative scenario, that is, gradual reforms, necessarily assigns a more prominent role to the state. This we shall examine in relation to (i) microeconomic links among enterprises, (ii) foreign aid and capital imports, and (iii) adjustment fatigue.

As regards (i), partial reforms abolish only some of the links between centrally planned enterprises; others remain intact and relations are conducted according to the old rules. For example, the collapse of COMECON trade has left many enterprises disoriented and without markets. But, on the other hand, the environment of collusive business behaviour can prevent new private entrepreneurs from entering to fill the vacuum. Moreover, this may strengthen the barriers impeding the emergence of entrepreneurs even further; barriers which some authors[12] consider to be already prohibitive.

(ii) Foreign help and capital imports (which will probably be much smaller than was expected only a year ago in East-Central European countries, when they raised false expectations) will not flow to those countries which have only partially transformed their economies. Preference will be given to those economies that have completed economic as well as political reforms, and which therefore provide a safer and more stable business environment. Also, this invested capital is more likely to have the political backing (and preferential treatment) of the governments of the 'capital donor' countries. The only capital that slowly-reforming economies can expect to receive is the capital which seeks high and quick profits based on speculative decision-making. Hence countries which are reluctant to implement radical reforms stand a much greater chance of 'staying out in the cold' than those which transform their economies in a rapid and comprehensive manner. The third reason, adjustment fatigue, will be dealt with under the heading of transitional costs.

The only possible argument for gradualism is the thesis that gradual reforms will minimize the (cumulative) social costs of transition. For this reason, gradualism is seen as a 'low risk strategy' in keeping with 'risk averse' behaviour in centrally planned economies. So far, however, few arguments in support of this idea have been forthcoming. Even so, governments drag their feet over reform, postpone decisions, and extend time-horizons. Examples can be found in all the East-Central European economies, but perhaps Yugoslavia is the most clear-cut case.

In our opinion, in East-Central European countries the state simply does not have the knowledge, skills and capacity to 'direct' and control gradual reforms over a long period of time while it maintains the level of economic activity at a satisfactory level.

Gradualism versus rapid change in relation to the role of the state can also be viewed in terms of privatization. Privatization is not an aim in itself, but a means to increase the efficiency of production. The evidence from the developing countries[13] suggests that privately owned enterprises are more efficient than publicly owned ones, and that typical public services (like water, telecommunications, health, etc.) can be provided privately as well. Even though the economic environment in developing countries (where markets do exist and private ownership generally predominates) is different from that of the post-socialist economies (where markets and private ownership are now emerging against considerable odds), we believe that these arguments are plausible and that they point to the comparative inefficiency of the state in managing production.

There are numerous theoretical models of privatization, none of which has ever been implemented on a large scale. Basically, two extreme types of privatization can be distinguished: the 'selling strategy' and the 'distributing strategy'. Each of these appear in a wide range of variations, options and combinations. We shall not embark on discussion of all possible modes of privatization and their pros and cons[14], but we do wish to stress that if privatization is not carried through quickly enough, the role of the state will remain over-large, bearing in mind that 80 per cent of those economies are state-owned.

In a slow programme of gradual transition the interregnum period is extended, and this creates major new tasks for the state. In these circumstances the state must oversee the privatization process, prevent major redistributions of wealth, and increase its supervision of production. The rationale of this argument is simple. If large parts of the economy remain in the hands of the state they will continue to be inefficient and will require large subsidies, state intervention, and so on. The state will devote its scarce resources (material as

slow page

well as human) to state-owned sectors, and it will be unable to pay sufficient attention to much needed reforms in other areas (specifically discussed in the following sections).

The experience of privatization in East-Central European economies by mid-1991 does seem to show more uniformity than the theoretical scenarios on offer. The state has played a very, and perhaps increasingly, prominent role in the privatization process, which seems now to be slowing down and taking longer than was initially envisaged - and this in spite of awareness that a changing ownership structure is a precondition for the efficient functioning of the economy.

In Poland, for example, the Balcerowicz Programme of 1990 planned to privatize half the state sector in three years and to achieve an ownership structure resembling that of Western economies in five. By the end of 1990, however, only five large enterprises had been privatized[15], and the new government announced a new privatization offensive including 'large' privatization in areas where disappointments had been greatest.[16] The process was to be supervised even more carefully, and privatization plans scrutinized even more closely by the Ministry of Ownership Transformation. Furthermore, the new government which came to power in 1991 is proposing further variants of the privatization procedure, including a voucher scheme.

In Czechoslovakia, the initial intentions of very rapid privatization, which relied heavily on the voucher system (although this was a scheme rather different from the Polish one), have now been modified. The legal framework for 'large' privatization was defined only in February 1991 and the Fund for National Property is to start functioning in mid-1991. This fund will play a prominent role in directing and overseeing privatization, evaluating plans and issuing permits. The voucher system has been scaled down, and the privatization process will take much longer.[17]

The Hungarian government underwent a major reshuffle in early 1991 when economists favouring shock-therapy left, and the new head of the State Property Agency (which is supposed to regulate, oversee and administer privatization) indicated that hasty privatization would diminish the state's revenues.[18] Towards the end of 1990, large-scale privatization slowed almost to a stop, and most of the securities issued were of large state-owned banks, largely to finance the losses of major state enterprises.

In Yugoslavia, only two republics have passed privatization bills, and the federal law, which placed great stress on the discounted sale of shares to workers, is not being applied on a large scale and across the whole country. Yugoslavia is a special case in that its undefined ownership structure based on 'social ownership' - a legacy of socialist self management - seems, in practice, to require first the introduction of state ownership and only subsequently privatization. Thus the state in Yugoslavia has taken on the major roles of owning and organizing production not only in the public sector. Albania and Romania have not even started to tackle the problem yet, and Bulgaria by mid-1991 has only started to privatize agricultural land.

At the time of writing, therefore, the feature common to all these countries is that the state (through a ministry, agency or fund) plays a prominent role in preparing and issuing permits for privatization, and it also assumes responsibility for production. Not only does this raise principal-agent problems, but it also encourages the idea that privatization must earn revenue for the government (an idea which seems to be spreading) and that commercialization must precede privatization, thereby prolonging the process.

Another important issue concerns the implementation of policy measures. Here the state must build and maintain a coalition for transition which imposes an economic policy involving unpopular decisions and policy measures: unemployment and a fall in real incomes, to mention just two. Moreover, this coalition must be sufficiently stable to enable the state to implement these decisions regardless of the social costs involved. The importance and difficulty of this becomes even clearer when the tradition of avoiding and ignoring laws and policy decisions, as well as a traditionally dynamic unofficial sector, are taken into account.

Transition paths and privatization strategies have very important regional aspects. The asymmetric effects of economic policies, the maintaining of favourable conditions and preventing unfavourable redistribution, providing protection against the unwanted consequences of policy decisions arrived at by majority voting: these are all factors which can induce increased state (federal or regional) control. These tendencies may be further strengthened by the economics of de-integration. The centre may attempt to prevent de-integration by increasing its control, and the regional authorities may try to protect their interests by appropriating control to themselves. Recent events in Yugoslavia, Czechoslovakia or the Soviet Union provide examples of both these processes. In Yugoslavia the republics have tended to take over entire sectors in the name of the protection of national (regional) interests; a strategy which has undoubtedly increased the role of the state. Similar cases may arise in other multinational post-socialist economies - Romania and China, for example.

Transition costs could provide an additional incentive for expanding the role of the state. Since two aspects (namely, capital shedding and institutional building) of these costs have already been dealt with, this section will briefly discuss the influence which labour-related transition costs may exert on the expanding role of the state. The risk-averse behaviour mentioned above, together with an egalitarian syndrome, could act as a major barrier against successful change: both of them are in conflict with the changes that a successful transformation would bring in the short and medium run. Unemployment, falling living standards, quasi-rents and property income, increasing inequality in income distribution, the major restructuring of household budgets and behaviour are some of the changes expected.

The pressure towards the adoption of populist policies, gradual change, and the maintenance of the existing social safety net of public services and its extension to include unemployment and poverty, will put additional pressure on the state. With the onset of stagflation, state funds will be very difficult to maintain without additional taxes causing budgets to increase.

2.3. 'New system' causes

The state plays an important role even in modern welfare mixed economies, and there is no reason to expect it not to be important in post-socialist ones as well. We offer four possible arguments for this: (i) market failures, (ii) legal and institutional underpinnings (iii) macrostability, and (iv) welfare policy.

(i) Since market failures are well-documented and analysed in the literature, we do not intend to pursue the topic further.[19] We would, however, like to draw attention to the fact that these activities require continuous government involvement.

(ii) The market economy is a well-organized system where the 'rules of the game' are known and sustainable. Even though the building of the institutions required for market exchange is a transitional issue, it is included here because of the time-horizon it implies: although laws can be passed quickly their acceptance takes time. The erection and maintenance of other institutions and underpinning an orderly market economy assign the state an important and unavoidable role. In today's post-socialist economies there is no legal structure for a market economy, the judiciary system has no experience in business law, and market institutions are non-existent.

(iii) Macroeconomic stability is a prerequisite for economic transformation. From the macroeconomic viewpoint, the situation in these countries can be broadly described as one of a slowdown of economic growth in the 1980s, with budget deficits, monetary overhang, inflationary pressures and the fear of rapidly rising unemployment. Post-socialist states do not have much experience (or likelihood) of achieving and maintaining macro-stability.

(iv) It is likely that welfare policy, and with it the state, will have a major role to play even in the long run; a role which is likely to be greater than it is in comparable economies. Not only will transitional costs be large (unemployment, a fall in the standard of living, etc.) but structural pressures (such as risk-averse behaviour by households, inequality preferences) will contribute to this development. The persistent crisis in the 1980s impoverished households[20] thus increasing probable pressures for welfare policy. Changes are expected both on the demand side (due to rising unemployment) and the supply side (institutional changes and financing) of existing social systems.[21]

3. State failure

Although the list of tasks which the state may end up by performing is impressive, it is obvious that the constraints on it prevent it from understanding too many things at once, especially if efficiency considerations are included. We have already seen the importance of the time constraint in implementing reforms. A predominant role of the state in the economy would create the inevitable danger that not even the most routine tasks would be carried out efficiently, and that there would be enormous pressure to increase the number of employees (which, of course, could only be financed through higher taxes or an inflationary budget deficit).

Can the state live up to these expectations? An answer can only be forthcoming if 'state failures' are taken into account. Interestingly, it seems that the problems of market failure have attracted more attention in the profession than has state (or government) failure, although development theory assumes that in developing countries state failures outweigh those of the market.[22] Although neither a clear definition nor an universal classification has yet been formulated of state failure, here we have been mostly influenced by Stern[23] and Krueger.[24] Of the long list of state failures the following should be mentioned:

(i) The state can commit serious mistakes in allocating resources (more serious than those committed by the market) in the economy by giving false directions. This can be done out of simple ignorance, but also because the taking of such decisions can be manipulated by powerful groups which act in their own interests and ignore wider issues. Narrow groups can influence state bureaucrats relatively easily, thus diminishing the welfare of society as a whole. Rent-seeking behaviour is common, and corruption may be widespread.

(ii) Economic conditions change rapidly and are complex. On the other hand, state decisions may be slow, rigid and inflexible, either because of an overlarge bureaucracy and/or because the components of this state decision-making process may be badly coordinated.

(iii) Individuals usually know more about their own preferences than the state does; hence the state cannot efficiently perform the 'information' function in place of the market. Although some markets (i.e. health insurance) suffer from imperfect information problems, the state cannot substitute the market and should instead complement it.

(iv) Too much state control may block private initiative (by raising legal barriers to entry). On the other hand, by providing subsidies (and a soft budget constraint) the state fails to offer the incentives to state-owned enterprises to minimize costs, to innovate and allocate efficiently that the market does.

(v) Although all state organizations have limited capacities, they usually do not know when to stop their activity, much of which is devoted to maintaining and increasing state power.

(vi) State intervention may cause price distortions. It has been estimated that the greater these distortions, the lower will be the rate of growth of the economy as a whole.[25]

4. Concluding remarks

The overriding economic goals of all post-socialist economies is the introduction of private ownership and a deregulated, efficient market economy. Paradoxically, however, it seems that the real-world economies will try to attain these goals by retaining a prominent, albeit changed, role for the state. We have discussed three sets of causes for the possible increase in the state's role: structural causes (size distribution of firms, underdeveloped services, risk aversion), path-specific ones (privatization, the timing of transition, the regional and transitional costs of chosen policy options), and 'new system' reasons (market failures, legal and institutional underpinnings, macro-stability and welfare policy).

One should bear in mind that forces do exist which could diminish the role of the state in post-socialist countries (for example, successful privatization on a larger scale, liberalizing prices, the deregulation of economic activity), but it seems that these forces are not yet strong enough to counteract tendencies in the opposite direction. Since they are very difficult to quantify and compare, the final result cannot be unequivocally determined.

It is very likely that the paradoxical development we have described (the important role of the state in a market economy) will reduce the probability of successful transition. The state cannot fulfil the tasks and expectations imposed upon it - not only because of state overhang, a negative inheritance from the past, and a credibility gap, but also because of the applicability of state failure as identified in development policy.

It is therefore essential in these countries that the state should transform (redefine) its role in the economy. And this is a very difficult task indeed. Although it seems that a rapid, efficient and comprehensive transition scenario, one which emphasizes fast and large-scale privatization, minimizes pressure for an increased role by the state (by bringing its role more in line with that of Western countries), we do not expect such a development to happen soon.

Notes

* This essay has benefited from discussions at the 1st EACES Workshop on privatization held in Trento, Italy, 1-2 March 1991 and the workshop at the University of Zagreb. The comments by Will Bartlett are greatly appreciated. Any errors or omissions are our responsibility alone, of course.
1 Chenery, 1979.
2 Nove, 1983.
3 Winicki, 1989.
4 Bićanić, 1988.
5 Vahčic, 1989.
6 See Petrin, 1986, for Yugoslavia; Laky, 1990, for Hungary.
7 Winicki, 1989.
8 Killick and Stevens, 1991.
9 Bićanić and Škreb, 1991.
10 Bićanić and Škreb, 1991.
11 Alessandrini and Dallago, 1988; Los, 1990.
12 Dallago, 1990.
13 World Development Report, 1983; Roth, 1987.
14 See Dallago, 1990; Dornbusch, 1990; World Bank, 1991.
15 Report on Eastern Europe, no. 1, p. 26.
16 Report on Eastern Europe, no. 12, p. 13.
17 Report on Eastern Europe, no. 11, p. 13.
18 Report on Eastern Europe, no. 11, p. 13.
19 See, for example, Stern, 1989; Datta-Chaudhuri, 1990.
20 Milanović, 1990.
21 Uvalić and Bartlett, 1991.
22 See World Development Report, 1983; Krueger, 1990.
23 Stern, 1989.
24 Krueger, 1990.
25 World Development Report, 1983.

Bibliography

Alessandrini, S., Dallago, B. (eds.) (1987), *The Unofficial Economy. Consequences and Perspectives in Different Economic Systems*, Aldershot: Gower.

Bićanić , I. (1988), 'Fractured Economy', in Rusinov, D. (ed.), 1988.

Bićanić , I., Škreb, M. (1991), 'The Service Sector in the East European Economies: What role can it Play in Future Growth?' *Communist Economies and Economic Transformation*, vol. 3, no. 2 (forthcoming).

Chenery, H. (1979), *Structural Change and Economic Development*, New York: Oxford University Press.

Dallago, B. (1990), 'Hungary and Poland: The Non-Socialized Sector and Privatization', mimeo, University of Trento.

Datta-Chaudhuri, M. (1990), 'Market Failure and Government Failure', *The Journal of Economic Perspective*, vol. 4, no. 3, pp. 25-40.

Dornbusch, R. (1990), 'Economic Reform in Eastern Europe and the Soviet Union: Priorities and Strategy', mimeo, MIT.

Jerovšek, J., Rus, V., Zupanov, J. (eds.) (1986), *Kriza, blokade i perspektive*, Zagreb: Globus.

Killick, T, Stevens, C. (1991), 'Economic Adjustment in Eastern Europe: Lessons from the Third World', paper presented at the conference 'Reforming Eastern European Economies', University of Surrey, 6th February.

Krueger, A. O. (1990), 'Government Failures in Development', The *Journal of Economic Perspective*, vol. 4, no. 3, pp. 9-24.

Laky, T. (1990), 'The Role of Small Enterprises and Privatization in Hungary', mimeo, University of Budapest.

Los, M. (ed.) (1990), *The Second Economy in Marxist States*, London: Macmillan.

Milanović, B. (1990), 'Poverty in Poland, Hungary and Yugoslavia in the Years of Crisis 1978-87', Washington: World Bank PRE, WPS 507.

Nove, A. (1983), *The Economics of Feasible Socialism*, London: George Allen and Unwin.

Petrin, T. (1986), 'Kriza male privrede', in Jerovšek et al., 1986

Report on Eastern Europe (1991), RFE/RL Research Institute, vol. 2, various issues.

Roth, G. (1987), *The Private Provision of Public Services in Developing Countries*, New York: Oxford University Press.

Rusinov, D. (ed.) (1988), *Yugoslavia: A Fractured Federalism*, Washington: The Wilson Center Press.

Stern. N. (1989), 'The Economics of Development', *Economic Journal*, vol. 99, no. 397, pp. 597-685.

Uvalić, M., Bartlett W. (1991), 'The Social Safety Net in Yugoslavia', OECD (forthcoming).

Vahčić, A. (1989), 'Prestrukturiranje jugoslovenske privrede pomoću poduzetništva', *Naše Teme*, vol. 33, no. 11, pp. 2906-15.

Winicki, J. (1989), 'Large Industrial Enterprises in Soviet-Type Economies: The Ruling Stratum's Main Rent-Seeking Area', *Communist Economies*, vol. 1, no. 4, pp. 363-84.

World Bank (1991), 'The Transformation of Economies in Central and Eastern Europe: Issues, Progress and Prospects', mimeo, Socialist Economies Unit, Country Economics Department.

World Development Report (1983), World Bank, New York: Oxford University Press.

Privatization in market economies and for building a market economy

Siro Lombardini

1. Privatization in the East and in the West

In the 1980s, privatization was a central topic of economic and political debate in several countries of the West, but mostly in the USA and Britain. After the fall of the Berlin Wall, privatization became associated with a market economy which, in its turn, has become associated with democracy. On closer scrutiny, however, privatization in market economies is a quite different matter from privatization conceived as a process by which a command economy can be converted into a market one (privatization to build a market economy). Yet the two issues have been assimilated into the general problem of privatization. And this, perhaps, for two reasons.

1. Economic theory - which can at most help us to understand adjustment processes in a market economy already established by exogenous events or state interventions - is taken to be the theory that explains how a market economy is to be built, how it works, and how it can be extended to solve those problems previously assumed to lie outside the scope and possibility of markets.

2. The economic system and the political system have been considered to be distinct entities, their only connection being those state interventions by which economic policy is implemented. To some extent - and this varies according to the school of thought concerned - they are required to make the market economy work, while, in the view of a quite substantial number of economists, interventions are necessary in order to gear the economy to the attainment of pre-established social goals.

The reasons adduced in justification of nationalization - in France in the

1940s and in the 1980s, in England in the 1950s and in Italy in the 1960s (the nationalization of the electricity industry) - were theoretical in character (increased efficiency of production, the attainment of social goals, a more stable economy). Today, similar theoretical reasons are again being advanced to justify privatization: if the market sphere is extended with new property rights, some economists argue, it will be possible to achieve certain social goals more efficiently.

The basic reasons why privatization is considered to be an issue fundamental to economies in both the West and the East link with a conception that has long dominated economic analysis: namely that the market mechanism is able to solve all supply problems, and that the only problems relevant to economic policy are demand problems, which are macroeconomic problems - they are, that is, essentially those that must be addressed when discussing the stability of the economy or its ability to secure a sustained rate of growth of employment.

Only recently has supply-side economics called attention to the possibility of improving the system's productive capacity by appropriate economic policies. Conceived in the context of neo-liberalist ideology, supply-side economics was restricted to a limited number of fiscal policy issues (the effect of reductions in income tax rates on saving, labour effort and entrepreneurial activity). But it is not difficult to envisage a broader set of possibilities for improving the efficiency of the system by state intervention: the field of supply side economics, therefore, is much wider than is usually thought.

2. State and market

A number of fallacies, which stem from the conceptions outlined above, have distorted debate on privatization in Western countries. These fallacies mostly concern the relation between state and market.

A market economy is deemed to be normally efficient, whereas all state regulation and intervention is judged to be normally inefficient. That this statement is baseless is evident. Let us consider the present condition of the Italian economy. Those well informed on the state of Italian industry are fully aware that the main reason for its loss of competitive advantage on international markets is the poor performance of a number of large firms, especially in product design and marketing. Yet in official debate the possibility that some private entrepreneurs may fail is ignored: the only issue regarded as relevant to the competitive advantage of Italian industries in the world economy is therefore wage policy.

The economic history of Italy has plentiful examples of the inefficiency of state intervention, but there are also numerous cases where state action has been more efficient than private activity. There is no doubt that, after the Second World War, the private car industry (led by Valletta of Fiat) proved to be more efficient than the state firms in the sector (Alfa Romeo in particular). At the same time the state steel industry achieved innovations in production technology (by means of the Sinigaglia Plan) which were far in advance of those in private industry.

If we are to frame the privatization issue correctly, we need an adequate understanding of the relationship between state and market. From the history of industrialization, it seems to me, the following two statements can be inferred:

1. No sustained process of development has ever occurred without some direct or indirect state intervention. (In some countries - Germany for instance - and at some stage of economic development, the state has been substituted by the financial system, which guides the market rather than being guided by it.) The boom in the United States during the 1980s would not have happened without an expansionary fiscal policy that had not only global but also structural effects. In fact, the industries that achieved the greatest success on an international scale were those that benefited most from government demand and from intervention to spur (and finance) research activities.

2. There is no sustained growth that can be maintained without a market: the USSR being the most salient example.

State and market do not correspond to two alternative ways of conceiving the economy: they act as complements to each other in determining how an economy can be structured and how it can work. To understand the role of the state we must free ourselves of the prevailing conceptions that the state is either a neutral *deus ex machina* (as some scholars of welfare economics assume) or the devil that contractualism seeks to exorcise.

We need, in fact, to revise our conception of the state. Contrary to current interpretations, Smith was well aware of the role of the state, which he saw as fulfilling a function which was not the mere satisfaction of certain collective needs. He listed the reasons why the state must create conditions for economic development: in particular, the production of those infrastructures whose productivity cannot be properly assessed within the excessively short time-horizon of entrepreneurs. Mill's position on this point was more radical.

Smith was also convinced that the pressure exerted on the government by merchants was against the public interest. Competition can frustrate the entre-preneurs' search for rent provided the state operates properly (not once and for all, by issuing an anti-trust law, but in all decisions of economic policy).

The minimalist conception of the state is unacceptable not only for theoretical reasons but for practical ones as well. The erosion of social cohesion due to the evolution of the economic and political system has reached such a critical point that the need for a strong state becomes crucial. Pressure on the government is exercised not only by merchants - as Smith pointed out - but by all social groups. A strong state is required to subordinate various contrasting interests to some common interest (the public good). Two interrelated problems arise here: how can the public good be defined, and how can a strong state be reconciled with a democratic system? These are not merely juridical-technical issues: they highlight fundamental social-cultural problems (concerning, in particular, the role of political parties).

While domestic needs require a strong state, if disruption of the international political and economic system is to be avoided, national states must renounce some of their powers; hence, for an international order to be rebuilt and maintained, weak states are necessary.

3. The real motives behind political programmes for privatization

Although most businessmen in Italy are in favour of deregulation, they have on several occasions exerted pressure on the government for financial help (or for the lira be devalued) and, eventually, for the transfer of some firms close to bankruptcy from the private to the public sector. In the United Kingdom, in recent years privatization has involved, not industries whose public management proved to be inefficient but those with better future prospects and therefore highly attractive to private entities: Cable and Wireless (1981), Amersham International and Britoil (1982), Associated British Ports (1983), Enterprise Oil and Jaguar (1984), British Telecom sold to Mitel, British Gas (1986), British Airways, Rolls Royce and the British Airport Authority (1987).

Businessmen, in fact, are interested in both nationalization and privatization, but their interest in either of these processes depends on the condition and prospects of the economy, not on scientific considerations. Likewise, neither are the interests of political parties and political leaders in nationalization and privatization based on theoretical arguments. De Gaulle was in favour of nationalization because of his resentment against French businessmen who had sympathized with Nazi Germany, and because he aimed to strengthen the power of the political system over the business community. In Italy, Fanfani's commitment to the nationalization of the electricity industry was similarly motivated. It comes as no surprise to note a positive correlation between the eagerness of certain political movements and political leaders for privatization and their relations with industrial and financial groups.

Both businessmen and political leaders seem to underestimate the fact that the new prospects for the world economy mean that relations between state and market will have to be revised.

4. New perspectives for the state and for the market

The recession in some Western countries will hamper the privatization process, for two reasons. First, big corporations and financial markets are in no condition to buy state properties unless an expansionary monetary policy is implemented (but in this case why hurry privatization?). Second, it is likely that new state interventions will become necessary. I hope that, in contrast to events in the USSR, Western countries will undertake proper diagnosis of the real conditions and prospects of the economy. They will thus avoid proposing unrealistic programmes which then oblige them to take sudden decisions with adverse effects on state-market relations; effects that can be avoided by a well-planned economic policy.

Unfortunately economists seem not to have developed an adequate analysis of real economic conditions and likely prospects. In fact, the reason why economists largely failed to explain the long boom of the 1980s, and seem incapable of assessing the present recession, is that they disregard changes in the structure of global variables because of the kind of theories and models they use. They have been unable to discover the reasons for the fall in the propensity to save and equally unable to make proper assessment of the impact of the change in income distribution on the level and the structure of demand.

The recession in the USA is not a wave in a fluctuating process akin to those that economists have examined. Short-period movements are constrained by those structural changes I have mentioned and which are inadequately analysed by economists. The relations between micro- and macro-structure turn out to be more complex than is assumed by both the Keynesian and the monetarist approaches.

It is not only the recession under way in most Western countries, but also the problems associated with the transition process from the command to the market economy in the East, that will pose the problem of the relations between market and state in new terms, even in the West. The transition process appears to be more complex than expected, and may even be of a different nature. It affects not only the countries directly involved but the whole world economic system.

Western and Eastern countries have a dramatic problem in common: their shortage of capital, a phenomenon that may be hidden by 'financiarization' processes. The USA is interested in exporting to Eastern countries. For this to be possible, apart from certain political conditions which we cannot take for granted, credit will have to be offered to those countries. This is credit, however, that they will probably be unable to repay, so that in a few years these countries will find themselves in the same position as those of the Third World. In the United States, too, debtors are unlikely to be able to repay their debts unless there is a strong devaluation of the dollar - which may come about as a result of the policy that Bush will, probably, adopt to lead the country out of the tunnel of depression. Most American economists now realize that the main obstacles to the revival of the economy are changes in income distribution (mostly caused by the low increase in wages as compared with other incomes) and the excessive indebtedness of both firms and households.

While America has to stimulate its economy, Germany has to accelerate the transformation of the eastern part of the country for political reasons. This requires policies able to attract capital from abroad.

I have shown how the prolonged boom of the 1980s was made possible by a harmony of disequilibria (American spending for the rest of the world, Japanese saving for America). Today, the prospects for the world economy depend on disequilibria which can no longer be harmonized.

5. New perspectives for privatization in the West

It is within this new world perspective that the problem of privatization must be reconsidered. We must address two problems which are considered in opposition but which, because of the new problems of economic policy, are becoming increasingly complementary. The conditions must be created for both more efficient markets and a more efficient state. Privatization is only one of the structural changes required.

Unfortunately, privatization has become a live issue in political debate for mostly fiscal reasons. The philosophy of Louis XIV - *Après mois le déluge* - dominates present fiscal policy in Italy: the dramatic state deficit is remedied (so to speak) by having people pay their taxes in advance and by selling state properties.

Standing prior to the problem of privatization is that of the conditions that must be fulfilled to achieve an efficient market. These cannot be visualized by applying the static approach on which the Pareto criterion for optimality is based. The most relevant problems are, in fact, those that concern the ways by which all potential entrepreneurial skills (also those of small businessmen) are exploited. The efficiency of markets depends to a large extent on the efficiency of certain services provided by the state. A remark, this, which suffices to show how market and state efficiency are interlinked.

Before the problems of privatization and deregulation can be addressed we have to deal with problems of state re-regulation. When I was head of the *Ministero delle Partecipazioni Statali* (Ministry of State Firms) in the first Cossiga Government (1979-80), I proposed that privatization should be implemented when private entrepreneurs can be reasonably expected to be more efficient that the state: a state of affairs likely to come about when firms' technology is of the kind I called 'commercial technology' - that is, when the success of the firm depends to a large extent on product features that are commercially viable (and can be made so by advertising). Food and textiles are two sectors characterized by commercial technologies. In the case of the other type of technology - engineering technology - it is less clear in advance whether private firms are more or less efficient than state firms, provided the latter are organized in such a way as to operate efficiently. This need arises not only as regards economic activities that can be run directly by the state, but also those activities that most economists agree are proper to the state.[1]

A new organization of the state bureaucracy is required. Some of the functions of the public administration should be transferred to agencies operating as private firms. These agencies would be controlled by the state, which, after setting the objectives of these agencies would exercise its power in similar fashion to majority shareholders in private companies. As for the firms directly controlled by the state, statutes should be drawn up to ensure their autonomy and to regulate relations between the different levels at which entrepreneurial decisions are taken (those of the controlling state-owned company or public body, like IRI, ENI and EFIM in Italy, and of the firms under their control). When the government wishes firms to pursue objectives that are justified within the framework of more general policies, it should offer compensation, so that what is most in the interest of society is also what is most advantageous to firms.[2]

6. Is a market economy a solution for the USSR?[3]

A completely different issue, however, is privatization in a system moving from a command economy to a market one. I shall confine myself to the case of the USSR. There is no doubt that the conversion of the Soviet economy to a market economy is essential for its structural crisis eventually to be overcome. But, precisely because of this, two preliminary questions must be answered. Is the market *the* solution for the structural crisis of the countries of the East, where the failure of central planning and the collapse of the political system (and its associated ideology) go hand in hand? How can privatization help to establish a market economy, and how can a market economy create the conditions for privatization?

Unfortunately, doubts concerning a possibly affirmative answer to the first question are well grounded. For various reasons, some of which may shed light on the problems themselves of privatization and marketization, others which will be better understood after my reflections below on the issues of privatization and marketization. I begin with some introductory remarks.

1. For the market mechanism to work, a proper interaction must be established between state strategy and agents' behaviour; a point that I made above in emphasising the complementarity of state and market. In the USSR, the problem of how the state should be institutionally equipped with the instruments it needs to manage the transition process and to create the conditions for a workable market economy has not been properly understood because of ideological prejudices (a dogmatic association of democracy with a market economy). The market economy has been conceived as being the spontaneous result of both price liberalization and privatization; and democracy as the spontaneous product of *perestroijka*.

2. The market can be the solution deemed to be appropriate only if it is competitive. Most of the debate assumes - more or less consciously - that the result of liberalization will be a competitive market. But, as we shall see below, this outcome is a difficult one to achieve.[4]

3. The creation of a market economy requires a process of cultural and social-institutional change. The most dangerous prejudice to have emerged in Eastern countries is the conviction that a market economy is simply a political option. The Shatalin Plan of 1989 envisaged demonopolization and destatization processes which would reach significant proportions within the first hundred days. Price liberalization was the second stage (the next 150 days). Budget reform, anti-monopoly laws and unemployment compensation, together with other social guarantees, were considered to be proper initiatives for economic policy. Monetary reform was set as the objective for the third stage (the subsequent 150 days). In the last stage (100 days) the process of denationalization and privatization was considered capable of decisive acceleration. The plan which opposed Shatalin's (the Ryshkov Plan) reflected awareness that transition is a much more complex process: unfortunately, however, it was unable to lay down rules for the combination of state strategies with the formation and evolution of a private market economy.

4. Building a market economy is a different matter from operating a market economy once it has been established. The market economies of the West evolved progressively, at least in Great Britain and in France. In the United States and Germany, financial markets and the banking system allow for a more rapid emergence of the market economy. The building of a market economy in the aftermath of the command economy entails specific problems, some of which have been identified by V. Pavlov, who has pointed out that the complexity of the first phase depends to a large extent on the fact that, on the eve of market, extremely heterogeneous economic

relations are still involved in the production of material goods - whether considered as a whole, or with reference to the various sectors, or within each of them.

Destroying the command economy has not been sufficient to achieve a market economy. The market economy must be built on the basis of changes implemented by a state which, within the new political framework, utilizes some of the instruments of the command economy and enters into joint ventures with foreign companies to create an efficient commercial network - one of the infrastructures most urgently required for a market economy to work.

Privatization must be implemented in the context of a more general structural policy designed to create the conditions for efficient state action and to transform enterprises from administrative units into economic firms. Privatization must go hand in hand with the building of the market economy, in particular with the new industrial structure.

7. Political obstacles

Broad consensus has been achieved in the USSR on the need for privatization. Yet such consensus has only hidden the political obstacles, not eliminated them. In order to understand these obstacles, brief discussion is required of the legacy of communism. The communism regime, in fact, was not without its consequences for the social system. The right to work was a real right: all young people were given jobs in firms, regardless of whether such firms were able to provide them with productive work. It is for this reason that Eastern countries possess an impressive amount of disguised unemployment. As we shall shortly see, the market allocative mechanism is unable to solve this problem; a problem, though, which it must indeed solve if the risk of upsetting *perestroijka* is to be averted.

The most significant effect of the old regime, in terms of its implications for the possible evolution of the processes considered here, is the creation of a specific political class.

The political class bred by the communist regime is likely to survive its crisis, especially in the USSR. Also, in the USSR there are links between the political class and people who perform roles similar to those of managers in Western countries. Because of the particular institutional structure concerned, we may consider these managers (in particular those in the military industries) to have become integrated into the political class. In fact, the radical reforms needed to overcome the economic structural crisis have provoked tensions within the political class, which has also assimilated intellectuals who fought against the old regime. The support enjoyed by the conservatives, both from sections of the army and from the directors of the military-industrial sector, is certainly a matter of serious concern for Gorbachev.

The privatization process involves not only potential managers and private citizens but also the present directors of the state firms linked with the political class. The initial conditions that I have described may induce the trade unions to react against the effects of marketization and privatization: a development that is especially likely in Poland. The outcome may be an alliance between the trade unions and the political class, with profound repercussions on both the economic and political systems.

The political class will act more or less consciously to offset the tendency of the market mechanism to eliminate inefficiencies should the consequence be a reduction of their income and a weakening of their power.

Economists cannot disregard the possible scenarios that these interactions between the political and the economic systems may engender. These inter-actions may increase the probability of the perverse effects, outlined below, on both the process of privatization and of marketization. Some of the effects produced by the old regime on the structure of the economy will survive political reform for a period long enough to create specific problems for the two processes.

There is a widespread conviction that, in the countries of the East, the structure of the economy is the one that *in theory* characterizes the centrally-planned economic system. This prejudice is the mirror-image of that held by many people in the West, namely that the actual structure of the economy is the one that our theory of the market economy allows us to conceive.

In the USSR, some of the present features of the economy are the result of an evolution which continued in spite of the central plan regime. I shall mention only two of these features:

1. Enterprises established direct links among themselves to ensure some system stability in the face of planning inefficiencies. This organization was more easily established in Eastern economies, where product competition was of little relevance and where the plan model inspired the organizational strategies of the big firms. The survival of these organizational features may be a by-product of the process of privatization and may become an obstacle to marketization.

2. In the USSR a large shadow economy has grown up over the last decades. The prospects for the development of small firms sectors may thus be more promising than those who ignore this phenomenon believe.

8. Marketization: the entrepreneurial problem

Marketization cannot be the result of the privatization process alone. For a market economy to operate effectively, economic activities must be run by entrepreneurs. In order to gain better understanding of this condition, we must divide the economy into three spheres:

a) the small firms' economy (personal enterpreneurship). Since a large part of this sector will grow out of the shadow economy, the problem of how it can be made to emerge must be addressed. A Schumpeterian process can be devised to help these entrepreneurs: a problem to which I return below;
b) medium-sized firms;
c) the largest firms (a few thousand in the USSR).

In the service sector, and also in small industries (and in agriculture), we may assume the existence of a substantial number of entrepreneurs (quite a few of whom already operate in the shadow economy). A large number of medium-sized firms can be privatized by transferring them to entrepreneurs - perhaps after their corporatization, which will enable financial institutions and the state itself to help finance the process of restructuring and development.

Weitzman has proposed a well-known scheme for transforming enterprises into cooperatives. He is well aware that - as Tugan-Baranowsky pointed out - cooperatives are intrinsically unstable.[5] Nevertheless, he argues, at least in a first stage, they may help to avert the negative effects that privatization may have on income distribution.

The opposite view has been advanced by Arrow and Phelps. 'A firm should not be operated for the convenience of its managers or its workers. When the economy is operated under worker-socialism or manager-socialism, the tendency is for inefficiencies arising from excessive job protection and under-pricing of products, which at first are manifested in shortages and later in slow growth of wages as well. The economies of Poland under Rakowski and Yugoslavia in recent decades can be cited in evidence'.[6]

I agree with the principle that firms should not operate in an institutional context which creates systematic advantages for their managers and workers. There is, in fact, the risk of increasing the probability of monopolistic behaviour (recall some effects of the closed shop clause involving the USA trade unions). But I am not as pessimistic as Arrow and Phelps. There may be some activities (agriculture and services) that can be undertaken more efficiently by cooperatives than by other kinds of firms. I am ready to recognize some specific role for the cooperative during transition, for reasons to some extent different from Weitzman's.

In the USSR, cooperatives have been proposed as a means to accelerate the privatization and marketization envisaged by the law but scarcely pursued. I personally think that the cooperative may be useful, not as a definitive organization model, but to ease transition. Cooperatives can be created in order to encourage those workers with entrepreneurial skills to emerge. This will lead to the transformation of the cooperative into a personal enterprise: an outcome perhaps judged negatively by those economists who believe that the cooperative system can represent an alternative to the capitalistic market system, but positively by those concerned with the efficiency of the economy - a precondition for the attainment of social goals.

The entrepreneurial problem is a different and much more serious matter for large firms. To assess the possible solutions we need to know how many of the present directors are potential entrepreneurs. My opinions on this differ from those of Soviet economists. Whatever the case may be, we must remember that it is not sufficient for potential entrepreneurs capable of running medium-sized firms to exist either inside or outside firms: they must be chosen.

This raises the problem of the influence exercised by the political class on the economy. Enterprise directors (perhaps also those who are potential entrepreneurs) will do everything they can to preserve their power after privatization. This is likely to occur if privatization is implemented through the purchase of the newly-created company by financial institutions established and controlled by the state. Pressures applied by the political class and the trade unions to avert some of the consequences of marketization (the reduction of employment) may make it easier for the old directors to keep their power. While the privatization of small firms can be achieved in a rather short period of time, the privatization of large firms takes longer. In the meantime, new links may be established between the managers of the new financial institutions, firms' directors and the political bureaucracy. The scenario may change if, in the new financial and credit sector, a certain freedom of entry is ensured and if foreign operators are ready to take advantage of it.

9. Privatization: financial and political problems

Fisher has suggested that '(s)mall firms should be privatized by sales almost immediately with some financing provided by the state. Larger industrial firms should be corporatized as soon as possible, moved out of the shelter of the ministries that now in principle control them, and put under the direction of corporate boards; shares should be distributed to some combinations of current workers in the firms, current management, mutual funds, holding companies, banks, insurance companies, pension funds, citizens, and the government'.[7]

There is no doubt that the government/enterprise relationship must be changed. This is not to imply, however, that we can envisage either firms operating independently of the government, or the government setting its strategies independently of firms. Certainly, one must avoid the Italian situation where the government plays the firms' role and the firms the government's. As we shall see below, the government should aim its strategy towards both long-run development and the optimization of transition. Its responsibilities should be distinguished from those of firms, and governmental relations with firms should be based on well-defined rules. When the rules are no longer sufficient to deal with the problems that arise, the exceptional situation must be isolated (with the transfer I have advocated of control of the firm to a special institution if necessary) and the special intervention given adequate grounding.

The power of the political class may make it difficult to obtain an institutional framework of this kind. Either this context must be established in the year of reform (thanks to the ideological reaction against the old regime) or it is likely to become wishful thinking.

Moving to financial aspects, I share Fisher's view concerning the distinction to be drawn between small and large firms. As regards small firms, privatization must go hand in hand with a solution to the entrepreneurial and accumulation problem. It is therefore advisable to stimulate interest in the private savings partly to be offered by people with the capacity to run firms. Credit institutions may be devised to finance these small entrepreneurs, according to the Schumpeterian model. Here, as we have seen, the cooperative may play an important role.

The problem is completely different in the case of large firms. Initially, I do not think it initially advisable for the shares offered to consumers (workers) to be placed on the market. They should be instead offered (possibly adopting the auction system) to the financial institution described by Fisher. In a second phase, when the market economy starts functioning, shares could be offered directly to households. The structure to be built at the beginning must be such that it offers the choice between the American model, which relies mainly on the secondary market open to everybody, and the Japanese model, which reduces the risk of takeover and thereby creates favourable conditions for groups to set up long-run strategies - even when they are not in a position to produce large profits in the short period and yet capable of producing desirable results in the long run.

There is another factor that militates against a system where the new corporations are allowed to offer their shares to everybody in the financial market. The most backward sector of the countries of the East is credit and finance. This does not mean that, given the opportunity, non-professional agents will not enter the sector. History abounds with examples of adventurers in the guise of financial experts. The Eastern countries have no need of this kind of experience.

If competent financial institutions are chosen as the counterparts to large firms in the process of privatization (thus possibly favouring the formation of a restricted number of rather large ones in the country and stimulating the interest of well-known institutions in other countries), then scarce financial skills will be better utilized. The financial institutions can be differentiated in order to take greater advantage of the specific expertise they manage to acquire.

The financial institutions must be encouraged to act according to economic criteria. Frydman and Rapaczynski are in no doubt that the plans proposed by some East European policy-makers, 'which envisage a mechanical or administrative system of allocating the shares of the privatized enterprises among the intermediaries [having the advantage of forcing] the intermediaries to accept the weakest enterprises among the strongest' is 'nothing short of disastrous'.[8] As I have suggested, it is preferable to have specific financial institutions for non-viable firms, which can be supported by the state, and to take action to liquidate or to restructure them in such a way as to minimize social costs.

The privatization process requires an adequate credit policy and a congruous monetary policy. Credit can play a Schumpeterian role by helping small firms and some medium-sized firms. Since bank deposits and government-issue vouchers can, for the reasons given below, be used to finance the privatization process or to buy government shares - the choice between the two alternatives depending on the real rate of interest - monetary policy has a role to play in guiding transition. It can thus be used as a tool in implementing the state's strategy; one which seems essential, as we shall see, for both the efficient attainment of long-term objectives and optimization of adjustment processes.

10. The effect of privatization on income distribution

Since Pareto, economists have usually distinguished between efficiency and distributive problems. The latter are no less important than the former: the behaviour of the political classes, their relations with the trade unions, the stability of privatization itself may depend on income distribution.

As Weitzman rightly points out, the working of a market economy has effects on income distribution which are socially undesirable. However, we must distinguish between the effects of the normal working of the market mechanism and those associated with speculative activities fostered by political decisions. Some substantial changes in wealth distribution are the result, not of the normal working of the market economy but of speculations made possible by the specific conditions of the social-political system. Recall the speculation that accompanied the strategies by which, midway through the last century, some states of the USA made the building of the railway system possible. Italy's powerful new capitalists grew out of the land speculation of the 1950s and 1960s.

Privatization may provide the historical opportunity for a class of a few, very rich people to emerge in the USSR. I share Weitzman's fears concerning the possible effects of a procedure which allows a new corporation to issue shares which are available for purchase by everyone on the financial market: '(V)arious *nomenklatura*, mafia types, speculators, profiteers, and other undesirables, as well as workers who happened to be in the right place at the right time, will benefit from such a procedure, while the public at large will lose out. Indeed, there is apprehension that the assets of some enterprises may already be in the process of being stripped away illegally or unfairly'.[9]

Since marketization will be associated with, at least, a temporary decrease in the welfare of large sector of the population, privatization may have devastating effects on the building of the new market economy should it end with the creation of a class of rich people which will restructure the political classes with undesirable consequences. There is in fact the risk - which I think is particularly serious in Poland - of a transition from a command system economy to a state capitalism bearing some resemblance to the South American Peronist regimes.

At this point, it is worth remembering the distinction that several economists favouring a free market economy have drawn between *business* and *finance* (to use Veblenian terminology) or between *entrepreneurs* and *rentiers*, to adopt the Keynesian classification. This distinction may be of some use - not only because it helps assessment of the effects on income distribution of the transition from the command system to the market economy, but also because the organization of the financial sector and the rules and pattern of behaviour determining the relations between this sector and industries differ among the various market economies (in Japan as compared to the United States, for instance). This raises the problem of choosing the best organization of finance; a problem which I discuss below.

Marketization has a direct impact on income distribution. If prices are liberalized, households with large bank deposits (and some of them have enormous bank deposits thanks to the privileges granted them by the old regime) will be able to purchase commodities as they become available. Arrow and Phelps have estimated that 'to eliminate the "monetary overhang" - for which a better term is the excess supply of real liquid, or paper, wealth in private hands - there must be a reduction of this real liquid wealth of about 100 billion rubles. ... That means that prices.... must ... increase... 25 per cent.[10]

There is a danger that the inflationary process caused by price liberalization may be much more substantial. Indeed, the price increases for some commodities may be huge. The reaction of public opinion, and of trade unions in particular, may be such that firms and government will be ready to accept wage increases.

This outcome has been considered (but in general undervalued). Most proposals on the matter have suggested that price liberalization should be a gradual process. In fact, two contrasting needs must be given joint assessment: avoiding such disruption in the price system and such a high rate of increase in the price level as to cause sectorial crises and dangerous public opinion reactions; offering as soon as possible a system of realistic relative prices which will make economic computations possible and allow people to make efficient choices.

The conflict between these two needs could have been mitigated by a transition process which provided the conditions for a rapid increase in productivity even in the industrial structures that worked in the old institutional system, and by proper monetary reform. All bank deposits should have been frozen, and the rules should have been established for the use of the purchasing power that these bank deposits represented in terms of a new ruble (with the introduction of a tax designed to reduce the inequalities entailed by the initial conditions represented by the cash properties). Vouchers could then provide compensation for the burden imposed by the monetary reform. Unfortunately, however, this has not been done. According to the Soviet economists to whose attention I have called this proposal, the measure was *too unpopular*. In January 1991 the government decided to withdraw small denomination notes (100 and 50 rubles). The measure provoked an unfavourable reaction and has not yet been a satisfactory substitute for the real monetary reform that, by freeing the new ruble from the bad legacies of the old, could have facilitated the strategy for transition.

Price liberalization, moreover, must be accompanied by measures designed to change the structure of industries and the working of firms, so that, in those industries characterized by hypermonopolization, prices cannot be set at a level which exploits consumers.

If prices are kept at a political level too distant from the real costs of commodities, the black market could grow in size and the transition problem become more serious. The situation has been further exacerbated by the differing attitudes adopted by the various republics towards the problem of price control.

11. The role of financial intermediaries in the privatization process

There is a link between the privatization process and general economic policy; one which will be better understood if we consider the more technical problems of how firms to be privatized can be valued. A number of economists have suggested that the value of such firms should be decided by the market. There are three possible methods available. The first is to let firms offer on the financial market a quota of the shares that will represent their capital after corporatization. The second is to hold an auction where shares are offered to financial institutions (investment funds, pension funds, etc.) authorized by the government. Alternatively, all financial institutions (the new national organizations authorized to operate on the financial market as well as foreign financial institutions) compete to obtain certain quotas of the shares of the various firms that have been corporatized. The third method is to transfer the corporations' shares to various intermediaries. The government could ensure that quotas of various corporations in different sectors and with different levels of efficiency are transferred to the same financial intermediary.

Pavlov has mentioned the government's interest in proposals by a certain number of foreign companies to create investment funds in the USSR that could provide services of various kinds associated with the financing of mixed firms and of cooperatives. The role of foreign financial intermediaries is a problematic one. Pavlov has stated very clearly that the financial independence of the USSR is of great significance and that there is no intention to lose it. The URSS needs financial expertise: once the financial expertise has been acquired, finance can always be produced (provided, as we shall see, accumulation is adequate). Financial expertise is different in kind from industrial-technological expertise. The latter produces objective results which are of value to everybody. A new microchip is a result of industrial technological expertise which has objective value. Financial expertise can help production indirectly: directly it aims to produce money wealth for the expert. Because of this direct goal, financial activities may cause instability in the system. Most economists in the West, and the large majority of economists in the USSR, are seemingly unaware of the actual role that financial institutions play. They are urgently needed but, as with medicines, we must endeavour to benefit from their positive effects while bearing in mind their possibly harmful side-effects. We must realize that special instabilities will occur because of their operation. A problem for economic policy is posed: how to keep the credit system under control.

In Western countries, households contribute substantially to the secondary (financial) market. This will certainly also be the case in the USSR at a certain stage of development. We must, however, take care when encouraging households to participate in the financial markets, both primary and secondary. It is difficult to conceive of an auction in which all families could take part. It may instead be advisable to offer them quotas of funds created by financial intermediaries, such funds comprising shares in various corporations. As Pavlov has remarked, one function of the financial market is to absorb some of the household money wealth that may be spent on the commodities market, thereby inducing accelerated inflation. Another function of the financial market - as we shall shortly see, one linked to the credit sector - is to create a flexible, self-regulating mechanism for interregional and intersectorial flows of monetary means and finance to be used for priority scientific-tecnological and social productive projects, as well as for those within individual sectors.

The financial system is closely linked to the credit system. The USSR has the problem of converting liquidity into finance. This may ease the growth of demand for real commodities, and it may facilitate solution of the accumulation problem. The result, however, may be rather unstable. If people really wish to increase their consumption and if, at the same time, they are induced - by a high rate of interest - to invest their money wealth in the financial market, there may be pressures for an increase in wages implemented by credit expansion. Unfortunately, analysis of the problem has been distorted by the essentially macroeconomic approach adopted by economists. The Central Bank must use its instruments to govern the high-powered money entering the system. But this does not ensure that credit will match the needs and the prospects of the economy: not only for the reasons adduced in macroeconomics (difficulties in controlling the velocity of money, the role of money-substitute performed by some financial assets), but also because credit policy is, to a large extent, constrained by the evolution of the system as a result of the market mechanism, by the behaviour of the trade unions (some economists - like Hicks and Caffè - have pointed out the trade unions' role as a monetary authority), and by the behaviour of the state. There are reasons to fear that microeconomics in the USSR have produced distorted views of how the market operates, whereas macroeconomics might justify a separation between monetary policy associated with fiscal policy and the other policies that affect the economy. This was of no help to the government of the Western countries: it could be disastrous in the USSR. The fear of macroeconomic prejudices increases when we read statements to the effect that the first measure required to balance the state budget is the implementation of a severe expenditure policy aimed at reducing expenditure in all directions but the sphere of social needs.

I do not intend to address the problem of what should constitute the quotas of the shares of the various companies to be transferred to private operators. For two reasons. 1. There is no single criterion: it all depends on the firm that has been corporatized and on the propensity of the intermediaries to acquire the company's shares. 2. The state may maintain legal control over the corporation but let private individuals manage the firm. The opposite case may arise where legal control is transferred to private persons while the state exercises a decisive influence on the firm's decisions (via the connections between the political class and the firm's management).

Some economists (Bogomolov for instance)[11] have suggested a system which transfers socially-owned firms, land and buildings to the people. This is the voucher system, versions of which are about to be introduced in Czechoslovakia, Hungary and Poland. It has two advantages. First, it provides a social (moral) justification for transition. Society's property will be given back to its members. Second, it may encourage the propensity to conduct entrepreneurial activities. One can envisage vouchers being used for four purposes: i) to obtain land and apartments (the preference of most peasant and working families); ii) to buy small firms, after further finance has been obtained from the credit system (which is the entrepreneurship-fostering Schumpeterian process I have already mentioned); iii) to obtain parts of the Funds which the financial intermediaries have created by buying shares of the various corporations; iv) to acquire state bonds.

12. Privatization and accumulation

Privatization and accumulation are two distinct problems. Yet, in the situation of the Eastern countries, they are interrelated.

Frydman and Rapaczynski have discussed the possibility of distinguishing between viable and non-viable enterprises.[12] It is my view that proper assessment can, at best, suggest a classification of firms into three classes: with a first category comprising the quite large number of certainly viable firms; a second, the largest, comprising firms which can be considered viable or non-viable according to the strategy to be adopted and, in particular, the level of forthcoming investments; and a third including those firms that are definitely non-viable.

Huge investments are required to ensure that the economy grows at a rate sufficiently high to bring unemployment - which will be increased by the gradual transformation of disguised into actual unemployment - to an acceptable level in a reasonably short time. The need for restructuring is extremely urgent. Pavlov has pointed out that, in present conditions, capital is insufficient. We must also take into account the fact that quite frequently the USSR's means of production have low qualitative features and that its labour supply cannot be fully utilized because the productive base does not grow at an adequate rate.

If a sufficient level of accumulation is ensured, restructuring can be accelerated and the prospects for privatization and marketization may become less gloomy.

One should not confuse the problem of accumulation with that of finance, although, of course, they are interconnected. As Pavlov reminds us, it is not sufficient to make finance available to firms. Firms, in fact, even if they had money at their disposal, were unable to spend it. Money could not be converted into capital and labour was often unavailable.

There are various avenues to explore in solving the problem of accumulation:

a) Family savings can be encouraged. This may have favourable effects on inflationary processes. Monetary policy (a high rate of interest), fiscal policy and education (through the mass media) may boost savings. Since 1st November 1990, the Central Bank of the USSR (Gosbank) has raised the rate of interest. Consumption is not easily curbed: the most we can hope for is an easing of its growth. There is insufficient production of consumption goods (and most of them are of poor quality). Only by affecting the orientation of consumer preferences can substantial results be obtained. As for fiscal policy, indirect taxes may have several advantages: they can be more easily implemented (people do not, generally, have an accurate idea of what they pay in indirect taxation); they may discourage certain kinds of consumption and reduce some disequilibria (price changes at the levels required to balance some markets may not be desirable). Pavlov has shown himself well aware of some of these effects and has stressed the need for consumption to be regulated during the transition phase by means of purchase tax. What happened to income tax - the average rate of which fell from 10.5 to 10.3 per cent - proves my point that direct taxes are not the most efficient means to control the growth of consumption. It used to be the commonly-held opinion that increased direct taxation reduces disposable income and therefore consumption. Today the more reasonable assumption is that increased direct taxation provokes a reaction which induces increases in monetary incomes.

b) Appropriate government strategies can encourage firms to save - both because they may be in a better position to draw up long-term policies and because shareholders may accept lower dividends more readily. The method adopted for financing firms (using either a Japanese-type system or an American-type one) will also have effects on their ability to retain

profits.
c) Foreign capital may be attracted by government strategy and because of
    generally favourable conditions in the world economy. Joint ventures
    between Eastern and Western firms may help, not only by transferring
    technology, but also by promoting competition in some industries (directly
    or indirectly affected) and by solving the accumulation problem. There is a
    danger here, however. The multinationals are only interested in promoting
    those few sectors which suit their strategies. This may create imbalances in
    the process of transition and therefore constitutes another reason why the
    government should establish a strategy flexible enough to compensate the
    effects of foreign agents. Those Western governments willing to help the
    Eastern countries should take steps to ensure that the financial means are
    assigned directly to governments in relation to their well-established
    strategies. Western countries should remember that the problems of the
    Eastern countries are also their own, for the failure of these countries to
    accomplish the transition to a market economy may have disastrous effects
    on a world scale.

13. A general strategy. Some political risks

A general strategy is needed not only for political reasons. The crisis of
communist ideology - which some leaders have tried to translate into a socialist
ideology - should not entail the disappearance of some of its social values;
values that many people believed justified the system. The instability of Soviet
society may, to a large extent, be explained by its divorce between the prevailing ideology and certain social values. A general strategy can help people to
regain these social values through new ideologies - which, of course, need not
be completely invented. Nevertheless, I do not believe that we can apply the
concepts of liberalism and socialism to the ex-Soviet societies, where the
situation is quite different, as we can to our own.
    Adopting a general strategy essentially means stating the following:

a) The priority ordering of those industries whose development should be
    encouraged, something which should have been done years ago. Priority
    should have been given to the distribution sector, the transportation system
    and to electronics and information technology. Joint ventures with foreign
    firms are urgently needed to develop these sectors. Land privatization
    should have been accomplished quickly to create - together with the
    building of an efficient commercial network - the conditions by which the
    food supply could be increased.
b) The conditions to be created so that marketization is possible in some
    sectors (like agriculture) in advance of the privatization process.
c) Measures designed to provide a satisfactory solution to the accumulation
    problem, and the problems concerning enterpreneurship and human capital.
d) Long-term objectives enabling the market economy to achieve sustainable
    growth (with limited pollution effects) and socially acceptable
    development. As Pavlov has stressed, the state will operate in the market
    through its plans and the associated orders to firms. Such operations

cannot be assessed on the basis of their macroeconomic effects alone: their structural effects are even more important. Some social goals (education, for instance) help to improve the conditions that determine the efficiency of the economy.

Apart from the general dangers associated with the interest and the behaviour of the political class, there are also a number of specifically political risks. The most serious of these is that control over firms may pass from the state to the local authorities. The danger of autarchy should not be under-estimated. There is a further problem, one more general than those already mentioned, which concerns the issue of property rights. Countries like the republics of the USSR face complex problems over the relations between the various republics, the central government and local authorities. The relationship among them must be settled in such a way as to secure those degrees of autonomy necessary to stimulate competition and efficient choices at various levels, and, at the same time, to ensure that a global strategy can be established.

Here we come to a crucial problem, perhaps *the* crucial problem. As Frydman and Rapaczynski have noted, '(t)here should be nothing surprising about the fact that governments in Eastern Europe may need as much restructuring and rejuvenation as the post-communist industry and the service sector'.[13]

If economists wish to benefit from the exceptional experiment being conducted by history in order to rejuvenate their science, they must pay as much attention to political and sociological aspects as to economic-technical ones. This may entail a profound revise of their paradigms: history can conduct experiments, it cannot provide the lenses with which to see them.

Notes

1 Lombardini, 1981.
2 These proposals were set out in two documents that I submitted to the Italian Parliament: see Lombardini, 1981.
3 This paper reached me a few days before the Minsk agreement (8/12/91), when the USSR disappeared as a state entity. This does not change the validity of the arguments discussed in the paper, which can be related, when they deal with the USSR, to the state of Russia. [Editor's Note]
4 There are in fact some economists - like K. Arrow and E. Phelps (1992) - who consider it possible that monopolistic firms may emerge from the privatization process. However, they assess the monopolistic firm according to the Cournot model for market forms (assuming that all firms operate in order to maximize profits, and that they thus solve the problem of the choice of productive technique and of organizational system in the same way). The reasonable assumption is that monopoly power will be used to remain in the market (below I shall more correctly use the term 'economic power', which is to a large extent political power). Therefore the alternative is not between a competitive market and acceptance of an efficient monopoly whose profits can be either retained or transferred to other agents. The alternative to the text-book competitive market is better in some respects (if the conditions for Schumpeterian oligopolistic competition are created) and worse in others (if inefficient structures are preserved).
5 Weitzman, 1992. If the cooperative is unsuccessful, its members (or their children) will find it convenient to leave. If it is successful they will be tempted to capitalize on their

good fortune and hire labour. In both cases the cooperative will eventually disappear. Pantaleoni was convinced that a cooperative must necessarily abide by the rules of the market.

6   Arrow and Phelps, 1992.
7   Fisher, 1991.
8   Frydman and Rapaczynski, 1992.
9   Weitzman, 1992.
10 Arrow and Phelps, 1992.
11 Personal communication with the author.
12 Frydman and Rapaczynski, 1992.
13 Frydman and Rapaczynski, 1992.

Bibliography

Arrow, K. J., Phelps, E. S. (1992), 'Proposed Reforms of the Economic System of Information and Decision in the USSR: Commentary and Advice', in Paganetto, L., Phelps, E.S. (eds.), *Privatization Processes in Eastern Europe: Theoretical Foundations and Empirical Results*, London: Macmillan.

Fisher, S. (1991), 'Privatization in East European Transformation', MIT Working Paper no. 578, April.

Frydman R., Rapaczynski, A. (1992), 'Evolution and Design in the East European Transition', in Paganetto, L., Phelps, E.S. (eds.), *Privatization Processes in Eastern Europe: Theoretical Foundations and Empirical Results*, London: Macmillan.

Lombardini, S. (1981), *Un tecnico al governo. Dall'esperienza di un ministro l'anatomia delle partecipazioni statali*, Milan: Rizzoli.

Weitzman, M. L. (1992), 'How Not to Privatize', in Paganetto, L., Phelps, E.S. (eds.), *Privatization Processes in Eastern Europe: Theoretical Foundations and Empirical Results*, London: Macmillan.

PART III

WESTERN EXPERIENCES

French privatization techniques and experience: a model for Central-Eastern Europe?

Wladimir Andreff

1. Introduction

Successful techniques of privatization were pursued in France over a rather short span of time, from late November 1986 to January 1988, fourteen months which were long enough to privatize more than one thousand enterprises. The techniques utilized for this rapid achievement were efficient, to say the least. In Central-Eastern Europe today equally rapid and efficient privatization techniques are badly needed, and I intend to examine whether or not the French experience may be taken as a 'model' in this respect.

Though impressive, the French privatization drive was not free from shortcomings and obstacles. Nevertheless, taken as a whole, the French experience may well provide enlightening ideas or useful guidelines for reformers and decision-makers as they undertake the far-reaching and rapid privatization of large state-owned trusts in Hungary, Poland and Czecho-slovakia. The political context, the economic environment and the institutional framework of these three countries obviously cannot be compared to France's in the mid-eighties, and even less to those of Canada, the United Kingdom or Japan.[1] These differences do not inspire optimism; indeed, we can expect many more obstacles to prevent the privatization process in Central-Eastern Europe from spreading to the same extent as it has in France. However, if we look at how French privatization proceeded, we can draw up a list of techniques providing the best chance of success in privatizing large state enterprises.

The present paper relies on an assumption which will not be debated here: I take it for granted that privatization is now a political 'must' in Central-Eastern Europe. Nor shall I discuss the appropriateness of privatizing small and big enterprises, although this assumption needs further elaboration on economic grounds as well as from a political perspective, as Grosfeld and Hare have stressed: 'Why have such rapid privatization programmes been put forward, and why would it not be possible to proceed more slowly? There is a political argument favouring a rapid transition, namely that it could prevent or minimise the risk of any return to the old centralized type of economic management'.[2] Unfortunately, economic and political momentum do not converge as far as changes in property and ownership are concerned, as will be shown below. Before arguing from this evidence that privatization should proceed at a very cautious pace, I feel that clarification is needed of what is meant by privatization and what is not. My purpose is to avoid the many misunderstandings of the notion of privatization that arise from a confusion among the different property rights covered by the same word.

2. Privatization: what are we dealing with?

Privatization is obviously the legal transfer or sale of state-owned or collectively-owned physical and financial assets to private owners. This definition is neither sufficiently comprehensive nor precise. It is not comprehensive because privatization may sometimes come about without the transfer or sale of state or collective assets: the share of private business in the economy may increase - which is strictly speaking a privatization drive as well - when new and already established private enterprises grow faster than enterprises in the non-private sector of the economy. The definition is not precise because it says nothing about the transfer of the prevailing property rights possibly involved in the transfer or sale of assets. In this respect, privatization implies that new private owners acquire three decisive rights over assets, namely the right to utilize assets *(usus)*, the right to appropriate any returns from assets *(usus fructus)*, and the right to transfer assets and to dispose of property *(abusus)*. Owners who cannot enforce all these rights on their assets enjoy only alleviated economic property. Their power of economic decision over assets remains limited; the privatization of assets has not actually been accomplished.

In the large joint stock companies of today, these three property rights of shareholders have to be defined a little differently. Shareholders enjoy non-alleviated economic property if, and only if:

a) they have the right to proportional participation in that part of profit which is earmarked for dividends,
b) they have voting rights at the shareholders meeting in proportion to their shares of total assets,
c) they have the right to sell their shares freely (colloquially, the right 'to vote with their feet').

Then privatization is defined as any legal decision which enforces the above-listed rights for private owners of an asset. This definition only makes sense if it is closely bound up with profitability and with increasing the value of assets. An enterprise that stays too long in the red will be unable to pay dividends and hence will eventually alleviate its shareholders' right (a). Because of right (c), several shareholders will sell their shares and therefore lose all their rights on assets; the enterprise might go bankrupt, thus alleviating or extinguishing all the rights of every owner. Private property in joint stock companies cannot last very long without profitability, or without erosion in the value of their shares.[3]

According to the economic literature on principal agent theory[4], as long as their property rights are not alleviated, private owners in joint stock companies enforce discipline on managers' behaviour. Well-monitored behaviour by managers consists of maximizing profit, not the maximizing of their own take-home gains or their non-wage benefits (large offices, pretty secretaries, retraining sessions in Bermuda, and so on). A well behaved manager works under the hard constraint of three types of discipline: contractual discipline in the employment relation enforced by shareholders; takeover discipline enforced by potential bidders; and bankruptcy discipline enforced by creditors.

Keeping in mind this more elaborated view of what we are dealing with, I shall eliminate several misconceptions which crowd the literature under the heading of privatization, and which have included privatization in various kinds of shift of economic activity out of the state sector. These misconceptions relate to different kinds of 'de-nationalization', and one should be mindful of the fact that state withdrawal does not guarantee that assets will actually be privatized or non-alleviated property rights enforced on private owners. There are many techniques for 'de-nationalizing' or decentralizing state property which are erroneously believed to be privatization techniques, and I shall now discard them from discussion. A first case in point is the contracting out of public activities to private enterprises, either through franchising or leasing. For instance, the technique of leasing assets to private producers, such as the *arenda* system in Soviet agriculture, is not *per se* a privatization technique. It has indeed been pointed out by Soviet economists[5] that leasing is the direct opposite of privatization and that it 'achieves the general character of State property'! In fact, in leasing its assets or land the state never loses the *abusus*, unless such assets or land are sold to the lessee at the end of the leasing contract. It is well known, for example, that Gorbachev is in favour of very long-term leasing (for 50 to 100 years) as against the privatization of land.

The technique of giving control over the firm to its employees for free, on the 'one employee, one vote principle', is not a privatization technique. Lewandowski and Szomburg[6] are perfectly correct to call it the 'socialization' of assets, which in itself has nothing to do with privatizing them. I would add that it is socialization with 'de-nationalization' which paves the way to either industrial democracy in the state-owned enterprise or self-management. Even in a self-managed enterprise, workers are allowed to decide on the internal division of labour *(usus)* and the distribution of take home gains *(usus fructus)*, but they do not have the right to dispose of property. Of course, property rights in a self-managed enterprise do not compare with the private monitoring of assets and the supervision of managers. There will only be real privatization if, instead of assets being transferred for free, they are bought by employees (or managers) of the former state enterprise in the context of a leveraged buy-out (LBO) or a leveraged management buy-out (LMBO). The success of an LBO or an LMBO implies, however, numerous preconditions: namely a high level of entrepreneurship among the employees, a rather sophisticated banking system, highly skilled financial engineering, a dynamic stock exchange, and a tight network of business lawyers, brokers, fiscal advisers, chartered accountants and auditors[7], which are hardly forthcoming in Central-Eastern Europe at the moment.[8]

Transfers of assets from the state to groups such as cooperatives, municipalities, trade unions, social and political organisations are again merely techniques for the collectivization, decentralization and socialization of property under continuing state ownership. The state does not usually relinquish *abusus* to the cooperators, mayors, unionists or politicians. Even if these people are then able to acquire *usus* and *usus fructus*, they will not be interested in the value of assets they cannot dispose of, and it is obvious that they will consequently not behave as profit maximizers.

The privatization of management in state-run enterprises seems to be a much more interesting solution for Central-Eastern Europe. The issue of how to manage the state assets that remain is high on the agenda in Hungary, Poland and Czechoslovakia[9] because it is increasingly evident that the privatization of assets proceeds slower than expected. The privatization of management seems to be a good interim solution when it is not feasible to privatize assets overnight. This technique involves the management of public enterprises according to the same criteria as those that operate in the management of private enterprises - especially the profitability criterion, which is thus given a first rank priority. Needless to say, in the absence of any shift in the ownership of assets, the privatization of management does not fulfil the conditions necessary for *abusus* to be removed from state hands. It cannot be regarded as fully-fledged privatization because the state still possesses the three major property rights, as well as the right to fire managers who do not achieve profitability. For instance, according to a 1988 decree in Laos, managers may be fired by the *tutelle* after three loss-making years. Nevertheless, separating ownership from the management functions of government is the scheme adopted by those countries still reluctant to alter the publicly-owned character of enterprises, and it continues to prevail in China and Algeria, for example.[10]

The last and most discussed technique under the heading of privatization is that based on the transfer of state ownership to holding companies, the shares of which are controlled and managed by financial institutions such as asset management bureaus (China), shareholding funds (Algeria, Poland), mutual funds (Czechoslovakia), banks, pension funds, and insurance companies - all of which are considered in formerly socialist economies to be the equivalents of institutional investors in (Western) fully-fledged market economies. A prerequisite here is the rapid commercialization of state-owned enterprises, so that their supervision can be distanced from the administrative process and enterprise guidance placed in the hands of persons interested in a return on the assets. By its very definition, commercialization is not privatization: the former usually involves the conversion of state-run enterprises into joint stock companies or other forms of partnership, with their shares initially held by a variety of organizations like those listed above. A joint stock company with numerous (even millions of) shareholders is the kind of 'socialization' of ownership, including private capitalist ownership, that Marx himself discussed and advocated a century ago.

If the organizations (banks, pension funds, insurance companies, etc.) that hold shares are themselves mainly state-owned or state-run, no real progress has been made towards privatization. The only outcome is a more dispersed ownership, which of course may ease the future re-allocation of assets between enterprises and industries still under state monitoring. Indeed, when private stakes are not involved, or when people have only limited access to the shares of holding companies, then these holdings are obviously still state-run and their managers may well receive instructions to 'go easy' on the dividends to be paid to shareholders. Publicly-owned holdings and state-run (mutual, shareholding, pension) funds have been implemented before all in those countries whose governments are unwilling to privatize, or in those countries where, for political reasons, it is necessary to find a proxy for a privatization which cannot be rapid in practice.

On the contrary, if these holdings are privately owned - which is not yet the rule in Central-Eastern Europe - then they are in fact institutional investors. However, too dispersed ownership does not provide owners with what I have called the contractual discipline enforced by shareholders on managers, although this is necessary for an efficient and profitable management. A process of ownership concentration will take place until a majority, or a substantial minority, of shares is held by a few core shareholders among the institutional investors who are ready and able to eliminate mismanagement (i.e. to compel managers to maximize profits). The outcome of this process is well known: it leads to the 'finance capital control' over big business exemplified by the links between pension funds, shareholding funds, banks, insurance companies and industry in the United States[11] and elsewhere in developed, fully-fledged market economies. The network of financial control is often paralleled by interlocking directorates[12], so that today 'big linkers' have replaced the tycoons of the last century. No doubt, in this case we have the genuine privatization of assets and management. Nevertheless, Kornai[13] is probably right to express doubts over this finance capital/big business complex as the private substitute for state monopoly over the economy envisaged in Central-Eastern Europe.

Probably in order to avoid the relatively undemocratic solution based on finance capital outlined above - certainly because it is not yet workable in Hungary, Poland and Czechoslovakia - the two latter countries have resorted to the last technique of privatization that I shall comment on here. This technique involves the free distribution of shares to the population or, as the scheme has been actually designed in these two countries, the giving away of property through coupons or vouchers distributed free to all citizens and redeemable as shares in new joint stock companies after a strictly defined span of time. Although democratic political forces are in favour of this scheme, there are, unfortunately, many economic obstacles which hinder the spread of this so-called 'citizen ownership'. First, the free distribution of shares or vouchers is not, properly speaking, a privatization process. If all citizens become the owners of privatized enterprises, there is a flavour of the socialization (or 'citizenization') of assets. Since each citizen acquires the right to sell shares, he or she enjoys the *abusus*. But they cannot enjoy *usus* and *usus fructus* without hiring professional managers to run the newly 'de-nationalized' enterprises.

With a maximum degree of property dispersal among the whole population, the two latter property rights are very likely to be alleviated by unmonitored behaviour by managers. On the other hand, monitoring managers would mean a concentration of ownership and a return to non-democratic control by concentrated financial stakes; it remains to be seen whether privatization and democracy can go hand in hand.

The second category of obstacles in the way of citizen ownership can be seen from the only experiment in free distribution of shares to be undertaken in the world. A large-scale free transfer was made to the general public in the Canadian province of British Columbia: 86 per cent of the population received shares, and they were satisfied in the short term as the value of each share climbed from 6 to 9 dollars; a success which was due to an aggressive promotional campaign in favour of privatization. However, the cost of privatizing was proportionally increased by 16.67 dollars for each shareholder, a cost in addition to the 30 dollars representing five free shares given to everybody. After a while, the distribution of shares was concentrated into fewer hands.[14] Poor investment decisions by the private managers operating in a highly politicized environment resulted in a significant decline in the value of the portfolio, and a loss of most of the value of the shares. It must be admitted that the free distribution finished in a mess.

The third problem is that free distribution to the population is not at all egalitarian, despite the claims sometimes advanced by the propaganda promoting popular capitalism. Citizens who obtain shares in loss-making enterprises will not be on a par with those who obtain shares in highly profitable companies. A last series of drawbacks to the free distribution of shares arise in a shortage economy, where the marginal utility of shares is low.[15] In this case, many citizens will soon sell their shares in order to finance the purchase of consumer goods, and the scheme will therefore fuel demand inflation in Central-Eastern Europe.

This is not to argue that all the techniques discussed above are irrelevant to the transition of formerly socialist economies. They could be effectively used as complementary instruments, but they are not techniques concerned with real privatization such as those that I list below.

3. The techniques of privatization

When studying the techniques of privatization, it is useful to distinguish between privatization 'from the top', privatization 'from below'[16] and 'spontaneous' privatization. The latter term refers to the transfer of state assets to their former managers by various means such as the exploitation of loopholes in new company laws, the setting up of joint ventures, and so on. Privatization 'from below' consists in both allowing new small stakes to enter private business and in offering small state-owned businesses for sale or lease to citizens. I shall focus on privatization 'from the top', as the process designed to change the ownership and property of large state-owned and state-run trusts, and for various reasons: this change is the main concern of most of the new governments in Central-Eastern Europe today; it is extremely complex to implement as far as techniques of privatization are concerned; and it is an area in which French privatization techniques have performed efficiently. Moreover, should it succeed on a large-scale, privatization from the top could introduce a kind of 'ratchet' effect into transition towards a market economy.

Five techniques are available for privatizing big state trusts, and I give a brief outline of them here.[17] Four of them presuppose that the state enterprise has previously been converted into a joint stock company. An auction sale of shares is the first technique, and implies that an active stock exchange is already in operation. The valuation of formerly state-owned assets is thus the result of floating shares on the stock market; that is, it depends on market price mechanisms. However, before the sale begins, it is advisable to compute a starting supply price, for instance on a price-earning ratio basis, from which trial and error will lead to the equilibrium price of the stock market.

A second technique can be suggested: a tender price offer. Shares are offered at a minimum price determined by a qualified privatization commission (or agency) after the auditing of each company to be placed on sale, and after professional advice has been gathered from chartered accountants, bankers and auditors. Would-be shareholders must propose a price higher than the minimum within a strictly defined span of time, at the end of which shares are sold at the striking price, thus soaking up all the issues of shares. This technique was used for the first five enterprises privatized during the Thatcherite period.[18] A possible mix of a tender price offer and an auction sale may be envisaged when the stock market is too small to soak up the whole supply of shares. Then a small proportion of all the issued shares is offered for auction, say 20 or 30 per cent of the total. The clearing price determined in this way is thereafter taken to be the tender price. The International Monetary Fund especially recommends this mixed technique for Third World countries.[19] However, neither a tender nor a mixing of auction and tender provides a satisfactory answer for the crucial issue of valuating the privatized assets in Central-Eastern European countries. None of the more usual valuation methods - price earning ratio, accounting value of net assets, discounted cash flow - can rely on accurate enterprise accountancy in these countries.[20]

One may also conceive of a non-market form of privatization. Under this third technique the state sells its entire stake in a company to an already private enterprise which is, for instance, interested in acquiring a backward or a forward linked activity in the public sector. This may be of some help in privatizing an unprofitable state-run enterprise, all the more if it can be split into several branches and sold to several buyers, with the state keeping the least profitable or the most loss-making affiliates of the firm. A fourth technique is merely a variant of the third one, although it operates more rapidly: here a private enterprise, either domestic or foreign, launches a takeover bid for, or attempts a merger with, a state-owned firm or affiliate. Needless to say, if the takeover or the merger succeeds, this is not without or against the will of the government embodying state power. A last technique paves the way for a very smooth and progressive privatization drive, although it is deeply rooted in market mechanisms. This technique has been used in France by the Socialist government since 1983, when it was reluctant to privatize public enterprises openly so soon after the 1982 nationalizations.[21] In this case, state-owned enterprises have been allowed to issue investment certificates or vouchers (*certificats d'investissement*) and 'participating securities' (*titres participatifs*).

These stocks are not actually shares, especially since their holders have no voting rights and hence have no say in management or power of supervision over the managers. However, whenever a state-owned enterprise does issue such securities, the share of private stakes in its total equity stock increases. Partial privatization thus proceeds smoothly from one occasion to the next, and again this solution seems appropriate to a small stock exchange which cannot absorb a large supply of securities. In France, people holding investment certificates or participating securities in state-owned firms later obtained the priority right to redeem their stocks in shares when, between 1986 and 1988, a right wing government decided on the wholesale privatization of several public enterprises.

4. The French privatization 'model': the technique mix and preconditions

In France, governments of both right and left have almost always rejected the fourth of the above-listed techniques. Whenever the potential bidder has been foreign, the French government has usually preferred at best to negotiate a non-market sale of state-owned enterprise, or, at worst, to forbid the merger or the takeover bid. With domestic bidders, a non-market sale has often been advocated for the purposes of industrial policy and the recovery of the internal market, or because it has been deemed as being in the national interest; that is, the sale has been conditioned by the endorsement of economic policy objectives by the buyer. The auction sale at a floating price is no longer utilized. Indeed, Mr Balladur himself described auction sales as 'shocking' when he was the Minister of Finance and Privatization between 1986 and 1988.[22] His argument was that, although auctions often maximize state income, they set prices so high that only professional and institutional investors can afford them. Highly uneven access to shares was contrary to the popular capitalism that Mr Balladur supported (and even more contrary to the social-democratic views of the political opposition).

The issue of investment certificates and participating securities has only been utilized by the Socialist government in order to initiate a process of creeping, though unavowed, privatization, which has never given majority share ownership to private stakes. Thus the French privatization drive in 1986–88 mainly relied on a mix of the two remaining techniques: tender price offers and direct non-market sales to already private firms. The choice of these two techniques obviously raised the question of how the price of shares was to be determined. In the last resort, the price was settled by the Minister of Finance and Privatization after his consideration of a minimum price established by a Commission of Privatization comprising seven eminent 'wise men': one former minister, one senior member of the Council of State, one former chairman of a Chamber of the Revenue Court, one professor of business law, one former chairman of Saint-Gobain, and two bankers. The Commission was appointed for five years with no revocation being allowed. For all privatized enterprises, the Minister of Finance and Privatization chose a tender price higher than the minimum price recommended by the Commission but lower than the would-be equilibrium price in the stock market. Indeed, for each privatized firm sold by tender, demand for shares exceeded supply, and there was no alternative but to ration each candidate's share-holding. For instance, the first privatization, of Saint-Gobain, generated a demand for 61.6 million shares as compared with a supply of 10.8 million issued shares. Slight underpricing has, of course, been the cornerstone of France's successful experience with privatization.

The results achieved were nevertheless impressive.[23] Fourteen large industrial, banking and financial state trusts were privatized between 24th November 1986 and 27th January 1988 (see Table 1). Twelve of these large firms were sold by tender, one by a non-market sale, and one privatized by special state decree. A fifteenth firm, the national bank *Caisse Nationale de Crédit Agricole* was sold a few weeks later to its regional and local affiliates. After their privatization, the fourteen big firms were monitoring a network of 1,082 commercial, industrial and financial enterprises, and supervising a workforce of 333,150 people. The value of the privatized assets amounted to around 125 billion francs, including 277 other sales of affiliates by the public sector to the private sector in addition to these fourteen large privatizations. Altogether, 1,359 state enterprises and affiliates were privatized within fourteen months. In the United Kingdom, Mrs Thatcher's government took six years to achieve a comparable score (assets of 7.5 billion sterling and about 400,000 employees in the twenty firms privatized between December 1979 and December 1985).

A second outcome of the French privatization drive was a dramatic change in saving behaviour. This change of course began with the Socialist government's deregulation of the French financial market in 1984, which provided new incentives for holding securities rather than deposits in savings banks. Privatizations altered the previously cautious saving behaviour of the French and gave a boost to somewhat bolder, though not reckless, shareholding behaviour: 16.6 million French savers bought shares in the twelve state firms sold by tender. Before the privatization drive, one out of twenty French households used to hold shares; the figure now rose to one in four. Moreover, almost all new shareholders (over 80 per cent) went on to hold shares in the long term; and they did not re-sell them even when the financial 'crash' occurred in October 1987. Shareholding was sustained by the gains accruing to shareholders as the market values of shares increased over their tender prices on the first day of quotation - from 6 per cent for shares in Société Générale to 80 per cent for Sogenal (see Table 1). Underpricing therefore appears to be a sensible approach. Only the shareholders in Suez, privatized a week after the financial 'crash', lost 21 per cent of share value at the first quotation. Nevertheless, despite the 'crash', the market value of all shares was largely over the tender price at the end of 1988.

Last but not least, the state budget secured an income from privatizations amounting to an overall sum of 81.7 billion francs as of 31st August 1989. This amount was much higher than the cumulative capital endowments by the state to all industrial public enterprises between 1982 and 1985 (50.9 billion francs), or the cumulative financial deficit of the public sector taken as a whole in 1984 and 1985, i.e. 69 billion francs.[24] One-third of state receipts resulting from privatizations was utilized to increase the capital endowment of the remaining state-owned enterprises and two-thirds financed repayment of the public debt.

Table 1
Privatization by Tender Price Offer (TPO) in France (*)

Companies	Employees	Date of TPO	Rate (+)
Saint-Gobain	140,000	24.11.86	310
Paribas	24,800	19.01.87	405
Sogenal	3,000	9.03.87	125
BTP (a)	420	6.04.87	130
BIMP (b)	400	21.04.87	140
CCF (c)	12,500	27.04.87	107
CGE (d)	240,000	11.05.87	290
Havas	15,000	25.05.87	500
Société Générale	43,600	15.06.87	407
TF 1 (e)	1,500	29.06.87	165
Suez	16,900	5.10.87	312
Matra	28,000	20.01.88	110

Companies	Amount (x)	Price 1	Price 2	Price 3	Price 4	Price 5
Saint-Gobain	6.300	369	415	414	615	677
Paribas	6.100	480	320	300	470	512
Sogenal	600	225	94	104	n.d.	n.d.
BTP (a)	100	176	138	128	n.d.	n.d.
BIMP (b)	100	170	188	194	195	n.d.
CCF (c)	1.700	125	107	114	190	209
CGE (d)	8.000	323	215	229	403	493
Havas	1.100	540	409	515	692	1.250
Société Générale	9.100	432	299	299	522	523
TF 1 (e)	1.200	178	170	185	410	381
Suez	6.500	261	279	240	312	390
Matra	400	123		136	253	4334

(*) Compagnie Générale de Construction Téléphoniques (CGCT) and Mutuelle Générale Française (MGF) are not included; these were not privatized by TPO
(+) Sale price of the share at the moment of the TPO in francs
(x) Total amount of the TPO in billions of francs
Price 1: market value of the share on the first day of quotation; Price 2: by the end of 1987
Price 3: market value on March 15, 1988; Price 4: by the end of 1988; Price 5: on October 5, 1989
(a) Banque du Bâtiment et des Travaux Publics
(b) Banque Industrielle et Mobiliére Privée
(c) Crédit Commercial de France
(d) Compagnie Générale d'Electricité
(e) TV channel

Source: Bizaguei , A., *Le secteur public at les privatisations*, 'Que sais-je?', no. 2414, Paris: Presses Universitaires de France, 1988. Haute Conseil du Secteur Public, *Le secteur public concurrentiel en 1987-88*, Paris: La Documentation Française, 1990.

If we wish to understand why French privatization was successful, we must go beyond the underpricing factor which proved to be so profitable for shareholders. The second factor in this success was the decision by the French government to diversify shareholding in newly-privatized enterprises into four blocks of shareholders. This second approach is particularly worth pointing out to Central-Eastern European decision-makers. The shareholding was divided as follows:

- Up to 20 per cent of total shares could be offered on international security markets. The aim behind setting this threshold was obviously to prevent foreign stakes from acquiring majority control over a newly privatized company - at least at the moment of its privatization. The first quotation shares might be traded and the majority share might even switch to foreign capital. The state, however, could retain a 'golden share' which would give the government the power to outvote all other shareholders on specific issues like takeovers and asset sales. This technique was used when privatizing Havas and Matra.
- A minimum 10 per cent of total shares were kept at a preferential rate for the wage-earners in the privatized enterprise. In each of the twelve tenders, there was excess demand for these reserved shares (from 1.3 times the supply in the case of Saint-Gobain to 3.4 times in the case of CGE). The rationing of wage-earners was thus necessary, each employee being allowed to buy extra shares at the tender price on general offer.
- A hard core of stable shareholders formed in each of the enterprises privatized by tender. The scattering of ownership was avoided, and this hard core was supposed to monitor managers and to impede any unwanted takover bid for the newly privatized enterprise. Each shareholder in the hard core was allowed to hold between 0.5 and 5 per cent of total shares, and all the hard core shareholders together were entitled to possess between 15 and 30 per cent of total shares. Shares have been sold to the hard core on a non-market basis, though at a higher rate than the tender price, this latter being then increased by 2.5 to 10 per cent of the surplus value resulting from the difference between the first quotation and the tender price. Moreover, hard core shareholders undertook to keep their shares for a determined span of time (usually two years) and to operate within a technological and commercial framework more or less imposed by the government.
- The fourth block of shares was placed on sale at the tender price and made available to every French citizen or resident in order to spread popular shareholding. Over 15 billion shares were requested during the first ten tenders, within one year; that is, an average of 1.5 billion by tender. All citizens and residents were allowed to order ten shares with priority at the tender price. However, demand was so high that the number of shares issued was insufficient to supply more than six shares per capita at the end of the Sogenal tender, four shares per head in the case of Paribas, and just one in the case of the *Banque du bâtiment et des travaux publics* (BTP).

A fifth type of shareholder, of course, comprised institutional investors, some of whom were involved in the hard cores and all of whom were able to buy shares in newly-privatized enterprises on the stock market when some individual shareholders (about 20 per cent of the total), disappointed by the 'crash' or otherwise, decided to re-sell their shares.

It is this mix of shareholders, in addition to underpricing, that made the success of the French privatization drive possible. Other contributing factors were the securitization of savings I mentioned above, a decreasing rate of inflation after 1984, the economic policy of the Socialist government aimed at financing industry with popular savings, and a new enthusiasm for entrepreneurship in French society, politics and government. The most fertile environment for successful privatizations, however, still remains the improvement in economic performance achieved by public enterprises. In 1982 only three out of twenty-one state-owned industrial enterprises were not in the red; in 1985 only five were not in the black (Table 2). By making public enterprises profitable the Socialist government paved the way for the successful privatization drive undertaken in following years.

Table 2
Deficits and Profits of Public Enterprises in France, in Millions of Francs
(1980-1985)

Companies	1980	1981	1982	1983	1984	1985
Nationalized before 1982						
EDF	84	-4,64	-8,363	-5,450	-900	1,012
GDF	49	-950	-2,560	-2380	-3,025	485
CDF	59	-67	-692	-768	0	0
SNCF	-675	-2,002	-5,300	-8,380	-5,540	n.d.
CGM	-360	-481	-736	-540	-380	n.d.
Aéroport de Paris	58	28	9	17	50	164
Air France	10	-378	-792	87	530	729
SNIAS	118	153	96	-357	330	-454
SNECMA	70	-65	-45	-39	40	n.d.
Renault	1,547	-690	-1,281	-1,576	-12,555	-9,600
CDF Chimie	-550	-1,213	-834	-2,760	-865	-1,300
EMC	10	-312	-946	-159	30	100
Sacilor	-1,300	-2,898	-3,737	-5,610	-8,100	-4,500
Usinor	-1,961	-4,240	-4,604	-5,456	-7,600	-2,000
Nationalized in 1982						
CGE	556	586	638	662	650	1,000
Saint-Gobain	932	566	-745	405	500	550
Thompson	502	-170	-2,208	-1,251	0	400
Rhône Poulenc	-1,184	-266	-787	159	1,989	2,311
Péchiney	607	-2,565	-4,615	-295	550	732
CII Honeywell Bull	180	-449	-1,351	-625	-500	110
CGCT	-150	0	-325	-555	-550	200

Decision-makers in Central and Eastern Europe must be reminded, however, that even French successful privatizations have not been without their faults and have not been immune to sharp criticism. First, in November 1989, a Parliamentary Commission estimated the 'cost' of underpricing to the state budget (i.e. in lower receipts) at 8.3 to 19.6 billion francs. We could, however, regard this state 'loss' as a gain for shareholders and as a precondition for success. And there has also been the political criticism of privatization: selling cut-price state assets is politically inappropriate, although it is one of the most unequivocal preconditions for success in privatization.

The Paris stock exchange is rather a narrow market compared with London, New York and Tokyo, and privatization is held to provoke a crowding-out effect on the bond market. An increase in interest rates has in fact been witnessed on the French bond market, and French enterprises did reduce their indebtedness in 1986 and 1987. On the other hand, profits increased after 1984 in the French economy, thus reducing bond issues, so that it is not clear to what extent a crowding-out effect actually affected that market.

Most small shareholders have behaved, and still do, as sleeping partners uninvolved in the privatized enterprise. They are unwilling to monitor managers, and they do not attend shareholder meetings. In a poll, 68 per cent of small shareholders confessed that they only looked at the market value of their shares and took no interest in the life of the enterprise. Although there are millions of shareholders, the management of privatized companies is monitored by the hard core of stable shareholders. Small shareholders have, ultimately, the choice between staying and voting like the hard core, or leaving and selling their shares. Even more striking is the fact that these sleeping partners are so dormant that they did not sell their stock even during the financial 'crash'. Could we expect greater involvement and monitoring from small shareholders in Central-Eastern Europe when they are completely unaccustomed to holding shares?

The financial 'crash' put a brake on the privatization programme, not because of the behaviour of small shareholders but mainly because of the government's appraisal of the risk of floating shares in a less than buoyant stock exchange. Only one firm, Matra, was privatized after October 1987. We must therefore single out a large but also confident stock market as a precondition for successful privatization. In Central-Eastern Europe, where this market exists it is tiny; how much will it have to grow before it reaches the size required by privatization 'from the top'?

There is another lesson to be drawn from the French privatization drive which is especially relevant to the situation in Central-Eastern Europe. The privatization of a large firm may sometimes only result in a shift in monopoly power from the state to private stakes. In Central-Eastern Europe, the supply side is in fact much more monopolized than in the French state sector. For instance, when CGE was privatized one might well have expected the emergence of a new private monopoly on such markets as, for example, high speed train (TGV) manufacturing. However, the real scope of CGE's activity is international, and hence it is deemed to operate on contestable markets for most of its products because these are international markets. Recall that a contestable market[25] is a situation of competition among the few in which 'hit and run' entry is possible; hence tendencies to monopoly or oligopoly do not kill strongly competitive behaviour. Unfortunately, in Central-Eastern European countries internal markets are now coming into being with a high degree of concentration on the supply side and with economies less open to international competition and markets.

The last critical issue in the French privatization process concerns the formation of hard-core shareholders.[26] The French Minister of Finance and Privatization was severely criticized because investors were not sufficiently diversified: the entire set of hard cores comprised no more than 10 foreign companies: among the French companies there were 12 industrial firms, 12 banks, 11 insurance companies and 10 other corporations. After 1987, the trading of shares on the stock market increased the weight of the remaining state-owned enterprises in the total equity stock of the privatized Saint-Gobain, Société Générale and Havas. Central and Eastern European decision-makers should therefore bear in mind that stock market mechanisms may also work in favour of a partial 'de-privatization' (or 're-nationalization'), and that the old *nomenklatura* may well rear its ugly head again in business. Mr Balladur has not escaped criticism for allegedly appointing political friends to the hard cores of newly privatized enterprises.

The final criticism aimed at hard core composition arose as the last firms were privatized, when it became clear to the political (Socialist) opposition that privatization had been conceived as a revolving and self-reinforcing process. The technique used was the following: in the hard core of, say, the first privatized enterprise numerous shares were sold to state enterprises which appeared on the list of firms soon to be privatized. When these were privatized, the privatization of the first enterprise was reinforced. Interlinking the hard cores of privatized enterprises is a way to lockstep the whole privatization process. Even the strong political will of Mr Balladur's successor (Mr Bérégovoy, Socialist Minister of Finance since May 1988) has not been strong enough to break this efficient stranglehold. A French-style revolving privatization of this kind is surely of interest to decision-makers striving to privatize from the top in Hungary, Poland and Czechoslovakia, particularly should they wish to avoid unexpected backsliding.

5. Privatizing in Central-Eastern Europe: Please, don't rush!

It is now probably correct to say that the French privatization experience can be taken, theoretically, to be one of the best 'models' for the privatization of large state enterprises in the countries of Central-Eastern Europe. However, it is also probably true to say that this model is impossible to implement because too many of the preconditions are absent for French techniques to work in these countries. By the same token, a privatization drive as swift and efficient as it was in France cannot be expected in these countries.

In brief, the Central-Eastern European economies lack a stock market of a significant size. They lack sufficient savings to invest in buying shares, first because they are shortage economies[27], second because deflationary and stabilization policies have shrunk much of the currency overhang that might otherwise have fueled the demand for securities. They lack a two-tier banking system and a tight network of banks prepared to loan money to would-be hard core shareholders. They lack sufficient numbers of profitable state-owned enterprises: most of them are still in the red and in any case would not be competitive on external markets whatever the rate of exchange might be. Thus the state cannot count on privatization to yield the receipts it badly needs to stabilize the state budget and to repay the foreign debt. They still lack a demonopolized supply side as well as contestable markets. They lack a full-fledged convertible currency, although the Polish zloty and the Czecho-slovakian crown are already convertible for residents. They lack a sufficiently large upper class of would-be entrepreneurs and even a new middle class willing to move up in social rank or at least to take the chance of going into business. And they probably lack (economic and, even more, political) know-how as regards the implementation of efficient privatization techniques.

It is the absence of all these preconditions that motivates my scepticism, if not pessimism, as to the feasibility of far-reaching and rapid privatization in Central-Eastern European countries. In the final analysis, these countries have much more in common with the developing world than any other economic situation where the issue of privatization has been raised ... And there are so many hindrances to privatization to reckon with in developing countries! Altogether, no more than 530 enterprises have been privatized in 90 developing countries with the aid of the World Bank. Working on a sample of 37 countries, Shirley[28] has shown that only two of them (Bangladesh and Chile) have been able to privatize more than twenty enterprises. How, therefore, can we expect a much higher number of success stories in the Central-Eastern European privatization drive? Furthermore, only twenty large firms have been privatized from the top in the Third World; all other privatizations have concerned small enterprises. Even more worrying, most of the privatized enterprises in developing countries have eventually gone bankrupt, and those that have survived are non-profitable and non-competitive to an extent that it would be advisable to liquidate them.[29]

It is not at all surprising, therefore, that the privatization drive in Central-Eastern Europe is developing more slowly than was expected at the beginning of the process, in an enthusiastic climate linked with the political transition to post-communism. In the Hungarian privatization programme, about 500 to 600 firms should be privatized 'from the top' during the period 1991-93, and it is expected that about 300 to 400 firms will choose to be privatized in the next three years.[30] This target is probably unattainable, and it is already anticipated that no more than 30 to 40 companies will provide business on the Budapest stock exchange by the end of 1991 - although over 200 tenders had been submitted by December 1990. In Poland, only five state-owned enterprises were privatized from the top in 1990, after the number of companies originally selected for the first wave of privatization had been reduced from twenty to twelve and then to seven. In Czechoslovakia, between 500 and 2,000 enterprises will be proposed for privatization in the first round of 'large' privatization. This is bound to fail, at least in the short and medium term, even though Czechoslovakia is in better economic condition for attempts at privatization than all the developing countries (530 privatizations altogether).

6. Conclusions

I shall not conclude with the magic formula for the optimal path to privatization
that so many economic advisers in Central-Eastern Europe dream of today; a
dream, perhaps, that is now turning into a nightmare. I prefer to suggest,
rather provocatively, a sort of check-list for those who regard privatization to
be a political 'must' in post-communist countries:

1. First of all, select a small sample of around 10 to 20 enterprises to be
privatized from among the most profitable enterprises in the national economy.

2. Do not contemplate dumping industrial 'lame ducks' by means of
privatization.

3. Give sufficient guarantees to private buyers of shares as regards their real
property rights by selling them at least 51 per cent of total shares, including the
same percentage of voting rights. The equity stock remaining in the hands of
the state and workers should not exceed 49 per cent of the total capital of the
privatized enterprise.

4. Sell shares instead of giving them (or vouchers) away free.

5. Sell shares on a cut-price basis utilizing a mix of auction sales (as soon as
the stock exchange is in operation) and tender price offers. For example, sell
about 25 per cent at the price that emerges from the auction. If demand is too
low, halt the privatization drive for a while, or pass to recommendations 6 to 9
on this check list.

6. Convince a hard core of stable shareholders to invest in each privatized
enterprise. If these cannot be found among political friends, call in former
communist leaders (who have usually accumulated money and wealth) and
former members of the *nomenklatura*, who are very adept at converting
themselves from *apparatchiks* into *entrepratchiks*.[31]

7. Remove any restrictions on foreign direct investment in the national
economy, although capital, even foreign, is a 'shy deer' not easy to tame.

8. Try to sell some of the less profitable or loss-making state-owned
enterprises on a debt-equity swap basis to foreign investors. Of course, this
will be a cut-price sale insofar as there is a discount on the international debt
market: a discount which is the price to pay for being stuck with a risky
investment climate at home.

9. Provide an improving and (if possible) welcoming and safe economic
climate for investment. This climate surrounding the privatization drive should
include:
-   prices and wages free from non-market constraints;
-   a stable national economy;
-   lax legislation on labour conditions;
-   emasculated, dismantled or even crushed trade unions and self-management
    organizations: the privatization of Japanese National Railways is the best
    known case in point;[32]
-   a fiscal system reformed in order to avoid any risk of over-taxing private
    capital;
-   the demonopolization of industries with backward and forward linkages
    with already private enterprises, by breaking up state trusts which might
    otherwise squeeze private profit through their monopolistic prices; some

economists suggest privatizing 'clusters' of interdependent activities;[33]
- no institutional barriers to restrict free enterprise and cut the national economy off from world markets.

10. Do not bet on your chances of winning the next democratic elections, even if wisely advised and even if safety nets have been provided to alleviate unemployment, income inequalities, poverty, and so on - these being the usual windfall costs of the first stages of any privatization programme.

In conclusion, two sentences should therefore be placed at the top of the privatization agenda for Central-Eastern Europe. The first: 'Please, don't rush!'. The second: 'Design the privatization programme using a telescope'. Privatizing hundreds and thousands of large state enterprises will take decades.

Notes

1 Abe, 1991; Curwen, 1986; de Croisset, 1986; Fitchett, 1985; Santini, 1986; Macavoy, 1989.
2 Grosfeld and Hare, 1991.
3 Van Brabant, 1990.
4 Grossman and Hart, 1983.
5 Berlin and Reznikov, 1989.
6 Lewandowski and Szomburg, 1989.
7 Biegala, 1988.
8 Andreff, 1991.
9 Grosfeld and Hare, 1991.
10 Lee and Nellis, 1990.
11 Chevalier, 1970; Pastré, 1979.
12 Fennema, 1982.
13 Kornai, 1990.
14 Jacquillat, 1985.
15 Filatotchev, 1990.
16 Kawalec, 1989.
17 See also Vickers and Yarrow, 1988.
18 de Croisset, 1986; Kay and Thompson, 1986.
19 Hemming and Mansoor, 1988.
20 Laszlo, 1990; Meyer, 1990.
21 Andreff, 1987.
22 Balladur, 1987.
23 Bizaguet, 1988; HCSP, 1990.
24 Andreff, 1987.
25 Baumol, 1982; Spence, 1983.
26 Hamdouch, 1989; Morin, 1989.
27 Kornai, 1980.
28 Shirley, 1988.
29 Nankani, 1990.
30 Grosfeld and Hare, 1991.
31 Bruszt, 1989.
32 Abe, 1991.
33 Day and Mikhail, 1990.

Bibliography

Abe, S. (1991), 'Privatization of Japanese National Railways and its Consequences', *Keiei Kenkyu*, vol. 41, no. 5/6, January.

Andreff, W. (1987), 'Les entreprises publiques et la modernisation industrielle en France', *Cahiers de la Faculté des Sciences Economiques de Grenoble*, no. 6, June.

Andreff, W. (1991), 'Techniques and Experiences of Privatization', communication to the Research Conference on 'Economics of Decontrol and Marketization in Europe. The Experience and Prospects of Eastern Europe', Davos: European Science Foundation.

Balladur, E. (1987), *Je crois en l'Homme plus qu'à l'Etat*, Paris: Flammarion.

Baumol, W.J. (1982), 'Contestable Markets: An Uprising in the Theory of Industry Structure', *American Economic Review*, vol. 72, no. 1, March.

Berlin, A., Reznikov, L. (1989), 'Arenda v otnocheniiakh sotsialisticheskoï sobstevnnosti', *Voprosy Ekonomiki*, no. 11.

Biegala, M. (1988), 'LMBO: mode ou besoin économique?', *Politique industrielle*, no. 13, autumn.

Bizaguet, A. (1988), *Le secteur public et les privatisations*, 'Que sais-je?', no. 2414, Paris: Presses Universitaires de France.

Bruszt, L. (1989), 'The Dilemmas of Economic Transition in Hungary', *Südosteuropa*, no. 12.

Chevalier, J. M. (1970), *La structure financière de l'industrie américaine et le problème du contrôle dans les grandes sociétés américaines*, Paris: Cujas.

Curwen, P. (1986), *Public Enterprise. A Modern Approach*, Brighton: Wheatsheaf Books.

de Croisset, C., Prot, B., de Rosen, M. (1986), *Dénationalisation. Les leçons de l'Etranger*, Paris: Ed. Economica.

Day, W. A., Mikhail, L. (1990), 'Propensity to Privatize Public Sector and State-Owned Enterprises in Hungary: A Conceptual and Strategic Framework', in *Economic Restructuring in Hungary*, Pecs: Studia Oeconomica, Janus Pannonius University.

Fennema, M. (1982), *International Networks of Banks and Industry*, Hague: Nijhoff.

Filatotchev, I. (1990), 'Prospects for Privatization in the USSR', Paris: DELTA, mimeo.

Fitchett, J. (1984), '"Private is Better" Idea Gaining Ground', *International Herald Tribune*, October 9.

Grosfeld, I., Hare, P. (1991), 'Privatization in Hungary, Poland and Czechoslovakia', Workshop on 'Economic Transformation in Eastern Europe', London: Centre for Economic Policy Research.

Grossman, S.J., Hart, O.D. (1983), 'An Analysis of the Principal Agent Problem', *Econometrica*, vol. 51.

Hamdouch, A. (1989), *L'Etat d'influence. Nationalisations et privatisations en France*, Paris: Presses du CNRS.

Haut Conseil du Secteur Public (1990), *Le secteur public concurrentiel en 1987-1988*, Paris: La Documentation Française.

Hemming, R., Mansoor, A. (1988), *Privatization and Public Enterprises*, Washington: International Monetary Fund.

Jacquillat, B. (1985), *Désétatiser*, Paris: Robert Laffont.
Kawalec, S. (1989), 'Privatization of the Polish Economy', *Communist Economies*, vol. 1, no. 3.
Kay, J. A., Thompson, D. J. (1986), 'Privatization: A Policy in Search of a Rationale', *Economic Journal*, vol. 96, March.
Kornai, J. (1980), *Economics of Shortage*, Amsterdam: North Holland Publishing.
Kornai, J. (1990), *The Road to a Free Economy. Shifting from a Socialist System. The Example of Hungary*, London: W.W. Norton & Company.
Laszlo, A. (1990), 'Some Problems with Privatization in Hungary', in *Economic Restructuring in Hungary*, Studia Oeconomica, Pecs: Janus Pannonius University.
Lee, B., Nellis, J. (1990), 'Enterprise Reform and Privatization in Socialist Economies', *World Bank Discussion Papers*, no. 104.
Lewandowski, J., Szomburg, J. (1989), 'Property Reform as a Basis for Social and Economic Reform', *Communist Economies*, vol. 1, no. 3.
Macavoy, P.W., Stanburg, W.T., Yarrow, G., Zeckhauser, R.J. (eds.) (1989), *Privatization and State-Owned Enterprises. Lessons from the United States, Great Britain and Canada*, Dordrecht: Kluwer Academic Publishers.
Meyer, M. (1990), 'Introduction à la comptabilité d'entreprise en Union Soviétique', *Revue Française de Comptabilité*, no. 211, April.
Morin, F. (1989), 'Le nouveau pouvoir financier en France ou "l'autogestion" du capital', *Revue d'Economie Industrielle*, no. 47.
Nankani, H.B. (1990), 'Les leçons de la privatisation dans les pays en développement', *Finances et Développement*, March.
Pastré, O. (1979), *La stratégie internationale des groupes financiers américains*, Paris: Ed. Economica.
Santini, J.J. (1986), 'Les dénationalisations britanniques: objectifs et réalisations', *Economie et Prévision*, no. 5.
Shirley, M. (1988), 'L'expérience de la privatisation', *Finance et Développement*, vol. 25, no. 3, September.
Spence, M. (1983), 'Contestable Market and the Theory of Industry Structure: A Review Article', *Journal of Economic Literature*, vol. XXI, September.
Van Brabant, J. (1990), *Remaking Eastern Europe - On the Political Economy of Transition*, Dordrecht: Kluwer Academic Publishers.
Vickers, J., Yarrow, G. (1988), *Privatization. An Economic Analysis*, Cambridge Mass.: The MIT Press.

The state ownership sector: lessons from the French experience

Dominique Redor

1. Introduction

'The choice between public and private enterprise cannot be analysed universally without taking into account the framework of political and social institutions, traditions and history, and the stage of economic development of the particular country to which the analysis is applied.'[1]

The place and role of the state in the economy, and more precisely the need to socialize some sectors in market economies, have long been the object of debate. In France, especially, much theory has been published on how to attain a Pareto optimum for activities in which some of the conditions of free competition are not met. When there are increasing returns ('natural monopoly') or external effects, for example, only a public enterprise will tend to fix a price equal to the social marginal cost of production.[2]

I shall not go into this debate in this paper. Instead, first of all, I shall examine activities where private and public firms coexist and where there is no monopoly - whether natural or the result of historical or political factors. Since the Second World War there have been public firms in nearly all activities in France (albeit to differing degrees): manufacturing industries, financial institutions, insurance companies.

Second, my study is a positive rather than a normative one: I intend to analyse the actual behaviour, management, and results of French state-owned firms during the last decade (1980-90). From a theoretical point of view, I shall refer to the 'evolutionary theory' of the economy[3] and investigate to what extent public firms have adjusted to the evolution of their 'environment', both national and international.

Chap 1. incorporate. (handwritten)

By 'environment' I mean:

> The ensemble of considerations which affects the well being of an organisation and hence the extent to which it expands or contracts. The selection environment is determined partly by conditions outside the firms in the industry or sector being considered - product demand and factory supply conditions for example - but also by the characteristics and behaviour of other firms in the sector.[4]

From the point of view of my treatment here, this environment is continually evolving in relation to competition among firms. In addition, in modern Western economies the state plays an important role (which varies according to the country considered) in shaping the environment of firms. This role has two aspects to it: on the one hand, economic policy (macroeconomic regulation); on the other, the economic, social and political institutions.[5]

When the French Left came to power in 1981, it implemented a major programme of nationalization. The percentage of people working in public firms compared to the total employed population (excluding agriculture) rose from 10.3 per cent (1980) to 14.6 per cent (1982). Employment in the competitive state sector increased by 600,000 people. The firms nationalized in 1982 were active in all sectors: the steel industry (Usinor, Sacilor), the chemical industry (St. Gobain, Rhône-Poulenc), electrical engineering (CGE, Thomson), and banking (CCF, Suez).

Among the sixty-five industrial and financial groups that the Chirac Government (1986-88) planned to privatize, only twenty-four were actually transferred to the private sector. These twenty-four groups amounted to 1000 firms and 350,000 jobs; the great majority of them had been nationalized in 1982 and only a few after the Second World War (for example the bank Société Générale).

I do not intend to describe these juridical, institutional and economic changes, however interesting the techniques of privatization used might be.[6] Rather, I shall focus first on economic analysis of the objectives and strategies of the firms which remained in the state sector during the decade under consideration (thus excluding the firms which were privatized in 1987) (Section 2). Second, I analyse the resources (mainly financial and human) that these firms used to develop their activities and how they managed them (Section 3). Finally, I examine how the environment of these firms has evolved, with particular emphasis on the state and European Community institutions and regulations. I also consider firms' responses and their capacity to adjust to variations in the environment (Section 4).

2. Objectives and strategies of the French public sector

2.1. *The criteria of the management of public firms*

Originally, there were three objectives behind the French nationalizations.[7] The first was to control the monopolist positions of large firms in the French economy: indeed, since the end of the 1960s concentration had been organized (in some cases) or at least encouraged by the state, and the aim of industrial policy has been to keep most of French industry free from foreign multinational firms. In addition, the concentration of the production system was considered to be a necessary condition for the attainment of international standards of efficiency through economies of scale. The 'rationalization' of declining firms and industries was coupled with this objective.

The second objective was to develop 'industrial democracy' within French firms. The public sector was supposed to play a leading role in promoting social progress and workers' participation in the strategic decisions of the firm. The underlying model was inspired by German and Scandinavian experiences and institutions.

Lastly, the nationalizations were supposed to combat the economic crisis which France (as well as other Western countries) was experiencing at the beginning of the 1980s. The aim was to increase capital investment through state-owned enterprises. The promoters of nationalization pointed out that, during the 1970s, industrial investment had relied increasingly more on public firms (22.3 per cent of gross investment in 1979 and 1980).

The management criteria of public firms in the competitive sector, compared with those in the private sector, have long been the subject of debate.[8] As early as 1982, in fact, under pressure from poor macroeconomic results and in particular because of an enormous disequilibrium in the balance of trade, the Minister of Industry J.P. Chevenement pointed out (in a letter to the president of the new nationalized enterprises) that: 'The traditional criteria of the management of firms must be applied to your groups without any restrictions. The different activities will have to achieve positive results and the profitability of the capital assets must be normal'. It is the final purpose of this paper to show to what extent these decisions have been respected by the public firms (see in particular Section 3 below).

2.2. The international growth of public firms

I begin with examination of the cooperation and international strategies of public firms. From a general point of view, during the 1980s the development and concentration of the French public sector, especially on an international level, was rapid in all sectors of activity. The following examples are among the most significant.[9] In 1988, Péchiney bought the American firm American National Can and in so doing became the leading world producer of packing materials. Péchiney is also the third producer of aluminium in the world and exports 73.6 per cent of its production abroad. In 1987, Thomson bought the consumer electronics division of the British firm Thorn EMI and, at the end of the same year, the consumer electronics division of General Electric (this production was exchanged for Thomson's medical electronics production). The French banking system (which was nationalized to a large extent after the Second World War) greatly internationalized its activities during the 1960s and 1970s, and continued to do so after 1981. The principal French banks (BNP, Crédit Lyonnais) bought foreign financial firms or cooperated with them, especially in the European Community. French insurance companies, however, are rather small by international standards (moreover, at the end of the 1980s the public insurance companies employed about 50 per cent of the total labour force in this sector). This is probably why there have been numerous international purchases and cooperation agreements in the public insurance sector. Thus public firms (AGF, GAN, UAP) have reinforced their influence, particularly in the European Community.

How can one interpret these developments? I suggest that the French public firms have followed the same management model as private multinationals; a model which has two interconnected parts. First, multinationals produce and sell in countries where demand is highest and/or increases most rapidly, that is to say in North America and Western Europe. Numerous surveys conducted on the behaviour of multinational firms in the 1970s and 1980s have reported this strategy. Second, such growth also has important consequences for the efficiency of production processes.

The modern economic theory of technical progress and innovation emphazises the size of a firm and the size of its market as determining factors in the division of labour and the mechanization and automation of production processes. In addition, the assimilation of innovation and new technologies depends on high and stable investments in both technical capital and, most of the time, in R&D and training. Firms increase the scale of their production by expanding on foreign markets, a process which has positive dynamic effects. At the same time, firms are able to collect more resources with which to finance their investments (both material and intangible).

2.3. *The managers of public enterprises*

In France, the presidents and managing directors of large private and public firms often have similar origins, backgrounds and careers.[10] They begin their careers in the public administration and after a time they enter a public or private firm; sometimes they move from one to the other.

The coherence of this system is founded on the *grandes écoles*, of which the most famous, the *Polytechnique* and ENA (National Schools of Administration), are financed by the state. On leaving their 'school', the new graduates must work in the public administration for a few years. Some of them remain in the administration, others are hired by private or public firms and often rise to top positions.

The fact that the leaders of the large public and private firms have the same university background and that they move easily from the former to the latter is certainly a factor which renders the management of private and public firms similar.

From a more general point of view, study of the behaviour of the top managers in large private corporations has shown that control by shareholders is often very limited. Whatever the status of their firm, managers tend to act in accordance with their own interests and not with the owners' objectives.[11] However, the concrete instruments of control vary greatly from one economic system to another and they influence managerial behaviour considerably. In the case of France, the ways and means of state control over public firms is of outstanding importance. Accordingly, I now turn to examination of the different forms of such control.

I first investigate the financial resources and the related constraints that condition firms. Second, I examine manpower and wage policy in the context of the various employment crises that affected France throughout the 1980s, and the state's struggle against inflation, an area where control over the public sector was particularly tight.

3. The resources of public firms

3.1. *Financial resources*

From a general point of view, public firms are limited in that they are not entitled to issue ordinary shares on the financial market. This exception apart, however, public firms use most of the financial techniques and resources that private firms do.

At the end of the last decade, in 1987 and 1988, self-financing (cash flow) represented more than 50 per cent (67 per cent and 61 per cent respectively) of the total financial resources of public firms. It must be said that the profitability of public firms in the previous years was less favourable, and that in 1986, for example, self financing amounted to only 30 per cent.[12]

Secondly, the state increased the capital assets of public firms. These contributions fluctuated a great deal during the period: for industry the highest level was attained in 1986 with a total of 21.8 billion francs (27 per cent of the total financial resources of industrial public firms), while the lowest level was reached in 1988 with a total of 4.7 billion (3.5 per cent of the same total).

One of the most important sources of financing throughout the 1980s was, in fact, the financial market. Specialists in 'financial engineering' devised new instruments to enable public firms to attract private savings on this market. Since it would go beyond the scope of this paper to study these new financial instruments in detail, I shall below make only brief mention of the new bonds and their place in the financing of public enterprises.

The law of January 3rd 1982 gave public firms the right to collect private savings on the financial market by creating 'participating certificates' and 'non-voting shares' *(certificats d'investissements)*. These participating certificates offer two kinds of income: either a fixed income (like straight bonds), or one which varies with the firm's results. Between 1983 and 1986 the public firms issued a total of 25.3 billion francs' worth of participating certificates. However, these certificates are costly for the issuer: in particular, they cost more than shares in a period of high interest rates like the early 1980s.

This is why public firms have increasingly preferred to issue non-voting shares. These are shares which do not entitle the holder to vote at the shareholders' meeting; a right which is necessarily reserved to the state or another public organization. Moreover they are 'preferred' shares, and their holders have the priority right to receive a guaranteed dividend (which represents a certain percentage of the nominal value). There was a rapid growth in the issue of these shares: in 1985 4.2 billion francs of non-voting shares were issued by public firms and 19 billion in 1986. During this period between 30 and 50 per cent of the financial resources of public firms were collected on the financial market.

This policy continued in 1987 and 1988, and other financial instruments were introduced: 'perpetual participating subordinated debentures' and 'perpetual cumulative subordinated debentures', which are a combination of shares and bonds and with payment linked to variations in the short-term interest rate. Some public firms also began to authorize their subsidiary companies to issue ordinary shares on the French financial market or on foreign markets.

It should also be pointed out that there are numerous financial inter-connections between the public and private sectors. These interconnections have two sources. First, for many years certain public financial organizations have been important operators on the financial market (especially the very powerful *Caisse des dépôts et consignations* which administers the deposits of savings banks), and for different reasons they have taken out shareholdings in private firms. Second, paradoxically, the privatization of 1987 increased the public sector's participation in various new private firms.[13] Indeed, the build-ing of 'hard cores' around new private firms linked various big French firms together.[14] Originally, the objective was to privatize most of these firms, but since the privatizations were rapidly stopped (see introduction), many private and public firms thus became closely interconnected.

3.2. *The employment and wage policy of public firms*

Initially, one of the objectives of the nationalization programme was to improve the employment situation, especially in the industrial sector which had been hit by the crisis of the 1970s. In fact, although in the public banking and insurance firms employment remained stable, it decreased rapidly in industrial public firms. Between 1983 and 1988 the latter lost 150,000 jobs, which led to a decline of 23.4 per cent.[15]

This decline can first of all be explained by the fact that the firms which were nationalized had been in difficulties for a long time. This was particularly true of the steel industry (Usinor, Sacilor) which lost 50,000 jobs during these five years (out of a total of 123,000 in 1983). It is a unique feature of the French system that employment was reduced drastically after the nationalizations, whereas in the 1960s and 1970s the steel industry, which was private, had been heavily subsidized by the state.

Second, the aim of state industrial policy during the 1980s was to rationalize the activities of firms in the public sector. Production which was not competitive on the international market was suppressed, and the specialization of each firm was increased. In addition, the new policy was designed to create a 'champion' in each branch or sub-branch and to concentrate the same activities of different firms onto a single 'development pole' (see my first point above concerning the objectives of nationalizations). This led to the suppression of many departments and productions which had previously existed in two (or more) firms; 'rationalizations' which were widespread in the chemicals and electronics industries.[16]

This period saw the improvement of social and economic measures in support of workers who had been laid off. A wide range of new measures were introduced. First it became possible to retire at 55 *(pré retraite)* or to benefit from retraining while receiving state subsidies or allowances. It should be noted, however, that these measures were generally not specific to the public sector; they were part of the legislation that covered all redundant workers, whether employed in the private or public sector.

As for wages, the government was very active in imposing new rules on collective negotiation in the public sector. From 1982 onwards the Prime Minister set the objectives of this negotiation for each year.[17] First, the mechanism linking the evolution of wages to consumer prices was severed so that targets for the inflation rate were set by the government at the beginning of the year, and wage increases had to be calculated on the basis of this anticipated rate. At the end of the year, if the observed rate differed from the anticipated one, certain adjustments were negotiated between the management of the public firm and the trade unions.

In general, the government sought to safeguard the purchasing power of wage-earners: this objective was achieved and wages increased very slowly (in real terms) in the public sector throughout the period (0.5 per cent in 1987 and 1.3 per cent in 1988, for example). In the private sector, wages (which were influenced by the results of negotiation in the public sector) increased slightly more. The deceleration of the growth of nominal wages was an important factor in slowing down inflation during the 1980s.

Analysis therefore shows that management of public firms drifted away from the initial programme of nationalization, and gradually came to resemble the management of private firms. One explanation for this convergence lies in the evolution of the economic and institutional environment of these firms.

4. The evolution of the environment of public firms

I shall focus on changes in the institutional environment - namely, the means by which the state exercises control over public firms, and the general regulation of the economy (at the national and European level).

4.1. *Administrative control by the state over public firms*

First of all, the state controls the management of firms through the usual hierarchical structure. Indeed, most public firms have a limited company status so that the representatives of the state are in the majority on the board of directors (the board also includes workers' representatives and possibly also consumers). In theory the chairman is elected by this board, but in practice the appointment is decided by the government.

Aside from this short-term control, the most important question concerns the coordination of the long-term strategy of these firms in accordance with the government's economic policy. Here too, the idea of linking the development of public firms to 'indicative macroeconomic planning' was rapidly abandoned. In fact, the 'contracts' signed by enterprises and the state progressively turned into very general strategic programmes, with firms at liberty to decide the ways and means to achieve their objectives.

The 'planning contracts' *(contrats de plan)* came into effect in 1982 and included objectives of a social nature (employment, worker retraining) as well as investment and profitability targets. Gradually, however, they became increasingly more global, so that they focused on profitability and the financial aspects of firms (the objective being, for example, to obtain a positive result or to reduce debts to a certain degree).

In 1988 planning contracts were replaced by 'objectives contracts' *(contrats d' objectifs)*. These, however, differed little from their predecessors, and were strategic plans for firms which were defined in very general terms jointly with the administration. In addition, there were no legal consequences concerning realization of the contract.

Thus it appears that, during the period under study, the state's formal control over public firms in the competitive sector weakened. However, the fact that the 'contracts' mentioned above did not include sanctions does not mean that such sanctions did not exist: they were in fact imposed by the financial results and the profitability achieved by the firms. Managers and even simple workers knew that if these results were poor, production would be 'rationalized'.

Furthermore, in addition to formal control by the state, informal controls must also be taken into account. Given the nature of the modern management of firms, important decisions cannot be incorporated into long-term 'contracts'. The decision to buy or to sign a cooperation agreement with a foreign firm, for example, is taken by the board of directors, that is, at the government level.

4.2. *The reduction of state intervention in the French economy during the eighties*

Despite political changes (J. Chirac was Prime Minister in 1986-88, whereas the rest of the decade was dominated by the Left), there was a continuous tendency towards a reduction in direct state intervention in the French economy during the 1980s. The example of credit control *(encadrement du crédit)*, which was suppressed in 1985 by P. Bérégovoy (Minister of Finance), is particularly significant. This resulted in the restoration of competition among banks[18], and particularly between private and public banks.

Another important change occurred in December 1986 with the passing of the law on 'prices and competition'.[19] This law, however, which was inspired by American legislation and designed to control economic concentration and restrictive practices, was suppressed when the Left returned to power.

But the most important factor behind the evolution of the environment of firms during this period was the growing international openness of the French economy and, especially, its integration into the European Community.

4.3. *French public firms in the European Community*

The EEC legal rules and the decisions of the High Court are based on a very narrow conception of free competition. In principle, private and public enterprises (in the competitive sector) are subject to the same rules and are supposed to behave in the same way. Problems, however, have arisen for public firms receiving important capital contributions from the state (Renault in France or Alfa Romeo in Italy, for example).

It must be noted that if the concept of 'neutrality'[20] of public firms promoted by the European Community prevails in years to come, the difference between private and public firms in the competitive sector will become increasingly less.

5. Some partial conclusions for Eastern economies

Many results of my analysis converge. During the 1980s French public firms in the competitive sector moved increasingly in line with the management and behaviour of private ones. This may appear paradoxical if we consider the programme of nationalization undertaken when the Left came to power, even more so since the firms under study retained the same legal status during the decade.

Thus the case of France demonstrates that the status of a firm (private/public) is not the only or even the most powerful factor determining its behaviour. The dynamic of the environment plays a fundamental role, and the French experience confirms one of the principal elements of the theory of economic change formulated by Nelson and Winter.[21]

During the period investigated, many elements determining the management of public firms have evolved: financial constraints, employment and wage regulations, the relations between the state and firms, and its control over them. These changes may be qualified as 'structural' in so far as they involve a large amount of the firms' environment.

Obviously, we must be careful when extrapolating from the French experience of the 1980s to the Eastern economies in the 1990s. First, we know that the hypothesis of 'all other things being equal' never holds, as attested by Kaldor's remarks quoted at the beginning of this paper. Also, since my study is quite general and needs completing on many points, the lessons learned here are necessarily partial and further investigation is required.

The lesson of the French experience for Eastern economies is not that they should follow (or drift away from) a 'French model' - the study of which is, in any case, beyond the scope of this paper - rather that, at the present time, attention should be paid to structural changes in the environment of firms. In addition, the dynamics of change (positive or negative), including the behaviour of public firms, will derive to a large extent from the reshaping of this environment.

Moreover, these changes should concern the principal factors in this environment simultaneously. If some factors are neglected, the risk of major disequilibria arises: think, for example, of the consequences of the suppression of state control over public firms or even of the privatization of firms if the conditions of competition are not met. It is fundamental, therefore, that all changes in the environment of the firms should be coordinated and programmed carefully.[22]

From another point of view, the French experience shows that there is a wide diversity of status, behaviour, and situation between the 'pure private firm' and the 'pure public firm'. This induces us to consider the 'mixed' economy as one stage (and maybe an objective) in the transition of the economies in Eastern Europe.

Notes

1 Kaldor, 1980.
2 Allais, 1959; Boiteux, 1956, 1960.
3 Nelson and Winter, 1982.
4 Nelson and Winter, 1982, p. 401.
5 Nelson and Winter (1982, ch. 16) cite the following factors as part of the environment of the firms: laws and policies regarding what is patentable and what is not; antitrust law and its administrative and judicial interpretation; public school systems; educational and R&D government support programmes.
6 See Andreff in the present book, and Durupty, 1988.
7 Stoffaes, 1983.
8 Leray, 1983.
9 Most of these examples are taken from Haut Conseil du Secteur Public, 1990.
10 Hamdouch, 1989.
11 For a comparative study of managerial behaviour in different economic systems see Moore, 1974.
12 Haut Conseil du Secteur Public, 1990, pp. 52-60.
13 Hamdouch, 1989, p. 208.
14 See W. Andreff's contribution to this book.
15 Haut Conseil du Secteur Public, 1990.
16 Stoffaes, 1989, pp. 606-8.
17 Faugere, 1988, pp. 102-8.
18 According to this regulation each bank had a certain quota of credit to grant each year. If the bank exceeded this quota it had to pay heavy penalties.
19 Chenot, 1988, pp. 185-97.
20 Haut Conseil du Secteur Public, 1990, pp. 167-88.
21 See also Kay and Thomson, 1986, on this point.
22 This latter point has been developed by Nuti, 1990.

Bibliography

Allais, M. (1959), *Cours d'Economie Générale de l'Ecole Nationale Supérieure des Mines de Paris*, Paris: Imprimerie Nationale.
Andreff, W. (1991), 'French Privatization Techniques: a Model for Central Eastern Europe?', Contribution to this book.
Boiteux, M. (1956), 'La Vente au Coût Marginal de l'Energie', *Revue française de l'énergie*, December.
Boiteux, M. (1960), 'L'Energie Electrique: Données, Problèmes et Perspectives', *Annales des Mines*, October.
Chenot, B. (ed.) (1988), *Les Déreglementations: Etudes Comparatives*, Paris: Economica.
Durupty, M. (1988), *Les Privatisations en France*, Notes et Etudes documentaires, Paris: La Documentation française.
Faugere, J.P. (1988), *Les politiques salariales en France*, Notes et Etudes documentaires, Paris: La Documentation française.
Hamdouch, A. (1989), *L'Etat d'influence: Nationalisation et Privatisation en France*, Paris: Presses du CNRS.
Haut Conseil du Secteur Public (1990), *Le Secteur Public Concurrentiel en 1987-1988*, Paris: La Documentation française.

Kaldor, N. (1980), 'Public or Private Enterprise: The Issues to be Considered', in Baumol, W. J. (ed.), *Private and Public Firm Management*, Macmillan.

Kay, J. A., Thomson, D. J. (1986), 'Privatisation: A Policy in Search of a Rationale', *Economic Journal*, March, pp. 18-32.

Leray, C. (1983), 'L'Apprehension de l'Efficacité dans les Entreprises Publiques Industrielles et Commerciales', *Revue Economique*, no. 3, pp. 612-55.

Moore, J. (1974), 'Managerial Behaviour in the Theory of Comparative Economic Systems', in Furubotn, L., Pejovitch, S., *The Economics of Property Rights*, Cambridge Mass.: Ballinger Publishing Company.

Nelson, R., Winter, S. (1982), *An Evolutionary Theory of the Firm*, Cambridge: Cambridge University Press.

Nuti, M. (1990), 'Stabilization and Reform Sequencing in the Soviet Economy', in *Recherches Economiques de Louvain*, no. 56 (2), pp. 169-79.

Stoffaes, C. (1983), 'Objectifs Economiques et Critères de Gestion du Secteur Public Industriel', *Revue Economique*, no. 3, pp. 577-611.

Privatization and quasi-markets in public sector service delivery in the United Kingdom*

Will Bartlett

1. Introduction

The privatization revolution began in earnest under Mrs Thatcher's government in the United Kingdom between 1979 and 1990. Yet, looking back over this period it is remarkable that one of the largest systems of public sector service delivery in the Western world went largely unaffected by this revolution until very late. Indeed, public spending on the Welfare State (including health, education, housing, social security and the personal social services) actually rose slightly from 22.9 per cent of GDP in 1979/80 to 23.2 per cent of GDP by 1987/8, under a system of state ownership and allocation. However, in 1988 and the two subsequent years, a set of legislative Acts was passed which promises to extend the privatization process throughout the whole area of public sector service delivery in the United Kingdom.

This paper describes this revolution in the making, a product of 'Late Thatcherism', and considers some of its likely consequences. Following a general introductory discussion of the introduction of the quasi-market reforms in the public services sector, the paper presents a detailed discussion of the privatization in public sector service delivery and the way in which quasi-markets operate in the areas of health, education, social services and housing in the United Kingdom. The concluding section provides an assessment of the likely effects on the efficiency of service delivery in the new system.

2. Quasi-markets in public services

In general terms, the quasi-markets revolution involves a process of separation of state finance from state provision of welfare services, alongside the introduction of competition in the provision of services between independent agencies. These agencies may be under private or public ownership, and may have profit or non-profit objectives, but they are no longer to be under exclusive public control. The agencies involved are to operate systems of service delivery that involve the extension of consumer choice and competition between private, voluntary or public suppliers within a framework of rules and funding set out by the state. Examples include provisions for 'opting out' of state control and/or ownership; the use of vouchers, or voucher-like arrangements; the development of internal markets in place of bureaucratic allocation; and competitive tendering within various sectors. In contrast to the privatization programme in the public sector, it is not envisaged that publicly owned institutions will be sold to private owners through a share issue. Instead, where a transfer of ownership to the private sector takes place, it is to be effected through a process of conversion of ownership to a new set of non-profit institutions.

The sectors involved include education, health, the personal social services and a wide variety of other government services. In the provision of health services, for example, 'self-managing' hospitals are now allowed to opt out of local Health Authority control and establish themselves as independent 'Hospital Trusts'. The first 57 such NHS Trusts were established in April 1991. Most of the Trusts comprise hospitals or groups of hospitals, although some Trusts provide other health services such as ambulance services, or community health services. They will earn their revenues through commercial operations on a quasi-market by competitive contracting for patients with Health Authorities and some General Practitioners, who will be the budget holders financed by the state. In personal social services, social service professionals will become 'care managers' and will be budget holders taking bids from competitive provider organizations (for example, old people's homes) so that resources will no longer be allocated by a central bureaucratic process. In education, schools may opt out of Local Authority control and, through the open enrolment system, compete for pupils with other independent schools in both the public and private sectors. Schools' revenues will be determined on a competitive capitation basis so that total revenue will reflect competitive success. As regards housing, non-profit Housing Associations will take on a larger role in the provision of housing to rent, and tenants of council estates will have the power to opt out of Local Authority control.

3. Health

By far the greatest part of health care in the United Kingdom is provided through the National Health Service (NHS). The NHS is one of the largest organizations in the world, employing over a million people throughout the United Kingdom. During the 1980s, the NHS increased its share of public spending, and the Department of Health is now the second largest spending department, with an expenditure of £21.57bn on the NHS in England alone in 1990-91. Moreover, by some measures the efficiency of service delivery improved during the 1980s: the number of patients per bed has increased from 16 in 1980 to over 23 in 1988-89; average bed occupancy stands at 80 per cent, compared to 55-65 per cent in the residual private health care sector.

Yet some problems remain. There is a large and growing waiting list, which passed the one million mark in 1990. Inefficiencies and inequities can arise in the way in which priorities are set to manage this large queue. More significantly perhaps, it is claimed by some critics of the system that there are high levels of microeconomic inefficiency in the allocation of resources, both spatially on account of the historically determined geographical allocation of resources, and across different types of health care, due to the implicit nature of decision criteria.[1]

The NHS and Community Care Act was introduced by the Thatcher government in 1990, partly in response to these criticisms and partly in reflection of the general policy trend towards the extension of the domain of operation of market forces into an area seen by Mrs Thatcher as one of the remaining bastions of 'crypto-Communism': the post-war Welfare State. More recently, the post-Thatcher conservatives have been at pains to stress the merits of the National Health Service, and have cast the reforms as an attempt to improve its efficiency, rather than as an attempt to replace it with something entirely new and different.

The Act, as with other elements of the quasi-market reforms, introduced both decentralization of control to independent provider units, and elements of a transfer of state ownership to organizations with a non-profit status. The decentralization of control is effected through a splitting of the NHS into two sets of 'purchaser' and 'provider' units. Firstly, in the new system, the District Health Authorities (DHAs) and budget holding General Practices (GPs) (still a minority of GPs) become the *purchasers*, along with private individuals, insurance companies and employers. Secondly, services are supplied by *providers* which include the hospitals which remain under DHA control (Directly Managed Units), GPs, and other newly independent 'provider units': the NHS Hospital Trusts.

Thus, to take one example, since April 1991 the Bristol and Weston DHA has purchased services from two newly independent Hospital Trusts (each comprising a group of several hospitals), as well as a directly managed Supply Unit. Two large GP practices will begin to manage their own budgets, although others will remain within the ambit of the local Family Health Service Authority.

It is intended that the new system will address some of the critics' concerns about the micro-efficiency of the system. For example, both DHAs and GP budget holders receive their revenue on a capitation basis: DHAs on the basis of their resident population, in line with previous trends towards a more consistent spatial allocation of resources; GPs on the basis of their patient list size, with the intention of offering a more effective system of incentives to stimulate GP effort.

The most significant new departure from previous arrangements, however, is to be found in the creation of a system of independent non-profit Hospital Trusts. The first wave of conversions of NHS hospitals into independent Trusts took place in April 1991, when some 57 Hospital Trusts were established. This first wave of conversions covers only 2 per cent of the 2,800 hospitals in the United Kingdom, but they are on average rather large and important ones. They account for 6 per cent of the NHS budget; 13 per cent of hospital beds; and £3.8bn of assets. They will be followed by a second wave of conversions in April 1992, when decisions will be made concerning a further 111 applications for Trust status.

A Hospital Trust is to be run by a Board of Directors, which consists of a chairperson, five non-executive directors, and five executive directors. The non-executive members of the board consist of two 'community directors' appointed by the Regional Health Authority, and up to three others appointed by the Department, and are likely to include people with top-level management experience in finance, information technology, legal services and personnel management. The executive directors, drawn from the upper echelons of the medical and administrative staff, represent the employee and professional interest and give substance to the Act's description of the Trusts as 'self-managing' units.

The Board will be able to run the Trust as an independent business, so that Trusts can establish their own input mix (type and mix of staff, materials, and so on), and to agree output levels with the various purchaser units with which they draw up contracts. They will be able to set levels of remuneration, bonus payments, and working conditions for their own workforce. They will be able to retain financial services, and re-invest such surpluses in the Trust. Income will be generated on the basis of contracts drawn up with a variety of purchasers, including DHAs (not necessarily entirely with the parent DHA), GP budget holders, insurance companies, employers, individuals and other Hospital Trusts and Directly Managed Units.

The assets of the hospitals and other service units which comprise a new NHS Trust will be transferred to its ownership when it is established. The Trust will become the new owner, free to dispose of any of the assets as the Directors see fit, and to purchase and develop new sets of assets. Sales of assets are subject to the veto of the Secretary of State for asset disposals valued at over £1m, whilst development schemes with a value of over £10m require approval from the NHS Management Executive.

At the same time the Trust will be debited with a debt equivalent to the current market value of the transferred assets. This debt will be held in two forms. The first part will be a fixed interest rate loan in the form of interest-bearing debt (IBD). The second part, however, will be a public equity stake in the form of 'public dividend capital' (PDC). The exact proportions in which these two types of debt will be held by each individual Trust will be declared by the Secretary of State at the time the Trust is established. It looks likely that the proportions will vary between a two-thirds/one-third split between PDC and IBD, to a fifty/fifty split between them. The important point, however, is that the dividend on the PDC is a form of (non-voting) equity dividend, payable only when the Trust is in financial surplus. In this way, part of the debt service payment is made contingent upon the state of the world prevailing at any particular time, and this has the effect of shifting a proportion of the risk involved in managing an NHS Trust onto the state.

Central to the operation and performance of the new arrangements for health care provision is the system of contracts which will link purchasers and providers on the new quasi-market, and on which the new system of resource allocation will rest.[2] It is envisaged that contracts will be of two types. The first type will be a cost-per-case contract. This, as one can imagine, sets a cost, or price, for each type of treatment. Contract prices can be set on an average cost basis, or on a marginal cost basis where there is excess capacity. Prices are regulated so that Trusts make a 6 per cent return on their assets, when entering into contracts with NHS purchasers, although they are allowed to exceed this target when entering into a contract with the private sector. The cost-per-case contract cannot be a complete contract, in the sense of specifying a separate price contingent on every set of circumstances. Nevertheless, any such contract is likely to require a far greater degree of price information than is currently available, since in most cases, individual treatment costs are just not known. In addition, such contracts are likely to be costly to write, implement and enforce, the more so the more complete the nature of the contract. It is not surprising, therefore, that a recent survey of the intentions of those units which applied for Trust status in the first round found that only 14 per cent of such applicants intend to operate mainly on the basis of cost-per-case contracts.[3]

The second type of contract which is expected to come into common use is the block contract. This is an incomplete contract under which the purchaser agrees to pay the Trust an annual fee in return for access to a broadly defined range of services. Broad performance targets, such as an increase in the proportion of day cases, maximum target waiting lists, reduced lengths of stay, and so on, are also laid down in the contract. The contract will also specify the mechanism by which quality will be monitored, and the remedies available if a Trust fails to meet the terms of the contract. However, such contracts will inevitably be incomplete, in the technical sense that they will not be able to specify a fee structure which is contingent upon every possible state of nature (i.e. every contingency). Moreover, an asymmetry of information will exist between purchaser and provider concerning the level to which the contract is fulfilled, despite the implementation of medical audit procedures designed to monitor service quality. Since block contracts are incomplete, and since information is asymmetric, they are open to the problem of what Williamson calls 'opportunism'.[4] This problem occurs once an incomplete contract is agreed, and purchaser and supplier are locked into the contract. The provider unit is then in a position to vary its performance strategy and to choose an imperfectly observed set of actions in pursuit of its own private interests, resulting in a level and mix of service quality which may not optimize the purchaser's interest. In the present context, this could just as easily be a level of service quality that is too high in some prestigious areas (relative to the efficient level), as a level that is too low due to an excessively lax set of working practices. This 'opportunism' effect (a form of moral hazard) may work to increase the costs of service delivery over and above that which would obtain under an integrated purchaser/provider system (such as existed before the reforms were introduced).

In addition, the existence of uncertainty about the exact costs involved in meeting an incompletely specified set of obligations can impose a high degree of risk upon the provider, given that under a block contract the contract fee is fixed, even though the delivery costs are variable and only partially controllable by the provider unit itself. In the case where Trusts are risk-averse, such uncertainty over cost outcomes may increase the desired fee for any specified quantity and quality of service delivery, since the contract fee will have to include an element to cover their risk premium. This may be an additional factor tending to increase the cost of operating a contract-based system of health service delivery, the more so the greater the extent to which risk is shifted onto the provider. In practice, an element of risk-sharing is built into the system through the use of Public Dividend Capital to fund the Trust's debt.

Thus the new system of health service provision is likely to have two offsetting effects on efficiency and performance. On the one hand, the inc-reased incentives provided to suppliers of service by the operation of market-type price signals, and by the possibility which the new arrangements will give to the independent provider units to appropriate financial surpluses, will tend to increase efficiency and reduce costs. On the other hand, there are a variety of factors which may work in the opposite direction. The likelihood that providers will adopt opportunistic strategies in the face of incomplete 'block' contracts, the increased administrative costs of fully specified cost-per-case contracts, and the increased labour costs which may follow the break up of the NHS monopsony on the labour market, will all tend to reduce efficiency and to raise the costs of supplying health services. The outcome of these opposing factors is as yet indeterminate, and careful theoretical and empirical research will be required to estimate and determine their relative impact.

4. Education

Education services in the United Kingdom have hitherto been provided and financed by 104 Local Education Authorities (LEAs). There is also a small private sector (accounting for more than 6 per cent of school children and 10 per cent of expenditure), and some schools are run by voluntary bodies, all of which are established as charities. Education is both free and compulsory from the age of 5 to 16, and organized into a primary sector (age 5 to 11), and a secondary sector (age 11 to 19) which is largely comprehensive (i.e. non-selective) in nature. Within the state sector, teachers are employed by the local LEA, and salaries are paid according to an agreed national scale (the Burnham Scale). LEAs manage administrative and advisory services for the schools in their area, and, before the 1988 Education Reform Act, had the power to allocate resources and manpower between their schools. They have also had the power to allocate children to schools in a school's catchment area, subject to an appeals procedure. Thus, although nominally under the direction of the Secretary of State for Education, in practice the locus of power over the allocation of resources in the educational sector has lain within the LEAs.

There has been much debate over the quality of education provided by the education system. Criticism has come largely from the right wing, which argues that resources are wasted through the system of administrative planning of education carried out at the local level by the LEAs. The criticism was especially vindictive in the case of the Inner London Education Authority (ILEA) which was actually abolished by the 1988 Act, and its powers trans-ferred to the London borough authorities. Few studies of the efficiency prop-erties of the education system have been undertaken - partly due, no doubt, to the difficulty of measuring the quality of education services. However, a cross section study by Lord[5] failed to find any correlation between expenditure patterns and performance.

Various reform proposals have been debated, although few have argued in favour of a completely private system of education, because of the absence of the standard conditions for the efficiency of a competitive market (such as perfect information and perfect capital markets). More widespread has been the advocacy of a voucher system. Under such a scheme, the voucher would cover the average cost of a place at a state school, and under some schemes its value could be topped up out of a parent's disposable income. Consumer choice would be enhanced through the ability of parents to send their children to the school of their choice, and schools would be free to select pupils and to organize waiting lists. Others, concerned with the adverse distributional effect of such schemes, argue that topping up should not be allowed and have suggested a modified scheme involving the use of discriminatory vouchers, whose value would be linked inversely to income levels, or to local property values.[6]

The privatization of the education sector has been a long-standing aim of the Thatcherite wing of the Conservative Party, and the first steps in this direction were introduced by the 1988 Education Reform Act. There are four main elements in the Act. Firstly, it introduces a national curriculum, which takes the power to set the 'output mix' out of the hands of the LEA. Secondly, it devolves the financial management of the school budget to the individual school's governing body. This arrangement, known as Local Management of Schools (or LMS), reduces the ability of the LEA to interfere in the day-to-day management of the school. Thirdly, it introduces a competitive system of capitation funding based on open enrolment at the level of the individual school. This funding system reduces the ability of the LEA to control the allocation of resources among schools, and introduces instead a form of voucher system. Fourthly, it makes provision for individual schools to opt out of LEA control altogether and establish themselves as independent Grant Maintained (GM) schools funded directly by the Department of Education and Science.

Even within the state system, the new arrangements will introduce elements of decentralization and quasi-market competition among schools. Budgetary devolution through LMS will enable head teachers to control the day-to-day management of the school, and it will allow school governors to make key strategic decisions concerning the management of the school, such as the appropriate level and mix of inputs (staffing, materials, heating, maintenance, etc), admissions policy, and educational priorities within the constraints set by the national curriculum. Quasi-market competition, associated with open enrolment and capitation funding, will mean that the more successful schools are in attracting pupils, the greater will be their capitation-based budget.

In addition, the LEA is no longer able directly to control the distribution of pupils among schools by administrative means. Under the new arrangements, schools will compete for pupils under a system of open enrolment which will enable parents to choose to which school to send their child. Schools will, however, retain some control over admissions policy, especially where demand for places is high and the school roll is full. The normal capacity of a school in terms of the number of pupils which may be admitted (known as the 'standard number') is set by the Secretary of State (rather than, as previously, the LEA). In most cases it is set at the number of pupils admitted either in 1979 or in 1988, whichever is the greater. Whilst this normal capacity may be exceeded by agreement between the LEA and the governing body in any year (or by appeal to the Secretary of State if no agreement can be reached between them), there is no obligation to exceed the standard number on account of an excess demand for places. Thus popular schools may be in a position to discriminate in their admissions policy in order to influence the quality of new pupil intake. However, school rolls have been falling since 1979 and there is a surplus of available school places; it is thus likely that most schools will have to compete strongly to fill their available capacity. It is intended that such competition will make consumer choice more effective, and will bring about a distribution of resources that will reward the more popular schools and penalize the less popular.

The dynamic properties of this system are worth considering. Since performance depends closely on the initial quality of the pupil intake, it is likely that successful schools will wish to screen out less able pupils, and thus enhance their likelihood of achieving high performance results, greater popularity, higher student numbers, and hence higher budget allocations, compared with less successful schools. Less successful schools are likely to be located in poorer areas, and so the selection mechanism will reinforce class-based differences in educational provision. Over time, these differences will increase as capitation funding allows successful schools to prosper and to become ever more appealing to prospective pupils. One way round such a process would be to allow genuinely free access to schools by removing the existing upper limits ('standard numbers') to open enrolment altogether. More popular and successful schools would find their teacher-pupil ratios falling, and without the power to restrict entry of new pupils, this would place a limit on their ability to increase quality by selectively admitting only the brighter and/or more socially advantaged pupils.

The most radical part of the new measures, however, is associated with the provisions which allow individual schools to opt out of LEA control altogether. Under these measures, schools which opt out, known as 'grant maintained' (or GM) schools, need not relate to the LEA in any way once they have become independent. Any secondary school, and any primary school with more than 300 pupils, can opt out of the state system following a secret vote among all the parents who send children to the school. Schools which an LEA proposes to close may also opt out, provided the closure has not been approved by the Secretary of State by the time the decision to ballot has been taken by the governors (or by a group of parents, the number of which must exceed 20 per cent of the number of children at the school).

The governing body of a GM school is composed of five elected parent-governors and either one or two elected teacher-governors. These governors serve a four-year term of office. In addition, the head teacher is an ex-officio governor. This group then appoints nine 'foundation' governors from the local community, including representatives from local business, to serve for a term which lasts between five and seven years. Thus, there is some element of employee participation in decision-making in the new system, although the majority on the governing body is held by lay parent and community representatives. Following the conversion, the governing body gains corporate status; it can enter into contracts and be sued; and individual governors become personally liable.

Privatization of the school is effected when, upon conversion, the ownership of the assets of the school is transferred to the governing body. This includes all the land, buildings and property used for the purpose of the school, with the sole exception of any property vested in the LEA or former governing body as trustees (in which case only the trustee rights are transferred). The governing body thus has complete rights over this property to use and to sell it. The governing body may also buy new property, and has the power to invest available liquid funds. In contrast to the case of the NHS Hospital Trust, however, there is no equivalent creation of an initial debt; in fact, any existing debts are retained by the LEA, which must continue to pay interest on any outstanding loans. GM schools have an added advantage over state schools in that they can apply for 100 per cent capital grants from the DES to support capital development programmes.

The GM school is financed directly by the Department of Education and Science, on a capitation basis which initially mimics what it would have received had it remained within the control of the LEA, plus its share of expenditure on central services. This amount is recovered by the Department from the LEA revenues. The GM school thus differs from a private school in that it does not receive its revenue from charging fees to parents, but by direct capitation payment from the state.

The governing body has complete discretion over admissions policy, up to a maximum limit of admissions specified in the articles of government. The admissions policy must, however, be consistent with the 'character' of the school as it was under LEA control (as, for example, a comprehensive school, or in its particular religious orientation). This character can be changed, but only with the agreement of the Secretary of State. Thus GM schools can adopt explicitly selective admission policies, and the dynamic consequences for the evolution of the quality of provision are thus likely to be even more pronounced as the GM schools 'skim the cream' of talented pupils off the state sector.

In sum, the introduction of quasi-market reforms in the education sector has been based on the separation of purchaser and provider functions primarily through the delegation of financial and managerial control to the individual schools' governing bodies (LMS). Schools' revenues are based on a system of capitation funding and open enrolment which introduces a voucher-type system designed to increase consumer choice and to encourage competition for pupils among schools. This has been backed by provisions for schools to opt out of LEA ownership and control and to convert themselves into independent grant maintained non-profit units. Privatization breaks the residual links between individual schools and the local education authority which under LMS continue to supply central services to individual schools and so retain a measure of influence over their performance. Consequently, grant maintained schools are likely to have greater flexibility than LMS schools over choice of levels of inputs and the input mix which they adopt. In each case the funding arrangements take the form of contracts which are linear in service output - in some respects similar to the health sector cost-per-case contracts discussed above. Under a system of this type the provider unit bears all the risk of financial losses, and reaps the benefits of financial success. In contrast to the arrangements of NHS Trusts, there are no provisions for sharing the increased burden of risk, which is shifted onto the provider unit in its entirety. On the other hand, the introduction of quasi-markets in education is likely to result in a closer and more direct relationship between consumers' choices and the flow of funds to provider units than is the case in the health sector. Parents can learn about the quality of the education services provided by an individual school over time through repeated sampling of quality performance. By contrast, in the health sector, often only a single sample of quality of service delivery can be taken by the direct consumer, who relies instead upon GPs and DHAs to act as their agents. These institutional purchasers have considerable power in influencing allocative outcomes and in creating a system of 'managed competition'.[7] Thus competitive forces are likely to have a greater influence on the provision of education services than on the provision of health services. Whether or not this leads to improvements in the efficiency of services depends largely upon the way in which the dynamics of the competitive process operate.

5. Social services (community care)

Changes to the system of provision of community care services (for elderly people, people with learning difficulties, physical disabilities and mental health problems) were first introduced by the NHS and Community Care Act of 1990. The main elements of privatization in this field relate to the encouragement of a separation between purchaser and provider roles at the level of the Local Authority social services department. It is intended that Local Authorities will no longer be responsible for the direct supply of all community care services but will take on more of an 'enabling' role through the allocation of funds. They will appoint 'care managers', at a local level, who may be autonomous budget holders, purchasing the best package of care for individual clients from a wide variety of competing agencies, only one of which need be the Local Authority.

A typical example of this process is the provision of residential homes for frail elderly people. When the legislation has been implemented, care managers will be expected to cast a wide net among competing Local Authority, private and voluntary sector providers. All providers will have to meet stringent quality control standards enforced through an independent inspectorate. The standards required in many cases exceed the existing practice in many Local Authorities. In addition, whilst the costs of care for clients in a private residential home will be met through the national Social Security budget, the costs of care in a Local Authority home will have to be met directly by the Local Authority itself. The policy envisages the encouragement of a high degree of private sector entry into an area which up until now has been largely dominated by public sector providers. However, partly because of the financial implications for Local Authority budgets during a period of reorganization and crisis in the system of Local Authority finance, implementation of reforms in this sector has been postponed until April 1993. Despite this delay, and as a by-product of the financial crisis, privatization in this area of community care provision is proceeding rapidly in many areas. Even though it was not a major intention of the reform of the community care services that existing provider institutions under public ownership would transfer their assets to the private or to the voluntary sector, in practice many Local Authorities are attempting to hand their residential homes over to Housing Associations and voluntary sector organizations. This process is occurring essentially because, in many cases, Local Authorities can no longer afford to administer their residential homes under the combined effect of the new financial regime and the new quality control constraints.

6. Housing

Since the end of the Second World War a large publicly-owned rented housing sector had been built up in the United Kingdom, owned and managed by the Local Authorities ('council housing'). Such housing was normally let at subsidized rents which did not reflect the current market value of the housing assets. Designed to provide for the basic housing needs of the poorer groups in society, security of tenure soon led to a situation in which there was little correlation between council house tenancy and the income level of a tenant household. As the average income levels of council house tenants rose, privatization on the basis of the direct sale of property to sitting tenants became a feasible policy. Legislation introduced in 1980 gave council tenants a statutory right to buy their rented accommodation. The policy was popular, and discounts were set at high enough levels to make purchase of a council house attractive to large numbers of households. In addition, public sector tenants were given a right to receive a mortgage loan from their Local Authority. As the privatization programme proceeded, the size of the discounts on offer increased, so that by 1986 they had reached a level of 60 per cent of assessed house value after thirty years tenancy (70 per cent for a flat). By 1988 the proceeds from privatization of council housing had reached £14bn. This figure should be compared to the £18bn raised from all industrial privatizations undertaken until that time, including British Gas, British Telecom, and Cable and Wireless.[8]

Eventually however, it became more difficult to increase the rate of privatization. The higher income tenants had bought their council houses, leaving predominantly low income, elderly households behind as a residual lump of public sector tenants. By 1988, some 57 per cent of council house tenants were in the bottom three deciles of the income distribution[9], and over half the heads of households in the public sector were aged over 60. In this situation a modified policy of privatization was introduced in the housing sector, reflecting the general trends of the quasi-markets programme.

The 1988 Housing Act offered council tenants the possibility to convert their entire estate, en bloc, into the ownership of voluntary housing associations. 'Tenants' choice' is to be a tenants' democratic ballot to strip the local council of ownership of their estates and to opt out of the public sector. The new landlord may be a Housing Association, a housing co-operative or even a private landlord. The new legislation seems to be designed to increase the variety of service providers in a locality and thus stimulate competition among them. Rents are to be set at levels the market can bear, and housing subsidies channelled through means-tested personal housing allowances

(Housing Benefit) to low income families, rather than through the directly subsidized rents of the earlier system. Transactions within the quasi-market in rental housing are to be actual market transactions, rather than contract-based, or voucher-based. Thus the new market which is being created in rental housing is much more like a real market than are the quasi-markets which are being set up in the other public sector services.

7. Assessment

The essential ingredient of the quasi-market reforms which have taken place in the period of 'Late Thatcherism' in the United Kingdom has been the transformation of a system of administrative state provision of welfare services into a market-type system based on the creation of new sets of institutions on both the demand side of the quasi-market ('purchasers'), and on the supply side of the quasi-market ('providers'). This separation between the functions of purchaser and provider supports the creation of a market in public services in which transactions are to be based variously on contracts (health), voucher-like arrangements (education), devolved budgets (community care), and market prices (housing). In several cases, but not in all, this has involved a process of privatization of the provider organizations. Often the mere separation of functions, and the devolution of budgets (as in the case of Care Managers, Local Management of Schools, Directly Managed Units in the NHS) has been thought sufficient to give providers a sufficiently increased incentive to improve the quality of service delivery.

Often, however, this separation of the two sides of the market has been supported by a process of privatization, as where ownership has been transferred to provider units such as Hospital Trusts, grant maintained schools, or housing association landlords. Privatization may support the incentive effects of quasi-market competition where the transfer of ownership results in an institutional arrangement where the provider organizations gain the right to claim the residual surplus (or loss) which results from their activities (i.e. from an improvement in productivity).

The separation of purchaser and provider functions gives rise to an increased asymmetry of information concerning the actions and performance of the provider units. Principal-agent theory suggests that in such circumstances an optimal fee structure (contract) will be linear in output, with fixed-fee contracts as a limiting case.[10] Further, where providers are more risk-averse than purchasers, an optimal contract will involve some degree of risk-sharing between the purchaser and the provider. This is because a provider's risk aversion increases the required cost of service delivery by an amount related to the provider's 'risk premium', and which is greater, the greater the share of risk the provider is asked to bear. This introduces a potential inefficiency into the system wherever contracts are not designed to achieve the most efficient means of sharing risk between purchaser and provider, and may offset the advantages obtained from the heightened incentives due to quasi-market competition. In addition the possibility that provider units may engage in opportunistic behaviour creates a potential further inefficiency within the new system which tends to increase the cost of service delivery. However, there is a trade-off between these two sources of inefficiency in terms of the variable degree to which risk is shared between purchaser and provider. Contracts which shift risk entirely onto the provider, such as a fixed fee (block) contract, minimize the incentives to providers to indulge in opportunistic behaviour, since they themselves bear the full amount of any resulting cost increases. They therefore minimize the costs associated with opportunism. On the other hand, such contracts, precisely by virtue of the fact that they shift the burden of risk entirely onto the provider, maximize the risk premium required to support the contract, and so maximize the costs associated with risk-shifting. This trade-off could be taken into account in the design of 'incentive contracts' in order to reduce the combined effect of the two sources of contract cost as far as possible. Such contracts would involve some optimal degree of risk-sharing so that the costs of financial loss and the benefits of financial success would be shared in the most efficient way between purchaser and provider. Such optimal incentive contracts balance the costs which arise from increased opportunism against the savings from reduced risk premia.[11]

This discussion suggests that the existing contractual arrangements which have been established in the United Kingdom quasi-market reforms have not always been designed to efficiently minimize the costs arising from these effects. For example, in the health sector, the cost-sharing arrangements associated with the system of 'public dividend capital' introduce a non-linear element into the reward structure of the provider units. When in financial surplus they must pay a dividend on such capital; yet when they make a loss they must bear the full burden themselves. The discussion of optimal incentive contracts suggests that efficient risk-sharing would require the purchaser also to bear some part of any losses made by provider units, and so share the risk of uncertain and unexpected cost increases. To take another example – education – the capitation funding system is equivalent to a contract linear in output, but it makes no provision for cost-sharing between purchaser and provider. An optimal incentive contract would, by contrast, involve some element of risk sharing. This could be instituted by creating an equivalent public interest in the independent provider units' financial structure by the creation of a 'public dividend capital' debt, perhaps held by the Local Authority. This would be similar to that created for the Hospital Trusts by earning dividends from financial surpluses earned by schools, but on account of which the Local Authority would also partially cover any losses which such schools realized in a particular year. In this way schools would share the benefit of success with the local education authority, but would also be to some extent (but not entirely) insured against the consequences of financial failure, which may be due in part to circumstances beyond their control.

Sometimes, however, the costs and inefficiencies involved in operating a quasi-market can be expected to be so great as to outweigh the improved incentives which might be stimulated by financial and managerial decentralization, even where such positive incentives are reinforced by privatization of 'opted-out' provider units. For example, the transactions costs involved in operating a quasi-market in health services may be excessive, due to the administrative costs of developing a satisfactory system of pricing, and the uncertainty surrounding the outcomes of particular treatments. Labour costs may be increased by a market system which replaces the monopsonistic position in the labour market previously held by the administrative agencies of the state, such as the NHS health authorities. Moreover, even if optimal contracts were to be designed, providers' opportunistic strategies could raise the costs of service provision. Similarly, in the provision of education services, even with effective competition among providers, market dynamics may permit inefficient outcomes when better endowed, and hence more popular, schools screen new pupil entrants to influence the quality of their intake. So, inequalities in service provision may be inefficiently widened by the introduction of the quasi-market. There are, therefore, a set of circumstances under which it may be relatively more efficient to forgo privatization and the quasi-market, and to operate services within an integrated system under public ownership and management. However, the way in which the balance of positive and negative incentives and effects works out in practice is essentially an empirical issue. Careful research of an empirical nature will be required to assess the comparative performance of the new varieties of privatizations which are emerging in the welfare sector in the United Kingdom in the 1990s.

Notes

* This essay is based on research undertaken for a project on 'Functioning of Markets: The Development of Quasi-Markets in Public Service Sector Delivery' at the School for Advanced Urban Studies, Bristol University. The research was funded by the Economic and Social Research Council within the 'Functioning of Markets' Research Initiative.
  I am grateful to Julian Le Grand, Carol Propper, Robin Menas and participants at the First EACES Workshop, University of Trento, Italy, for their valuable comments and discussion.
1 Barr, 1987.
2 Bartlett, 1991.
3 Newchurch, 1990.
4 Williamson, 1975.
5 Lord, 1984.
6 Le Grand, 1990.
7 Appleby, 1990.
8 Forrest, 1991.
9 Forrest and Murie, 1988.
10 Ross, 1973.
11 Laffont and Tirole, 1986; McAfee and McMillan, 1988.

Bibliography

Appleby, J. et al. (1990), 'The Use of Markets in the Health Service: The NHS Reforms and Managed Competition', *Public Money and Management*, (winter).

Barr, N. (1987), *The Economics of the Welfare State*, London: Weidenfeld & Nicholson.

Bartlett, W. (1991), 'Quasi-Markets and Contracts: A Market and Hierarchies Perspective on the NHS Reforms', *SAUS Studies in Decentralization and Quasi-Markets*, no. 3.

Forrest, R. (1991), 'Privatization and Housing under Thatcherism', SAUS mimeo, and forthcoming in *Journal of Urban Affairs*.

Forrest, R., Murie, A. (1988), *Selling the Welfare State*, London: Routledge.

Laffont, J. J., Tirole, J. (1986), 'Using Cost Observations to Regulate Firms', *Journal of Political Economy*, 94(3): pp. 614-41.

Le Grand, J. (1990), 'Quasi-Market and Social Policy', *SAUS Studies in Decentralization and Quasi-Markets*, no. 1.

Lord, R. (1984), *Value for Money in Education*, London: CIPFA.

McAfee, R. P., McMillan, J. (1988), *Incentives in Government Contracting*, Toronto: University of Toronto Press.

Newchurch (1990), *The Newchurch Guide to NHS Trust Applications*, London: Newchurch & Co.

Ross, S. A. (1973), 'The Economic Theory of Agency: The Principal's Problem', *American Economic Review*, 63(2): pp. 134-39.

Williamson, E. O. (1975), *Markets and Hierarchies: Analysis and Anti-Trust Implications*, New York: The Free Press.

PART IV

EASTERN PROCESSES

Comparative analysis of privatization variants during the period of transition

Ruben N. Yevstigneyev

All privatization processes in the world can be divided into two large groups. The first of these comprises processes which take place in a market economy. In this case economic agents switch their roles within the framework of the same rules of the game. Neither the transformation of public into private property, nor the transformation of private into public property, entails changing the entire socio-economic model.

The second group consists of processes which take place in a non-market economy. Here, privatization is one of the elements that establishes a qualitatively new socio-economic model. It is understandable that simultaneously creating new economic agents, establishing a new economic environment for their functioning (a market), and transforming the political system means that this kind of privatization is much more complicated than a partial change of proprietors within a market economy. The complexity of the process stems not only from the fact that it is necessary to resolve the various mutually connected problems mentioned above, but also from the fact that such a task is now on the agenda for the first time in history.

Everything involved in the undertaking is new. For example, in discussion of privatization in a non-market economy, the basic issue has been the notion of state (public) property. Does this belong to all the people whose interests are represented by the government? Or is it in the hands of the party-governmental *nomenklatura*? This is not an idle question because the answer determines to a large extent the form that privatization should take, as well as the nature of the future public sector (should it remain unchanged or should it be turned into something else?).

We need to compare the two approaches to privatization carefully in order to forestall attempts to shift the Western experience of privatization mechanically to the USSR and the East European countries. This warning, however, relates only to the transition period; it has nothing to do with the socio-economic model itself to which all the post-communist countries aspire. I do not intend to discuss whether the nature of this model now is capitalist or socialist, since, in my opinion, today both adjectives are inadequate. It would be more correct to talk about a movement towards a modern civilized society in the forms established in the developed states, and about the natural stages that this movement passes through: industrial, post-industrial, information, post-information. Here I wish to deal with only one problem, that of the transition from universal state ownership to prevailing private ownership in the countries which have been called, or (as in the case of the USSR) are still called, 'socialist'. Since privatization in the Soviet Union is still only sporadic (the package of laws on this subject has only recently been adopted, and only in some republics), I shall deal mostly with the experience of a number of East European states.

Let us begin with more precise definition of the notions of 'state property erosion' and 'privatization'. The first term is not sufficiently clear. More than thirty years ago it was widely used in Yugoslavia, where it meant the transformation of state property into so-called 'social' property. Although this latter was proclaimed to be non-state property, it could not be converted into either group or, especially, individual private property. The 'self-governing socialism' built on such unstable ground was unable to demonstrate its superiority, and as a result Yugoslavia now faces essentially the same problems as the other post-communist countries. It would be a great mistake to repeat this experiment - that is, to limit changes by delegating some of the rights of state bodies to new economic agents (by which I mean self-governing, managerial or mixed types of enterprises) and not to privatize them. This approach, which was typical not only of Yugoslavia but of other countries as well, can only swing the pendulum of the management of the economy from the hardline approach to decentralization and back again, thus dismantling all the country's economic structures. This is why the 'state property erosion' ('commercialization') of state enterprises is justified only as a temporary measure enabling transition to privatization.

Only by changing the social model as a whole - i.e. by democratizing political life by moving towards a modern market, and by demonopolizing and privatizing the economy - can a serious crisis be averted. By privatization I mean not only the appropriation of property by an individual, but the transfer of state property into any form of non-state ownership. Only two principal forms of property are really viable in a market economy: private property in all its various forms[1] and state property. Unless private property exists, neither the capital market nor a full-fledged market economy is possible. Thus the term 'capitalistization' seems to be synonymous with the term 'privatization'.

The majority of the post-communist countries have recognized that they must privatize in the above-mentioned sense of the word; but they initially underestimated the prime importance of establishing an order of priority in their objects. Only recently have the notions of 'small' and 'large' privatization appeared, and only recently has the importance of China's experience in this field been realized. It is difficult to find anybody who doubts the rationality of giving priority to agriculture, light industry and services in order to accelerate the saturation of the market with foodstuffs and staple commodities and thus reduce social tension. This is not the only reason, however. In these sectors the rate of circulation of capital is especially high, and resources might therefore be accumulated to reinforce privatization in other industries. Furthermore, 'small' privatization can be carried out relatively more easily than 'large' privatization because it does not require enormous financial resources. This is perhaps why the relative laws have been little discussed.

There are different forms of 'small' privatization. First, one can cite the redemption of enterprises by their collectives (a sort of Employee Stock Option Programme system). A second form is the auction sale of small enterprises to individuals or collectives, including foreigners (in Poland, permission for foreign investment agency should be given to the latter if their endowment exceeds 10 per cent of the cost of fixed assets). Another form is the conversion of state enterprises into joint-stock companies of an internal character.

The characteristic feature of this kind of privatization is the prevalence of intermediary types of small enterprises consequent on an unprecedented shortage of consumer goods and other commodities. For instance, about 80 per cent of newly-created small enterprises in Romania last year [1990, Editor's Note] were of this type. On these grounds, governments are often accused of legalizing profiteering and corruption. The accusation seems to be justified, but if we look more closely at the subject we perceive that the real reason for it is that the first steps towards privatization have not been backed by the introduction of a real competitive market.

In order to avoid stifling privatization from the very beginning[2], taxation on the first private enterprises is reduced. In Hungary a special bank for the preferential financing of entrepreneurs has been established with assets of 4 billion forints and 100 million marks has been granted for this purpose by Germany. It is interesting to note that the only part of an entrepreneur's assets liable for this debt is his initial capital.

These measures have encouraged the emergence and further development of a middle class to provide the basis for a future civil society.

'Large' privatization has encountered many difficulties in all the countries concerned; primarily, the danger of non-controlled or so-called 'spontaneous' privatization. I shall again use a Hungarian example. After Hungary's adoption in 1989 of its first laws on privatization (the law limiting the number of hired workers, the law on transformation of economic units, the law on securities), the sale of state enterprises began. Enterprises were sold for next to nothing, either to party and state officials trying to retain their positions, or to foreigners, or to both (through joint ventures). To prevent this situation, a special law in defence of state property was passed in mid-1990. According to this law, the sale of any state property, including land, is now permitted by so-called 'property control commissions' established in the capital and all the provinces and comprising representatives from different parties as well as specialists.

However, this measure has proved to be inadequate; and to control the course of privatization, special all-state bodies have been founded in all the ex-socialist countries. These institutions are subordinated either to the parliament (as in Hungary), or to the government (as in Bulgaria and Romania), or to finance ministries (as in Poland and Czechoslovakia). It is obvious that the problem of subordination of these institutions is important, but much more important, I believe, is the problem of their functions. Should these bodies 'grant' the property to the future proprietors they decide to choose, or should they facilitate the privatization process? The East European countries have given preference to the second approach, the reason being that the first could dangerously politicize the privatization process by being compulsorily implemented in the interests of the structures formed under the command economy. Here I am referring both to the use of privatization in order to accumulate additional resources in the state budget, and to the possibility of various kinds of machination and corruption. As regards the second approach, this means not only that the privatization process must be regulated, but that it must be implemented in accordance with the laws of the market. In this case, however, the agent of privatization at the macro-level should not be the state, since its power is based on the reproduction of budgets revenues. These agents should consist of state holdings, property funds, special investment banks, stock exchanges, and other components of the capital market. In Russia, for instance, it is expected that about 80 groups of industrial enterprises will have been created by winter 1991. Each of these will be organized as a holding company which temporarily represents citizens as proprietors.[3]

All attempts to leap immediately from the previous condition to a new one should be qualified as mere adventurism. This is why methods for the successive and smooth (which is not equivalent to slow) implementation of 'large' privatization have been devised. At the beginning of this process, as has already been mentioned, the different variants of state property erosion (such as leasing, small enterprises, and concerns) are possible and even desirable. These intermediate forms can promote the flexibility of central management and the demonopolization of the economy. It is worth noting here that as one of the preconditions for privatization today, demonopolization can be considered one of its consequences in the future.

As experience has shown, along with 'commercialized' state enterprises, there exists another important step in privatizing enterprises. In this case a holding company performs the role of owner of the capital. Current and prospective activities are kept strictly separate in the enterprise, as well as labour and capital revenues. The real prerequisites for participation in stock exchange activities are created, and foreign capital is stimulated to take part in development, including the joint venture form.

It seems to me that the greatest success in this sphere so far has been achieved by Hungary and Poland. In Hungary, for example, investment societies with predominant state participation have been created under the aegis of the State Property Agency. These societies buy the property of liquidated state enterprises and then sell it to new proprietors after its full modernization with the help of not only domestic but also foreign capital. The government tries to accelerate these processes. Thus, to this end, the Budapest Stock Exchange (the first one in Eastern Europe) was restored in summer 1990 as a self-regulated financial organization. The founders of the Hungarian stock exchange were forty-one banks, several financial institutions, and brokers' companies. The second such stock exchange was founded in 1991 in Warsaw, and in its first weekly sessions the shares of the privatized large enterprises were traded. In countries where stock exchanges do not yet exist, shares are sold by banks. Thus in Romania public subscription for the shares of the first five enterprises intended for privatization was opened in November 1990. Four banks and two hundred bank divisions participated in this campaign.

The desire of the ex-socialist countries to move more rapidly from state property erosion towards real 'large' privatization is quite understandable. Unfortunately, however, there are numerous obstacles in the way. One is the highly inefficient structure of the economy, especially in the Soviet Union where it is dominated by heavy industry and the military-industrial complex. There are also social barriers to 'large' privatization, primarily strong egalitarian traditions. Among political impediments, one should mention the absence of reliable guarantees against infringement of the rights of private owners.

I now turn to the obstacle which most urgently needs dealing with today: the financial obstacle. According to market logic, the appearance of real owners of what was formerly 'nobody's' property is inevitable. But where will these owners appear from? Can they be created artificially - that is, by distributing state property to everybody, in equal shares and free of charge? Although very attractive in social and political terms, this approach cannot withstand the slightest criticism from the economic point of view - apart from the organizational difficulties involved or even, perhaps, the effective impossibility of the solution. The head of the Romanian government, P. Roman, has called such approach 'an attempt to force Stalinism in through the back door'. The Minister of Industry of the Czech Republic, M. Gregr, has labelled it 'nationalization inside out'. At first sight, this measure looks like social justice, but in fact it means the consolidation of a notorious lack of responsibility and, again, a lack of competition. It is quite clear that even the distribution of the state property itself will not create entrepreneurs, although this is the main task of privatization - and nor will the distribution of state property create real stimuli for personal enterprise.

The opponents of the voucher system point out that its introduction will provoke hyperinflation on the consumer market: joint-stock companies and holdings will not obtain additional money, but will be obliged to pay dividends, with either a cut in budget revenues or an additional monetary issue as the result. Besides, the rapid devaluation of the vouchers through inflation will nullify all these expensive arrangements.

'As to the justice', the chairperson of the Moscow property commission, E. Kotova, has written, 'such an approach may be not so bad theoretically, but in actual life this principle will fail for sure. The possibilities of different people to invest their vouchers will distinguish one from another. The *nomenklatura* will invest its money in the most profitable business. Thus, this policy is to become a policy of a postponed social outburst'.[4]

In my opinion, the paid distribution of state property will have a twofold effect. Firstly, the receipts could be used to pay off the state debt, to reconstruct and modernize present enterprises, to provide aid for the socially weak sections of population. Secondly, the appearance of real entrepreneurs will boost production and establish the preconditions not only for overcoming the crisis in the economy, but for its stable development in the future.

Does this not mean, therefore, that the sale of state property is the most realistic decision, even from the point of view of social justice? This question immediately comes up against the counter-question raised by the advocates of free privatization: where will potential buyers obtain the money? The fact is that the people of these countries have no money (according to some calculations, in the USSR they could redeem only 7 per cent of state property, in Poland only 3 per cent); and nor do enterprises have sufficient sums of money available.

Nevertheless, the Eastern Länder of Germany as well as Hungary, for instance, have rejected the variant of free-of-charge privatization in favour of any form involving the attraction of domestic and foreign capital. Last year, the Hungarian government agreed to the proposal by the Hungarian Socialist Party that workers should be given the right to redeem their shares with the help of long-term credits charged out of future dividends.

If we take the case of privatization of the first five large enterprises in Poland at the end of 1990, their property was estimated at 470 billion zlotys. About 80 per cent of their share capital is to be sold by subscription. More than 90 per cent of buyers will pay by means of state bonds at a discount of 20 per cent. It should be noted that, in Poland, workers in privatized enterprises have the right to buy 20 per cent of all shares at a reduced price. In Bulgaria, the government has removed all restrictions on the circulation of shares between private firms and individuals. The revenues that citizens obtain as dividends are not taxed for the first five years. In Romania, most state property is privatized in the joint-stock form and only 30 per cent is to be distributed free of charge among individuals aged 18 and over.

These various examples show that paid privatization is always accompanied by various preferences and privileges. The voucher system is used by almost all the countries, especially Czechoslovakia, where citizens redeem shares not only for cash, but also in exchange for 'property vouchers' (investment money) distributed for symbolic payment. Every adult citizen receives a voucher as a certificate of his/her right to be an owner of a proportion of the national wealth. The vouchers can be spent on the following: 1. the purchase of shares in a state joint-stock company (holding), the workers in which may obtain 15 per cent, and the members of the board 20 per cent, of all shares; 2. the purchase or lease of municipal property; 3. the purchase of shares in one of the privatization banks (i.e. banks acting as an intermediary when vouchers are exchanged for the holding's shares).

The effectiveness of this or that method of transformation of state property will be proved by time. But one thing is already obvious: none of these methods can function properly without the simultaneous development of a market and a market infrastructure. Moreover, every step towards the market and privatization is at the same time an effort to escape the crisis and to stabilize the economy. I am convinced that the idea of economic stabilization as a preliminary step to privatization and transfer to the market is deeply misguided. The proponents of stabilization as this first step fail to understand that the issue is not the replacement of the planning mechanism of reallocation of resources by the market mechanism, but total transition to a market-type economy. In a market economy, production by society is no longer represented by the simple sum of separate economic units tied to the central authorities, but by a pattern of circular movements of the society's capital, products and income. Thus stabilization must comprise the formation of the market and privatization as its major components.

Notes

1 The notion of private property was officially recognized in the Soviet Union by the Law on Property adopted by the Supreme Soviet of Russia in December 1990. See *Rossiyskaya Gazeta*, 11 January, 1991.

2 Attempts of this kind have taken place in the USSR in particular, not only in the form of 'equal rights' for the different sectors of economy, but by discriminating, for instance, cooperatives against other sectors.

3 See 'Programma pravitel'stva RSFSR po stabilizacii ekonomiki i perekhodu k rynochnym otnosheniyam', *Rossiyskaya Gazeta*, 21 May, 1991.

4 E. Kotova, in 'Business, Banks, Stock Exchange', Moscow, no. 4, 27 May, 1991.

A microeconomic approach to large-scale privatization in the transition from a centrally planned economy to a market economy. The case of Czechoslovakia

Brigita Schmögnerová

The project for 'large-scale' privatization in Czechoslovakia has been strongly affected by the intellectual and ideological arguments presented in the writings of Friedrich von Hayek and Milton Friedman. As a result, some 'communist dogmas' - for example, that 'private ownership is inferior to state ownership' - have rapidly faded. On the other hand, the lack of criticism has given life to new dogmas or misunderstandings. Among these is the unprecedented overvaluation of private ownership; the neglect of the other forms of ownership including Employee Stock Ownership Programmes, worker-owned firms, producer cooperatives, and similar, considered to be a 'radical alternative to capitalist and state-owned firms'[1]; a strong reliance on schemes of 'fast privatization'; and adherence to the idea of the need for 'a redefinition of state property rights' which is believed to be a precondition for privatization. A characteristic feature is that there has been little attention paid to the economic environment of privatized enterprises and to the internal mechanism of firms. The possible outcomes of this may be the low efficiency of privatized enterprises, and negative effects on the modernization of the production and competitiveness of Czechoslovak enterprises. A more pragmatic approach to privatization as a response to challenges of transition is urgently required.

1. 'Rapid' versus 'gradual' privatization

In the first half of 1990 two schemes for privatization were discussed in Czechoslovakia: rapid and gradual privatization. These two schemes differ over the rate of privatization, the techniques to adopt and their macro and microeconomic implications.

'Rapid privatization' assumes the implementation of non-standard techniques of privatization: the free distribution through vouchers of a portion of state assets to individuals. The vouchers will be used to bid for shares in state-owned enterprises in a computer-simulated auction. This approach makes it possible to privatize rapidly and to remove a capital barrier which hinders privatization in previously centrally-planned economies, except for East Germany.

Gradual privatization assumes the standard techniques of privatization; and a long period of implementation, it should be said, is not entirely excluded from the project. However, the rapid approach greatly predominates in privatization policy. The group of enterprises for which privatization by standard techniques is envisaged comprises 10-20 per cent (between 400 and 800) enterprises, while 50 per cent (2,000) are expected to be privatized by non-standard techniques ('voucher privatization').

The microeconomic effects - both positive and negative - of the two schemes vary considerably. The advantage of rapid privatization is that the danger of government interference in enterprises will be considerably reduced in the short period. However, the belief that rapid privatization will enhance the efficiency of the privatized enterprises within a brief period of time is rather debatable. It is very likely that rapid privatization will result in a very diffused ownership which will provide low incentives to owners and less effective control over managers. In a joint-stock company with diffused ownership, most individual shareholders will not bother to improve the firm's efficiency and will prefer high dividends to a long-term allocation of investment. The more diffused the ownership, the more acute the principal-agent problem becomes. If insufficient attention is paid to the development of an efficient internal and external corporate control mechanism[2], the conflict of interest between owners and managers may become uncontrollable and the failure of privatized enterprises inevitable.

It must be said that the short-term prospects are not particularly encouraging. External, market-based control mechanisms cannot be employed efficiently unless the market for corporate control is well developed. This is not the situation as the transition from the centrally-planned economy to a market economy begins. There is some hope that mutual funds, investment funds, and so forth, will make the control of managers depend on different types of funds and the number of shares of the firm owned by the fund.

Some negative effects of gradual privatization are unavoidable (for example, the relatively slow formation of a private sector), others are not: the government's interference in enterprises could be limited by granting autonomous status to state-owned enterprises. Gradual privatization need not lead to the inevitable failure of transition unless it turns into a very slow process - that is, if privatization in a low capital-intensive sector like services is postponed or if foreign capital is not permitted to enter. Gradual privatization can be accelerated by macroeconomic measures promoting both the growth of domestic capital (through higher interest rates, anti-inflation policy, etc.) and foreign capital inflow (legal framework, etc.).

2. The project of ownership restructuring

The government's programme for privatization involves a case-by-case (i.e. firm-by-firm) project for ownership restructuring. Some authors[3] warn that this approach could give the enterprise an opportunity to bargain with the government (e.g. to demand a cut in the enterprise debt) and suggest a common approach to privatization. There are negative and positive aspects to both the case-by-case and the common project approach. The former include the danger of bargaining when the case-by-case approach is adopted and the danger of the enterprise's uncooperative attitude when a common project of privatization is forced upon it. A firm-by-firm approach (each firm drawing up its own privatization project) makes it possible to adjust privatization to the position of the firm in the market, to the firm's restructuring project, to incentives for workers and managers, to foreign capital inflow, and so on. The enterprise chooses to whom and how to sell; a choice which is restricted by the law and subject to government approval.

However the Large-Scale Privatization Act and other recent government legislation on privatization have eliminated many of the potential positive effects of a case-by-case approach. For example, no employee share ownership or manager ownership is envisaged, and foreign capital inflow is excluded in the first round of sale under the rapid privatization scheme. In particular, the neglect of an interest structure within the enterprise may have a negative impact on enterprise behaviour and in the short run provoke an uncooperative attitude towards privatization.

3. What comes first: restructuring or privatization?

3.1. *Organizational restructuring.* The benefits deriving from the dissolution of large firms - improved competition, the easier privatization of small state-owned enterprises, etc. – suggest that dissolution should precede privatization. On the other hand, some negative effects of dissolution prior to privatization have soon emerged: the increasing number of loss-making enterprises and enterprises lacking capital after their dissolution could endanger privatization, since these enterprises are difficult to privatize. As a result the government has refrained from massive enforcement of the dissolution of large firms. In most enterprises, internal organizational restructuring has taken place more as a response to a changing economic environment than as a preparatory step towards privatization.

3.2. *Industrial restructuring.* The priority given by the government to privatization has received intellectual backing from the property rights approach to the efficient allocation of resources[4], which closely relates allocative efficiency with private property rights.

The outcome was the government's negative attitude towards the industrial restructuring of state-owned enterprises before privatization. Government policy did not try to create a stable and stimulating economic environment to encourage such restructuring. The priority given to privatization and privatization policy increased uncertainty, including expectations of managerial 'parachutes' and the dismissal of workers, which further discouraged the restructuring of state-owned enterprises.

It is clear the government underestimated the importance of the industrial restructuring of state-owned enterprises. The poor economic indicators of enterprises at the end of 1990 and at the beginning of 1991 show this quite clearly.

3.3. *Financial restructuring.* Since August 1990 the insolvency of Czechoslovakian enterprises has dramatically increased, and the indebtedness of firms has also grown considerably. The financial restructuring of troubled enterprises prior to privatization has been recognized as an urgent priority. Since massive financial restructuring may have negative implications for macroeconomic stability, the government is strongly opposed to the writing-off of all debts, 'to nationalizing' the obligations and the 'dubious property' of enterprises. The concept of the 'redefinition of property rights of the state' - which was applied a year ago by a new law on state-owned enterprises giving to them less autonomy than in centrally-planned economies, as had been advocated by some economists[5] - turned out to be completely impracticable. On the other hand, in reducing enterprise debt in order not to endanger the privatization programme, various forms of financial restructuring have to be reconsidered and applied (lowering the interest rate, reducing enterprise debt by partially writing it off, repaying some debts out of the proceeds from the sale of state assets).

4. The economic and political environment for large-scale privatization

4.1. *Economic environment.* Ownership structure is undoubtedly one of the factors in enterprise allocative and productive efficiency. Nevertheless, analysis of enterprise behaviour cannot be limited to one factor, even if it is the most important.

Two groups of factors must be taken into account: a) the economic environment of enterprises; b) the internal mechanism of enterprises. I shall restrict myself to the economic environment.

Generally, successful state-owned enterprises are easier to privatize. This is true as regards standard techniques of privatization. The success of the dominant non-standard technique of privatization depends on desired demand (as opposed to effective demand in a real sale of assets), which may decrease considerably when loss-making or heavily indebted enterprises are on offer. Enterprises with no strategic thinking and no adjustment programme are also less attractive. It is clear that the more the preparatory stage of state-owned enterprises is orientated to the proper organizational, industrial and financial restructuring of enterprises, the better the prospects for privatization will be. This task requires a suitable economic environment.

Equally, the privatization of state-owned enterprises does not constitute a positive danger to production costs or allocative efficiency unless the economic environment lacks a number of attributes.

To some extent, the necessary attributes of the economic environment *before* and *after* privatization may differ; nevertheless they comprise the following: stability and low uncertainty[6], the existence of a strong motivation to act, which may be endangered by a heavy tax burden, optimistic expectations, which are undermined by an extremely tough restrictive fiscal and monetary policy, competitiveness, and avoidance of a 'regulation trap'.

Instability and uncertainty discourage long-term thinking in state-owned enterprises and privatized enterprises. The negative motivation of state-owned enterprises is relatively higher if no additional government subsidies are expected and if the threat of liquidation exists. Positive motivation is in negative ratio to the tax burden. The role of market competition is generally accepted. The more competitive the market, the more profit-oriented behaviour by enterprises can be expected, irrespective of ownership. The government regulation of state-owned enterprises (derived from the assumed necessity for a 'clear definition of the property rights of the state') as well as the regulation of privatized enterprises justified by 'emergency measures', can endanger the entrepreneurship of enterprises with negative consequences for efficiency - and to a profound extent.

4.2. *Political environment.* There has been little controversy on the importance of forming a non-state private sector in the transition to a market economy. The opposition has advocated equal opportunities for all forms of ownership, including worker-owned forms of producer cooperatives, efficiency being the only criterion for existence. The leading party has gradually adopted a more conservative attitude, giving preference to 'capitalist ownership'.

The government has not tried systematically to gain public sympathy for the voucher scheme of privatization, while the opposition has emphasized the negative aspects of a voucher scheme: the dangers of corruption and abuse, the preferential status of a well-informed state bureaucracy, etc. It has pointed out that a rapid passage from an equal to an unequal distribution of wealth would soon follow a 'voucher privatization' because the majority of people would prefer to sell shares in order to raise their low standards of living.

No major campaign by the trade unions which emphasizes the negative effects of a large-scale privatization on employment in the short term has been placed on the agenda. This cannot be explained solely by lack of experience or imagination. The general support for a market economy and private sector is a more accurate explanation.

The most widely disputed issues have been a large-scale, mostly politically motivated restitution, the extent of the institution, and the forms that compensation should take. A political compromise has finally been reached. On the other hand, the commitment to return property to its former owners has been further criticized by enterprises as an obstacle to foreign capital inflow and to fast privatization.

This does not mean that state-owned enterprises have welcomed a large-scale government privatization programme unanimously. A large group of predominantly profit-making enterprises, with capital-intensive strategic programmes prepared, considered privatization as a way to escape from government interference and to attract strategic investors from abroad. The previous antagonism of a large group of enterprises, which reflected a trade-off between their fear of government interference and their desire for government paternalism, has changed as a result of a halt in subsidies, premiums, etc. The predominant attitude of the state-owned enterprises at present is to reserve judgement on whether privatization will help to improve their position. This is the case of many loss-making enterprises which face closure or are undergoing structural crisis. Except for small enterprises privatized under a 'small-scale' privatization scheme, no significant group of market-oriented state-owned enterprises defending the *status quo* can be found.

On the other hand, the government has not sought to attract more support for privatization in enterprises through employee shares, additional compensation in case of dismissals of workers or managers, or managerial buy-outs.

5. Conclusion

Privatization is a very complex issue. The success of privatization is closely related to the success of the transition policy of which it is part, and to a favourable political environment where there is social consensus on the most controversial issues.

Notes

1 Jones and Svejnar, 1982.
2 Walsh and Sewart, 1989.
3 Lipton and Sachs, 1990.
4 Furubotn and Pejovich, 1972.
5 Lipton and Sachs, 1990.
6 Rodrik, 1990, proposes sustainability.

Bibliography

Furubotn, E., Pejovich, S. (1972), 'Property Rights and Economic Theory: A Survey of Recent Literature', *Journal of Economic Literature*, vol. X, no. 4.

Jones, D., Svejnar, J. (eds.) (1982), *Participatory and Self-Management Firms*, Toronto: Mas.

Lipton, D., Sachs, J. (1990), 'Privatization in Eastern Europe. The Case of Poland', Brookings Papers on Economic Activity..

Rodrik, D (1990), 'How Should Structural Adjustment Programmes be Designed?', *World Development*, vol. 18, no. 7.

Walsh, J., Seward, J. (1990), *On the Efficiency of Internal and External Corporate Control Mechanisms*, mimeo.

What is the real performance of Czechoslovakian industry in the start-up period of radical economic reform?

Marie Bohatá

1. Introduction

Since 1948, the Czechoslovakian national economy and its structure have been shaped by the demands of the Soviet Union and of other socialist countries. With minor exceptions, the Czechoslovakian national economy is characterized by high energy, material and investment inputs; by the extensiveness, obsoleteness and age of its production facilities and technology; and by the resultant low effectiveness of its industry in comparison with the advanced world.

The Czechoslovakian economy has a low export and import share, and a low export efficiency which attains approximately half the level of kilogram prices and productivity, and operates with substantially higher costs and inputs. At the same time it struggles with price and value deformations.

The efficiency of Czechoslovakian industry is generally unsatisfactory. Exports per worker in US dollars in the late 1980s (1988) amounted not even to 50 per cent of Austria's level in 1985, and was a third of that achieved by the Federal Republic of Germany. During the 1980s, a mere one-quarter of Czechoslovakian manufacturing plants (excluding the fuel and energy industry) managed to take advantage of the development of world import demand to raise the average annual growth of their exports until it at least equalled the annual growth rate of world demand. Moreover, between 1985 and 1988 there was such a dramatic decline in the export efficiency of Czechoslovakian industry, as compared with world standards, that only a hundred enterprises - that is, 10 per cent of the overall gross production in the manufacturing industry - could be considered successful.

It is well-known that there are marked variations in individual Czecho-slovakian enterprises; differences that are also apparent at the level of the constituent republics. The indices showing the relationship between aggregate production, number of workers and the volume of fixed assets are largely similar, but the export efficiency of industry in the Slovak Republic is markedly lower than it is in the Czech Republic. According to estimates by the Research Institute for External Economic Relations (VUVEV), exports by the Slovak Republic should increase by more than 5 billion crowns to bring them up to Czech standards. And almost 70 per cent of these exports should go to countries other than those of the former socialist bloc.

Bearing in mind the initial situation required in the enterprise sector for the successful start-up of economic reform by the Czechoslovakian authorities and, of course, for the reform of the enterprise sector as well, let us try to give more specific characterization to the present efficiency level of individual manufacturing enterprises.

2. Assessment of enterprise efficiency

The performance of a non-market economy is difficult to measure because there is no generally accepted performance (efficiency) rate. Any assessment is, understandably, heavily dependent on existing prices as the only available means of measurement.[1] In this type of economy it may be possible to solve the problem by means of a simulation of real prices, i.e. those that are valid in the world and in international trade. Consequently, in the case of Czechoslovakia, it would be useful to assess the efficiency of enterprises in terms of Czechoslovakian foreign trade. A number of indicators are available, but in order to be as objective as possible, the use of a multiple-index criterion assessment is recommended. By combining several indicators, this approach makes it possible to attach a more appropriate importance or weight to each of them individually. I shall leave methodological problems aside and examine the results of assessment which uses this approach.

Table 1 presents the figures for 1988. Efficiency is measured by a multiple-index criterion.[2] Table 1 indicates that over half of the enterprises showed unsatisfactory efficiency, 37 per cent belonged to the medium level, and only 9 per cent of enterprises achieved excellent results. However, it must be emphasized that, in Czechoslovakian terms, excellent efficiency may be estimated at about 50 per cent of that attained in developed countries, as far as the indicator of the share of exports in production is concerned. Efficiency in terms of production per worker in US dollars is a little worse: here Czechoslovakia reaches about 45 per cent of the European standard. As regards the export efficiency of investment (the value of exports per 1,000 currency units of investment), the country achieved only about 65 per cent of the European standards.

Table 1
Efficiency of Enterprises in Various Industries

Industry	Total number	Number assessed	low	Efficiency medium (per cent)	high
Engineering and electrotechnical	370	292	41	47	12
Iron and steel	38	30	70	30	0
Chemicals	80	59	54	41	5
Textiles	78	60	50	40	10
Clothing	14	12	58	42	0
Leather and shoes	23	16	25	69	6
Glass and ceramics	34	28	46	43	11
Woodwork	47	36	39	53	8
Paper	26	21	76	14	10
Pharmaceutical	28	22	54	32	14
Non-ferrous metallurgy	27	22	50	45	5
Building materials	78	60	68	27	5
Printing	20	18	66	22	12
Food	142	135	70	21	9
Others	59	46	74	24	2
Manufacturing industry	1064	847	54	37	9

Source: VUVEV, 'Export Efficiency of Czechoslovakian Manufacturing Industry in 1988', *Economicka informace*, no. 103, June 1989.

3. Assessment of enterprise competitiveness

Apart from this assessment, which places more emphasis on volume indicators, an evaluation of competitiveness has been made that seeks primarily to reflect world parameters in both the costs and the outputs determining labour productivity. This is expressed as the ratio between value added measured in world and Czechoslovakian prices. This analysis - as an attempt to transfer Czechoslovakian enterprises into the harsh conditions of world competition - was conducted in a sample of more than 300 enterprises. However, its results are representative, covering as it does almost two-thirds of output in the manufacturing industry under examination.

The competitiveness rate (K) within industries is shown in Table 2.[3] The assessment of K values is based on the principle that the economic results of an industrial enterprise should at least maintain the officially given exchange rate of the Czechoslovakian crown (K=1). Enterprises which are absolutely uncompetitive i.e. those with costs expressed in world prices higher than their output in world prices[4] are characterized by the so-called (lower) 'limit coefficient of the necessary increase in labour productivity' (to surpass the zero K value).

It is possible to regard those enterprises which show a coefficient of K>1 as 'prospective'; a group which includes 133 enterprises, i.e. 42 per cent. As one would expect, the engineering sector predominates.

Table 2
Competitiveness of Selected Enterprises in Manufacturing Industry

Industries	K	K value interval	Limit coefficient of the necessary increase of labour productivity in the worst group
Metallurgy	0	(1.61;0)	3.47
- ferrous metallurgy	0	(1.04;0)	3.47
- non-ferrous metallurgy	0.89	(2.2;0)	0.23
Chemical and rubber industry	0	(2.2;0)	6.37
Engineering	1.42	(3.42;0)	1.18
- metal-working	0.936	(2.03;0.21)	
Electrical industry*	0.93	(2.42;0.17)	
Wood-working industry	0.59	(1.30;0)	0.21
Paper and pulp ind.	0.24	(0.91;0)	5.7
Light industry overall	0.83	(2.16;0)	1.49
- glass, ceramics and porcelain	1.00	(2.16;0)	1.49
- textiles	0.62	(1.20;0)	0.22
- ready-made clothing	0.96	(1.03;0.83)	
- leather goods	1.15	(1.26;0.59)	
- printing	0.83	(1.00;0.61)	
INDUSTRY OVERALL	0.70		

* The sample is not sufficiently representative. Moreover, world prices lower than domestic ones markedly reduce the share of material costs (these are converted into import prices, whereas output is converted into export prices), and this improves actual efficiency.

Source: See Table 1.

The group of so-called 'conditionally prospective enterprises' includes the fifty enterprises with K values ranging between 0.75 and 1.00. Enterprises showing a lower rate of competitiveness are considered to be 'non-prospective', whereas those with figures near 0 should be subjected to the most radical solutions. This latter group includes seventy-five enterprises i.e. 24 per cent.

A variant quantification of the impact of changes in the crown's exchange rate on competitiveness was also carried out (see Table 3).

Table 3
Impact of Exchange Rate Changes on Competitiveness

	1 USD= 15 Kčs	1 USD= 20 Kčs	1 USD= 25 Kčs	1 USD= 30 Kčs	1 USD= 32 Kčs	1 USD= 34 Kčs	1 USD= 10 Kčs
Number of non-competitive enterprises	181	123	91	79	74	72	154
%	60.5	41.1	30.4	26.4	24.7	24.1	85.1

Source: See Table 1.

Devaluation increases the number of competitive enterprises. Hypothetical calculations prove that with a shift of the exchange rate of 1 USD from 15 Kčs[5] to 20 Kčs, the share of uncompetitive enterprises drops from 60 per cent to 41 per cent, under the exchange rate of 25 Kčs to 30 per cent and under the rate of 30 Kčs to 26 per cent.[6] The number of uncompetitive enterprises thus decreases by more than two-fifths when the exchange rate changes from 15 to 30 Kčs.

On an industry basis, devaluation considerably strengthens the competitive abilities of enterprises in the machine industry and a number of enterprises in light industry. Its effect is least felt in metallurgy and the paper and cellulose industry. It appears that the main movement begins in the vicinity of a rate of 20 Kčs per USD (especially in the machine industry) and continues in the interval of 20-25 Kčs per USD. A further drop below 25 Kčs per USD has no effect whatsoever on the problematic industries (metallurgy, wood-processing, paper and cellulose) and thus benefits, in fact, only the textile industry and, partially, the chemicals industry.

On the other hand, if Czechoslovakia's currency were revalued, for example by 10 Kčs per USD, 15 per cent of enterprises would remain competitive (in the engineering and glass industries).

When analysing competitiveness, special attention should be paid to labour costs. Since very low labour costs in Czechoslovakia are considered an important comparative advantage, how can a realistic comparison be made? The key point is the exchange rate value. If we take the existing official exchange rate (28 Kčs per 1 USD), Czechoslovakia only reaches 40 per cent of the level of Portugal (which has the lowest labour costs in the group of developed countries). Considering the real costs of exports (20 Kčs per 1 USD), Czechoslovakia reaches 60 per cent of the Portuguese level. The most objective method may be to use purchasing power (10 Kčs per 1 USD) which gives a result close to the Portuguese level. Nevertheless, low labour costs (wages) are a weak motivation factor. Detailed calculations on the group of competitive enterprises show that there is some likelihood of labour costs increasing to the level of Portugal. If we follow the effect of this increase on costs (by variant value of the exchange rate), respectively 15 per cent, 25 per cent and 75 per cent of enterprises would still remain competitive (out of the 100 per cent originally competitive).

4. Enterprise size, decentralization and demonopolization

Recently, there has been wide-ranging discussion on the strength and size of population units, and on the decentralization and demonopolization which are assumed to bring about increased efficiency. It is well-known that enterprises with between 1,000 and 5,000 employees predominate in industry, their average size being about 2,800 workers. No state enterprise has fewer than 100 workers and the largest one (SKODA Plzen) employs about 40,000 people.

An analysis of the position of enterprises in the Czechoslovakian 'market' (carried out by the former Federal Pricing Office) found that, on 30th June 1989, of the 538 enterprises examined in the productive branches of industry, there were 185 which had a monopoly status in the production of commodities and a share in the overall production of the particular branch exceeding 80 per cent. In 38.8 per cent of all branches of industry, 100 per cent of production was concentrated into a maximum of four enterprises. The picture was as follows:

- in 37 branches (7.6 per cent) there was only one enterprise;
- in 56 branches (11.6 per cent) there were only two enterprises;
- in 52 branches (10.7 per cent) there were only three enterprises;
- in 43 branches (8.9 per cent) there were only four enterprises;
- in 287 branches (61.2 per cent) there were more than four enterprises; but there was usually specialized monopoly production in these branches.

Let us deal first with the largest enterprises (more than 4,000 employees). There are 121 of these in Czechoslovakian manufacturing industry, 81 of them situated in the Czech Republic and 40 in the Slovak Republic. Most of these enterprises belong to the engineering and electrical industries (57). Metallurgy is represented by 11 enterprises, the chemicals industry by 10, the textiles industry by 14, the clothing industry by 6, the glass industry by 8, the woodworking industry by 4 enterprises, and so on.

The importance of these enterprises, from the point of view of the national economy, can be seen from the following figures:

- their share of the production of the overall industry amounts to 38.5 per cent;

- their share of employment is 36.5 per cent;
- their share of fixed assets totals 33.6 per cent;
- their share of the overall exports is 51.4 per cent;
- their share of exports to developed countries is 57.8 per cent.

Over 12 per cent (14 enterprises) are practically monopoly producers (more than 90 per cent of commodity production) in one or two branches, with production that amounts to at least 100 million Czechoslovakian crowns. 18 per cent of the enterprises produce over 75 per cent in one branch or another. A mere quarter of the enterprises do not exceed 25 per cent of overall Czechoslovakian production in the branch concerned.

More than a third of enterprises are very strong units indeed. They not only account for more than 50 per cent of commodity production in their particular branches, but a number of them cover two or even more branches. For example, CKD Prague is a monopoly producer in six branches, VCHZ Kosice in four and the tube rolling-mill at Chomutov in three branches.

Eighty-one enterprises show a high export capability (share of exports in final sales exceeding 50 per cent). The majority of these enterprises are located on the territory of the Czech Republic (61). In relation to developed countries, this strong involvement is shown by twelve Czech and three Slovak enterprises. It may be of interest to note that, in Czechoslovakian manufacturing industry with a predominating export-oriented engineering sector, only two of these enterprises are purely machine-tool plants.

As for monopoly producers, 16 of these (40 per cent) reach a share of their exports in the overall production of the respective branches that is lower than 20 per cent, whereas 3 enterprises do not exceed even 5 per cent.

Within the group examined, there is a quarter of monopoly producers which produce largely for the domestic market. About half of these turn out machines, equipment and electronics.

Understandably however, even the multiple-criterion assessment cannot embrace all aspects of enterprise economics: above all, entrepreneurial management and its ability and desire to do business, take on certain risks and 'operate' within the market. But those enterprises assessed as 'very good' (even though mainly hypothetically)[7] could withstand competition even under harsher conditions. This group comprises 31 large enterprises which have already operated in a competitive environment (although with some kind of protection from the state).

As regards Czechoslovakian monopoly producers[8], only 7 per cent of these meet the most stringent criteria. The negatively assessed group of 46 enterprises represents about 370,000 workers. The worst situation is to be found in the metallurgy, paper and pulp, chemical and textile industries while, geographically, problems in efficiency of large enterprises are concentrated in the regions of North Moravia, Central Slovakia and Central Bohemia. This group also includes 13 monopoly producers.

The present structure of Czechoslovakian industry is the outcome of rigid and highly unresponsive relations which prevailed in all branches for many years. The present-day pattern of industry has been heavily influenced by Czechoslovakia's position of dependence within the CMEA integration framework (raw material imports, machinery exports, and exports of consumer goods), by the over-inflated size of heavy industry, and by the low value of the tertiary sector. Industry reflects the persistence of the inertial, negative influences of the old structures with manifestations of uneconomic material- and energy-consuming operations, technological backwardness and a low rate of utilization of national labour. All these phenomena have been inevitably accompanied by a strong pre-established investment drift and by a large number of unfinished construction projects. Persistent deficiencies include the low degree of adaptability of economic subjects, unsubstantiated claims for financial coverage from centrally administered financial resources under conditions of market and monetary imbalance and strong monopolization.

There are two main conditions for the economic recovery of the CSFR, apart from the structural adjustment of its industry:

1. The realization of systemic changes which reflect the scenario of economic reform.
2. The implementation of a flexible economic policy.

5. Privatization as a means to achieving higher economic performance

I shall conclude with a number of remarks concerning the concept of the privatization process in Czechoslovakia. Prior to the introduction of an extensive process of large-scale privatization, so-called 'minor' privatization is currently being implemented in accordance with the provisions of the Amended Decree of the Federal Ministry of Finance and on the basis of an agreement between the federal and national governments. The aim is to lay the basis for the subsequent rapid privatization of enterprises of trade and services.

Within the framework of the minor privatization programme, property (with the exception of property subject to restitution) is auctioned off to Czechoslovakian citizens, with payment in cash. The sales are regulated by local committees appointed for the purposes of privatization and restitution.

Concurrently with minor privatization, in cases involving the same type of property, such property will be returned to its original owners and/or their heirs. This applies to property appropriated from the original owners during the nationalization process.

Simultaneously with the promotion of small-scale and medium-sized entrepreneurial activities, efforts are being made to solve the problems of the large state enterprises. The purpose of the process of organizational restructuring is to establish economic units possessing solid capital and with strong competitive potential. Throughout this process, attention will be paid to the need to demonopolize the Czechoslovakian economy.

An important step forward in the process of major privatization involves the appraisal of enterprises and their transformation into a legal form conducive to privatization. Most frequently, this will involve the formation of a joint-stock company.

The sale of property shares in state enterprises (within the framework of major privatization) is beyond the reach of the Czechoslovakian population: personal savings in the country are far too few to meet such requirements and most are destined for current consumption. The full-scale use of such savings for privatization purposes would, moreover, jeopardize the viability of the Czechoslovak banks and savings banks.

The only way to involve the broadest section of the population in the process of major privatization within a relatively brief period of time is to offer shares to the population 'below cost'. The technical aspect of this operation is the so-called 'investment coupon' method.

A list of enterprises which could be privatized by means of coupons is currently being drawn up. There are three main reasons why an enterprise should not be included on this list.

1. The state is interested in preserving full control over the enterprise or the stock company. This means that there is some rational reason for maintaining state ownership (public services, etc.). The government estimates the maximum share of state ownership at about 30 per cent.

2. There is an acceptable (rational) project for privatization by means of a standard method. It may be realistic to privatize about 10 enterprises in this way every year.

3. The enterprise belongs to 10 per cent of the best enterprises or to 10 per cent of the worst. There is, evidently, no reason for privatizing these latter enterprises, which may be expected to go bankrupt. The best enterprises are candidates for the application of standard methods.

The number of enterprises that will undergo non-standard privatization can be estimated at around 2,000 (about 50 per cent of the economic units existing today). This number is also acceptable from a 'technical' point of view.

Apart from this non-standard privatization strategy, standard strategies will also be used. In particular:
- the priority sale of shares to employees and/or to the property funds of towns and villages;
- the sale of property shares or of the entire value of privatized enterprises to native and foreign investors at market prices;
- the investment of joint-stock capital in joint ventures with foreign capital participation;
- leasing arrangements involving parts of enterprises or entire enterprises, open to groups of employees or to private entrepreneurs.

Notes

1 Although attempts have been made to measure the efficiency, or rather labour productivity, in terms of the time consumed, these are tied to the so-called complex coefficients of consumption based on input-output analysis. Therefore they cannot be generally applied to the enterprise sector.

2   (i)   overall exports per worker;
    (ii) overall exports per 1,000 crowns invested;
    (iii) share of overall exports in gross production;
    (iv) share of overall exports in final sales;
    (v)   share of exports to developed countries in final sales;
    (vi) ratio between export and domestic prices (exports to former socialist countries);

      (vii)   ratio between exports and domestic prices (exports to developed countries);
     (viii)   overall average year-to-year index of export prices;
      (ix)   average year-to-year index of exports to developed countries;

3 Figures for 1987.

4 It stands to reason that there is no economic interpretation of a negative K value. Therefore I use symbolically K=0.

5 Situation at the end of 1989.

6 There were three devaluations in 1990 - respectively of 18, 24 and 28 Kčs per USD (with the aim of preparing for internal convertibility) - as one of the principal reform steps undertaken.

7 Primarily because of the competitiveness of enterprises with not fairly representative exports and their low share in overall production.

8 Enterprises with a more than 50 per cent share in commodity production within the whole national economy.

Privatization in Hungary: debates, developments and risks

Eva Voszka

Introduction

Privatization in Eastern Europe has been discussed in numerous publications inside and outside the countries concerned. A great variety of approaches, empirical descriptions of a given stage of the process, and attempts to model the events or the procedure recommended are available. This paper will focus on the dynamics of the process in Hungary.

After a short discussion of the issues involved, I shall describe the main dilemmas faced by the transformation in ownership structure; dilemmas which have not changed in the recent past and have not been resolved. Nevertheless, there have been some shifts in methods and concepts, and by analysing these shifts, this paper will try to demonstrate and explain the continuity in, and the eclectic character of, the changes in ownership structure as they are reflected both in debate and in practice.[1]

1. Debates on ownership structure before 1990

In Hungary, unlike other East European countries, discussion of ownership rights and structures began well before the free parliamentary elections held in March 1990. This discussion followed two main lines of thought.

The first concerned the spheres lying outside state property and which dominated the whole economy. The equality of rights of non-state ownership - that is, cooperatives and small private entrepreneurship - was offically declared in the early 1970s to be part of economic reforms. Ten years later a new impetus was given to the extension of these sectors by legislation and regulation, which made it possible for private entrepreneurship to be established in several organizational forms. At the beginning of the 1980s the signs of economic crisis became more and more evident, and a fall in the standard of living now threatened. The liberalization of private production may be considered as a compromise designed to create opportunities for people to compensate for their falling incomes from the state sector with their own activity. By this time there was consensus among economic advisers and leaders of the party-state that small private firms were important components of the national economy.

Nevertheless, an axiom accepted until the end of 1988, even by the most radical reform economists, was that the dominant sector of the economy must remain in state hands; that is to say, nationalization was irreversible. The second main line of debate concerned this sphere. The question was how to exercise ownership rights within state property, and this, broadly speaking, was the main issue of the entire economic reform process. There was, however, a specific organizational approach to the problem.

At the first stage, after the reform of 1968, a number of specialists working in government commissions put forward the proposal to incorporate state enterprises and to create state holdings as the owners of their shares. Debate during this period was dominated by the question of capital allocation, since the aim of the changes would be to rationalize investment decisions by decreasing direct redistribution from the state budget.[2] On this basis, other proposals were made to set up special 'owner organizations' without shares or company form.[3] The idea behind both these measures was to separate ownership functions from the management of enterprises on the one hand, and from the government bureaucracy on the other.

These proposals were rejected by the political leadership as too complicated and ideologically unacceptable ('not socialist forms'). Presumably, behind this rejection lay the fear that direct party and state influence at the enterprise level would be lost. Nevertheless, the idea of separating the different economic functions had by now established itself when a second wave of debate started in the early 1980s.

This second stage can be described as a stage of enterprise control, since the aim of the reform economists was to abolish the state-bureaucratic character of ownership rights. There were two main competing ideas: the holding concept, and some type of self-government at the enterprise level.[4] The latter proposal was accepted by the politicians, and enterprise councils were set up in 1984-85. These bodies, which consisted of managers and workers' representatives, were given the right to determine organizational structure, the right to appoint the chief executive, and powers of decision over merger and de-merger and over the establishment of joint ventures and partnerships involving state property.

This approach followed the traditional line taken by the reforms. It increased the independence of enterprises from central control by extending the *de facto* ownership rights of enterprise management, which dominated the enterprise councils. However, these self-governing forms were in contradiction of all the other aims of ownership reform: they did not separate the role of the owner and the manager; and they did not rationalize capital flow and organizational structure.

Debate continued in 1987-88, in a third stage which can be characterized as 'changing form and decentralization'. The new proposal was to transform state enterprises into groups of companies, where a holding would be formed from the enterprise centre and would possess the majority of shares.[5] This conception still did not remove the dominance of state property. On the contrary, all the reform economists as well as the reformist wing of the Communist Party emphasized that the company form in itself would not threaten the role of the state as owner. This was a very important factor in the passage of the law on companies in 1989; a law which, although it did not regulate the transformation of state enterprises into companies, did not exclude it either.

It was precisely the company form that led directly to the next stage of debate after 1988, namely the privatization stage. Shareholders could now be not only state organizations but private persons or institutions as well. The easiest way to introduce privatization, argued its proponents, is to transform enterprises and to sell their shares. Since that brings us to a new cycle of discussion, I shall comment on the first stages of debate before moving on to examine these new aims and issues.

The relatively long history of discussion on ownership rights and structures displays considerable continuity. Although the ideas and proposals have principally addressed property rights within the state sector, their aims and the organizational framework proposed have also been suitable for the removal of state ownership as well. Thus the practical task of privatization found theoretical precedents in Hungary, since the idea of large-scale privatization had appeared prior to the political upheaval, in the last years of the old regime. What is even more important, some of the proposals put forward in the previous two decades were followed by practical decisions and changes. Moreover, the events of the last three years, too, have had their precedents or special preconditions.

2. Transformations in ownership structure: 1988-90

Three main lines of action have been pursued in changing the ownership structure in Hungary.

The first has been the establishment of new private enterprises, as the development 'from below' of the private sector. I have already mentioned that this process started well before the dominant role of state ownership was called into question. Owing to a rather liberal environment (first deliberately created to maintain the reform-image of the system, later the consequence of a deepening economic crisis) a great number of small entrepreneurships and half-legal nuclei of private units emerged in the 1970s and, especially, from the early 1980s onwards.

Since 1988 a surge in the creation of new companies can be observed, and the number of economic units has increased from ten thousand to nearly thirty thousand in the last three years. The rate of growth was 50 per cent in 1989 and more than 90 per cent in 1990. The driving force behind this rapid expansion has been the limited liability company; the number of traditional enterprises and cooperatives has remained practically unchanged.

Unfortunately, there is no system for registering ownership structure in Hungary; hence nobody knows to what extent units are privately owned. We can only assume that the smallest units (employing fewer than 20 people) and founded 'without any precedents' (i.e. not previously included in the records of the Central Statistical Office) are private firms. This would mean that 40 per cent of the economic organizations existing at the end of 1990 were private.

This is an encouraging phenomenon, even if we must bear two facts in mind. First, although the number of private firms increased rapidly, the size and weight of their activities remained small. The share of the whole private sector in the GDP - including agriculture, services and the widespread second economy - is usually estimated at 10 to 15 per cent. Second, a considerable number of the new units registered in 1988-90 were presumably private units established in previous years without registration or legal entity which were legalized or had their organizational form changed. Continuity here signifies a less dramatic change in the number of market actors than official statistics would seem to show. On the other hand, continuity means that thousands if not millions of Hungarians became familiar with entrepreneurial attitudes even under the old system, and this fact provided the basis for a new wave of changes.

Independently of evaluation of this 'bottom-up' development, it should be made clear that the founding of new private firms led to the expansion of the private sector, but since these firms were mostly established by the pooling of private capital, they emerged independently of the privatization of state assets.

The second main line adopted in changing the ownership structure has mostly involved privatization - as the founding of joint ventures comprising state enterprises and foreign capital. This type of development has also had a long history. the first legislation on joint ventures was passed in 1972 during the early stages of reform. Administrative control over the founding of joint ventures was eased and financial preferences were progressively extended during the 1980s. In most recent years, the process of involving foreign capital has also accelerated. According to a recent announcement by the Registration Court, nearly 4,000 joint ventures were founded in 1990 with more than 70 billion forints of initial capital. The foreign investment involved was about one-third of this sum.[6] Of course, not all the Hungarian partners are state enterprises, but the majority (if not in numbers then in terms of capital involved) may be considered as privatization in the strict sense of the word.

Here it should be noted that the term 'privatization' is used in Hungary with different meanings. Apart from the strict sense (i.e. the handing over of state property to private persons or to companies with majority private ownership), it is often applied to all changes that alter the traditional forms of state ownership. Under this broad definition, the transformation of state enterprises in 1988-89 was called 'spontaneous privatization', although in most cases (apart from those of joint ventures with foreign capital) it did not result in the appearance of private owners.

The process of this third main line of change has usually involved the transformation of factories, plants, central divisions (trade, computing, product design) attached to large enterprises into independent joint stock or limited liability companies. Most of their shares have remained in the hands of the residual state enterprise created out of the former enterprise centre. The new owners, where any have appeared, are state-owned banks and the business partners of the given enterprise - again state firms.

Transformation of this type was mostly (but not always) initiated by the enterprise management. The reasons for this are numerous: to gain tax concessions or other preferences and at the same time to achieve greater independence from governmental organs; to avoid a state-led privatization; to achieve a compromise with those factories inside the enterprise that had traditionally fought for their autonomy; to avoid bankruptcy by making a debt-equity swap with the banks; and so on.[7]

Whatever the motives, such types of transformation were executed by the management following the previous establishment of enterprise councils. These bodies had the right to decide on the organizational form of the enterprise. Legislation in 1988 and 1989 gave further impetus to these changes. Nevertheless, in my view, the existence of these frameworks was not the reason for 'spontaneous privatization'. Both the establishment of enterprise councils and, through them, the transformation into company form were instead the consequence of the increasing power of the enterprise management which resulted from (as well as being a driving force behind) previous economic reforms. In this process, by the time the political change had come about (i.e. when a mass privatization process could begin) most state property rights had already devolved to enterprise and company management. The inheritance from the former political system, however, was not one of strong and stable ownership, but a dispersed model where property rights were divided among different types of organizations and social groups.[8]

This is one of the circumstances affecting the possibilities and characteristics of privatization; one of the reasons why there has been continuity not only in discussions but in the real changes as well. Continuity exists not only for the period before the political turnover but also for the first year of the new system. The three main lines of action in changing the ownership structure remained the same even after March 1990. This means that the privatization process did not speed up, and that there was no social consensus on the general framework to adopt in eliminating state ownership. Thus dilemmas over the privatization process became more evident, and the methods proposed to solve them did not remain the same.

3. Dilemmas of privatization: 1990-91

The main questions concerning privatization - and the transformation of the economy as a whole - are the following. What forces will drive and conduct the process? How rapid should it be? Which social groups will be preferred and which discriminated against in the shorter and longer run? What will the social and economic nature of the new structure be? As we shall see, all the solutions put forward have their favourable and unfavourable consequences in general, and for different social groups in particular.[9]

3.1. *Centralized versus decentralized methods*

The first dilemma is whether transformation should be led by a strong government, on the basis of a detailed programme, or by the individual initiative and self-governing movements of economic actors themselves. In other words, is it possible to set up a liberalized, decentralized market system by means of centralized decision-making mechanisms?

Serious doubts can be raised about the intentions of the economic actors concerned. It is probable that they will prefer to preserve or to create monopolistic and protected positions rather than enter into market competition. The government can state, not without good reason, that a spontaneous process does not lead in the direction of a market system.

On the other hand, it is obvious that the creation of a free market means that the government will have to relinquish a significant amount of the power it exercises over the economy. The parties and politicians that have recently come to power may find it difficult to refrain from influencing processes directly.

Nevertheless, strong central control has evident disadvantages. The centralization of economic decisions may reproduce the traditional bargaining mechanisms characteristic of the centrally planned economy. These methods are familiar both to the government apparatuses and to the economic units. The experience of several decades has shown that transformation conceived and led by central political organs proves to be ineffective. This method may even undermine the legitimacy of the new government by providing support for those who criticize the old style of the new regime and the lack of fundamental changes.

There are various other factors that render the centralization of economic transformation not only dangerous for the government but also technically difficult. One problem is the initial situation inherited from the old system: the decentralization of property rights from the central level to enterprise management. I have already argued that this decentralization reflected the real power relations within the economy and strengthened the positions of the enterprise management. If this is true, the situation will not be altered simply by declarations and decisions on the part of the government.

The second problem is the present shortage of individuals and organizations able to prepare and execute a comprehensive programme for the government. After political transition, the state apparatuses were reorganized. The distribution of different functions is still unclear, and ministers, for example, are often not specialists but politicians. Also, the experts who previously worked on reforms have been dismissed because of their involvement in the old system. At this point we have to refer to the specific feature of changes in Hungary: the continuity of the process - which, in this context, means that the members of previous governments and the staff who worked for them were not necessarily communists: many of them were simply specialists. Now that they have been dismissed, it is difficult to find replacements with the same amount of knowledge and experience.

Thus the government may find it more rational from both an economic and political point of view to use decentralized methods for transformation.

What has actually happened in Hungary in the last three years is a formal shift from spontaneous to centralized methods, and thence to the decentralization of the decision-making mechanism. We have to use the adjective 'formal' here, because the real shifts have been less dramatic than the declarations and intentions.

First, the so-called 'spontaneous privatization' of 1988-89 was not particularly spontaneous. The state organs forced enterprises to begin to transform themselves into the company form by providing negative incentives (a restrictive economic policy, tighter controls on financial sources, a cutba ̄ on subsidies) and positive encouragement (normative and individua preferences, tax concessions, the liberalized regimentation of companies). In several cases, especially where bankrupt enterprises were concerned, transformation or privatization was carried out directly by government organs. Ministries were able to bring self-governed enterprises under direct state supervision. The ministry representative was legally present at sessions of the enterprise councils, which meant that the supervisory body received information on the transformation plans of enterprises in advance. Ultimately, the top managements of firms consulted representatives of the state administration even if they were not formally obliged to do so.

Despite governmental interference, the process has been sharply criticized for its 'spontaneous' character on account of the decision-making powers assigned to enterprise managers. The main arguments against have been the following.[10] The process does not necessarily create new and real owners, and thus the rights of management appointed by the old political system are extended without administrative or strong market control. State revenue has not been increased by the transformation, even if some assets have been sold to foreigners. There has been a lack of competition for new owners and a lack of public control. Therefore the suspicion that assets have been 'sold off' at a cut-rate price and allegations of corruption cannot be ignored.

These arguments may be well-founded. Consequently, the last government of the old regime made efforts to control the process by setting up the State Property Agency (SPA) and by setting out directives for the selling of state assets. Nevertheless, it was the new government that tried to centralize in order to concentrate the rights of disposal into its own hands; to be able to distribute state assets to new owners; and to assign the important posts to its cadres. The first and most important step was not the elaboration of a comprehensive privatization programme or the identification of the groups of new owners, but deciding who the real owner was (and thus the seller). The significant issue for the new government was renationalization in order to restore its powers which had been much reduced by its predecessors in government.

The SPA was subordinate to the government, not to the Parliament, and its rights were extended. Between July 1990 and 1991, no transformation or privatization could be implemented without control or approval by the Agency. The management of the state enterprises were able to draw up programmes for changing the ownership structure and to negotiate with potential partners, but all contracts had to be confirmed and signed by the SPA.

This centralization proved to be rather formal in nature, and led to no clarification of roles. In the autumn of 1990, the SPA considered that its most important achievement was that it had not altered the pace of enterprise-initiated transformations. The SPA stressed that the firms were ready to cooperate and that they often themselves requested state assistance.[11]

This view is also confirmed by the experience of the enterprises. The managements of state enterprises devote most of their energies to finding the relevant person at the SPA, identifying intentions at the highest level and, in possession of this knowledge, working out the appropriate bargaining strategy with which the enterprise's specific aims can be achieved. In this situation all the elements of transformation and privatization (form schedule, selection of

ers) may be part of a bargaining process where enterprises
‌ over the outcome. Centralization, therefore, has remained
‌ than half of the proposals put forward by enterprises have
‌ any adjustment by the SPA; in the remaining cases the
‌ reverted to the initial plans. The programmes begun by the
‌ privatizing the retail trade and twenty big enterprises) are still to
‌ented.

‌ view of these disadvantages, discussions started in spring 1991 on the
‌ecentralization of privatization. Apart from economic factors and the informal
pressures applied by enterprises, conflicts were exacerbated by struggles
among the governmental apparatuses. The overwhelming power of the SPA
was sharply criticized by the Ministry of Finance (which seems to be the
dominant organization in economic policy) and the branch ministries. Thus it is
the pull towards decentralization that seems to be winning, together with the
increasing influence of ministries and 'self-privatization' - that is, the
reappropriation of decision-making rights by enterprises. Recent debate has
concentrated on the scope of these latter. The aim of the SPA is to apply the
method only to small enterprises (employing fewer than 300 people) while the
Ministry of Finance proposes self-privatization as the rule, not to be used only
in the case of the smallest firms.

Whatever the final outcome may be, one should bear in mind that
decentralized privatization may produce the same disadvantages as spontaneous
privatization. These problems will probably provoke the same counter-
arguments, and the process may swing back to a more centralized line again.

3.2. *Selling versus redistributing*

A specific feature of Hungarian privatization usually cited by comparative
studies is the state's intention to sell and not to redistribute its assets.[12] Indeed,
there is no comprehensive programme comparable, for instance, to the Czechoslovakian voucher system. It is also obvious that the first programmes implemented by the government emphasized the 'British method' of privatization.

There are political, ideological and economic arguments on the side of
redistribution. Clearly, those political parties which propose free or preferential
access to state property may gain additional votes and support. The
redistribution of assets may compensate for such unavoidable economic
problems as high inflation and unemployment. The ideology here is one of
social justice: namely, egalitarianism. Whether one becomes an entrepreneur
should not depend on previous social status, which is supposedly connected to
loyalty to the old political system. Last but not least, the proponents of
redistribution see the main obstacle to privatization as the lack of capital and
liquidity, an obstacle that only this method can eliminate.

Arguments in favour of selling have been based on the other aims of
privatization: revenue for the central budget, and the creation of 'real owners'
who invest their own money in privatization. According to this logic, people or
organizations who receive assets or shares as a gift would be less averse to
losses. They would create a weak ownership structure, in the sense that they
would be unable to control the management because of the diffusion of
ownership.[13] Doubts have also been raised as to the equality of redistribution.

Depending on the method applied, certain groups would receive preferential treatment because their former property was nationalized, or they would have access to inside information through their previous or actual positions.

Despite the counter-arguments and the declaration of the sales system as the general rule, some elements of redistribution have occurred, even in the initial programmes of the new government. Handing state assets over to local governments and pension funds has always been part of these proposals. The benefit to the state in these cases would be a saving in subsidies out of central funds. Similarly, giving preferential treatment to employees by allowing them access to their firm's shares has never been excluded as a possible method of privatization. Indeed, it was the last government of the old system that prepared a version of the Employee Stock Ownership Programme (ESOP).

There has been an observable tendency towards increasing the role of redistribution in recent months. Almost all the legislation on ownership structure passed or debated by the new Parliament supports this statement. The first measure was the Compensation Law which returned agricultural land, or a voucher proportionate to its value, to the original owners. (Among other possibilities, the vouchers can be used in the privatization of any state asset.) As a consequence of a decision by the Constitutional Court, compensation was extended to all types of property up to a certain limit of value. The second law, passed in 1991, provides for the return of a significant part of Church property. There are proposals under discussion for handing over state assets to local governments, and an Employee Ownership Programme is envisaged. Social security organizations are supposed to receive state shares or enterprises as well.

The reason for this shift in privatization methods seems to be predominantly political. The two smaller parties in the coalition have pledged themselves to some form of redistribution. The Smallholders Party made an electoral issue out of the reprivatization of land, and the Christian Democratic Party has close links with the Catholic Church. The opposition parties have criticized these proposals, arguing that they would slow down the privatization process, would produce an economically irrational ownership structure, and would increase the burden on other social strata. Nevertheless, in the competition for votes, they themselves have come up with other ideas on redistribution. The Socialist Party has argued for employee ownership, and the liberal party, the Free Democrats, has proposed equal redistribution to all citizens, but only up to a limited extent.

However, as a consequence of a pact between the largest coalition party and the strongest opposition party, all laws on ownership need only a simple majority to pass.[14] The coalition therefore has a convenient majority in Parliament, and the trend towards redistribution could not be interrupted even if the opposition wanted it to be. The political aspects of privatization may push the process away from the initial emphasis on selling.

3.3. *The shape of the new ownership structure*

The dilemmas concerning the new ownership structure are perhaps the aspect most widely discussed in Western analyses. Models and descriptions have concerned themselves with potential owners, concentrating on such issues as internal versus external ownership (i.e. groups inside and outside the enterprise), foreign versus domestic ownership, and institutional versus natural ownership. Another line of analysis addresses the future functioning of the new system and examines dispersed versus concentrated structures, the treatment of monopolies, and the control and management of remaining state property.[15]

These latter issues seem to have been rather neglected in Hungarian discussion: the main goal is to privatize, and all other questions about forthcoming economic mechanisms have been set aside. Problems to do with the new ownership are discussed mainly in connection with the role of the state and the methods of privatization.

It is obvious that decisions on these latter questions have their impact on the ownership structure. Redistribution is by definition a centrally-led process. The state takes the decisive role in the first stage, and then hands over to redistribution sub-centres (such as local government). Selling off state assets can be done by both centralized and decentralized methods; in the former case, the state as seller decides on the new ownership structure directly by choosing the buyers, or indirectly by giving preferential treatment to applications by various groups.

Bearing in mind that the dilemmas mentioned above have not been resolved, it is not surprising that the framework of the new ownership structure is still uncertain. Government programmes usually list all the possibilities, without coming out in favour of any particular one. Nevertheless, changes in the concepts of centralization and redistribution have been followed by a shift of emphasis as regards the desirable ownership structure.

The first government programme on privatization, introduced in August 1990, advocated institutional ownership and argued that it would be irrational to go back to the initial, anachronistic forms of the 'romantic capitalism of the 19th century'. It is desirable, and even possible, to jump several stages and to make use of modern forms of institutional ownership, such as pension funds, insurance funds and various types of financial intermediary. However, the government has done little to establish the framework for institutions of this kind. Indeed, the first law it passed was on 'small' privatization; a law which gave priority to small-scale natural ownership and excluded foreign capital from the purchase of retail units. This tendency was strengthened by an overall shift towards redistribution, induced primarily by the Restitution Law. Because of this change of emphasis, both natural and domestic owners were envisaged by the new government proposal of April 1991. Redistribution may thus lead to a significant amount of internal ownership, i.e. ownership by employees as well.

In parallel with the emphasis on natural and domestic ownership, the government has taken its first steps towards institutional ownership by passing a law on church and local government property. Similarly, despite recent attacks on foreign capital and the curtailing of their tax concessions, attracting foreign investment is still the main priority for both government and firms. The so-called First Privatization Programme - the selling of twenty large enterprises by the SPA - although still not complete, seems to prefer foreign buyers.

The conclusion to be drawn as regards these dilemmas over future ownership structure is that both programmes and practice are rather eclectic.

Slight shifts in concepts have had no significant impact on actual developments; and shifts in the latter have not matched the programmes declared, which continue to derive from political debate and social pressures.

3.4. *Rapid versus gradual privatization*

The fourth dilemma concerns whether changes should be made gradually or rapidly - in one great leap. A marked feature of Hungary after two decades of economic reforms is that it has fewer illusions about step-by-step solutions than any other East European country. The Hungarian experience shows that the results of this approach are limited. Moreover, Hungary tried to decentralize and liberalize even before the political upheaval, and had introduced several market-type institutions. What remained intact was the dominance of state ownership. Hence the conclusion can be drawn that the key issue in transformation is privatization: without a rapid rebuilding of the ownership structure, no significant changes will occur.

There are two other political arguments against slow transformation. First, a freely elected government has to demonstrate that it is different in nature from its predecessor - otherwise it will lose legitimacy. Second, it has become obvious in recent months that slow transition preserves the traditional power structure within the economy, including the bargaining power of large enterprises vis-à-vis the central government.

However, there are serious factors of a political nature which push the government in the direction of step-by-step changes. As experiments in 'shock therapy' undertaken by other countries show, rapid transformation provokes enormous problems, including a rapid fall in living standards for broad sectors of the population. Here one has to consider factors such as growth in unemployment, even higher inflation, and the reduction in social redistribution from central budget funds. People whose standard of living has been deteriorating for more than ten years, whose savings are exhausted, or who are surviving on the threshold of poverty, even by East European standards (nearly one quarter of the population), would not tolerate such a strategy. The relatively affluent middle-class has become accustomed to its standard of living and to its exemption from shortages. They have something to lose - more than their counterparts in other East European countries. It is apparent that the legitimacy of the new regime would come under threat from these social strata if quick transformation were attempted.

Nevertheless, the new government has declared its intention to proceed with rapid privatization and to reduce the proportion of state ownership to under 50 per cent within three years. The rationale of this plan is based on decisions taken to deal with the basic dilemmas of centralization, redistribution and the new ownership structure.

One of the government's declared reasons for centralization was to speed up the privatization process. The method it used was the introduction of such 'active programmes' as small privatization and the First Privatization Programme. These initiatives have proved to be rather slow (at the time of writing, both of them are just at their beginning after more than six months), and in many cases enterprise-initiated transformations have been slowed down by the state bureaucracy.

The decentralization of decisions, the return to self-privatization, is supposed to give new impetus by eliminating SPA interference in transactions. There are some doubts about the consequences of the new method. First, those enterprises willing and able to transform themselves have already done so by now. The remainder will presumably find it more difficult to find investors. Therefore, secondly, they will obviously resort, not to privatization but to self-transformation into company form without private partners. We should not forget that the main line of the 'spontaneous privatization' which preceded decentralized privatization was precisely this.

Shifts in the methods used to resolve the second dilemma, redistribution, may speed up changes in the ownership structure without creating private owners (for instance by giving state assets to churches or to holding companies and pension funds not established by private investors). The extent of privatization thus depends on the terminology used. If every type of denationalization (i.e. liquidation of traditional state ownership) is considered to be privatization, independently of the identity of the new owners, the process may be formally rapid.

Other types of redistribution, such as restitution of land, bonds acquired as compensation for buying state assets and the preferential treatment of employees, may also speed up privatization. However, they create a diffuse ownership structure; a structure that is unable to control management.

Even if privatization proves to be as rapid as the government predicts, a huge amount of assets - nearly half of them - will remain in state ownership, and these are assets which have been neglected for a long time. In recent months, however, several proposals have appeared in government documents, all to do with some kind of holding form but with different frameworks and functions for the new organizations.

One type of holding would be created out of the shares remaining in state majority ownership, as in the electricity or oil industries. These holdings would exercise direct control because they would have the right to decide on all aspects of enterprise activity. Discussion continues as to whether they should be subordinate to branch ministries or to a special ownership organization.

The other type of holding would exercise ownership rights over enterprises not yet privatized, but with the longer-term intention of selling them. These would be mainly financial organizations. It is not clear, however, on what basis they could be formed (on that of the former large enterprise centres or with new apparatus acquiring shares in different sectors and firms), and their subordination is uncertain as well.

4. Some risks in present transformation tendencies

These dilemmas and the shifts in the manner of handling them reveal some contradictions with a competitive market system.

The first danger is non-privatization, with a slowing down of ownership change due to the institutional framework, a lack of demand or a lack of supply. Although the creation of organizations to take temporary control of the assets still in state ownership is necessary, the actual establishment of this type of holding may hinder further privatization. It will obviously be in the interest of these owner organizations to preserve their positions and not to sell state assets.

Although I consider slow privatization to be a danger, the speeding up of the process by using artificial methods may also be harmful.

We may call this outcome 'quasi-privatization'. Quasi-privatization may occur as a consequence of centralized decision-making mechanisms, when state property is handed over to institutional owners without a private background, or without close control by private owners. But the consequence of decentralized methods may also be that enterprises, since they are unable or unwilling to involve private capital, transform themselves into the company form without privatization. As the experience of 'spontaneous privatization' has shown, in this type of transformation new owners may emerge that are entirely or majority state-owned (enterprises, banks and other institutions). This would lead to the development of new redistributive centres, the mutual dependence of the organizations concerned and, as a social consequence, to the formation of influential networks ('clans') in top decision-making positions.

On the other hand, centralized methods can be applied not only through redistribution but by selling state assets. In this case the danger arises that the new owners will not be chosen primarily on the basis of economic rationality, but on the basis of political influence or other types of pressure. As a consequence, a new group of owners may form which is dependent on its connections with the state and parties and which will constantly obtain state contracts and preferential treatment.

Finally, if the centralization of decision-making powers implies redistribution as well, and if privatization is not quasi but real, the outcome may be diffuse ownership. If this structure does not emerge as the result of a long-term, market-type development but is artificially created by the state, and if there is no fully-fledged market economy with all its institutions and behavioural norms, there may be serious consequences: diffuse ownership will be unable to control management, and the situation (and economic performance) may be very similar to that of the decentralized and weak state ownership of previous decades.

Since all the trends mentioned above - the centralization and decentralization of transformation process, the sale or redistribution of state assets, different types of potential new owners - are present in Hungary, none of these dangers can be excluded. Nevertheless, it is hard to predict the likelihood or the significance of certain of them precisely because of the eclectic and constantly shifting character of the transformation process as a whole. This is why models of privatization are of only temporary relevance, valid for only a certain period of transformation. I am sure that we shall have to wait for years, if not for decades, before we can begin comprehensive evaluation of the privatization process in Eastern European countries. Until then, all that researchers can do is take 'snapshots' of this operationally and intellectually fascinating process.

Notes

1 My empirical analysis is based on case studies written by A. Havas, G. Lamberger, S. Pasztor, J. Revesz and E. Voszka for a research project by Penzugykutato Rt and *Közgazdagtudományi Intézet* in 1990.
2 For a summary of debate during this early period see Hoch, 1990.
3 Kopatsy, 1969; Tardos, 1972.
4 For an excellent summary see Sarkozy, 1986.
5 See, for example, Matolcsy, 1988.
6 Konjunkturajelentes (Conjuncture-report) 1990/3, *Konjunktúra és I·iackutató Intézet.*
7 For more detailed analysis of the reasons for this see Mora, 1990; Voszka, 1991.
8 Szalai, 1989.
9 An earlier version of this section was presented at the CIRIEC conference "Public versus Private Enterprise", Liege, April 1991.
10 For an excellent summary in English see Stark, 1990.
11 *Jelentés az Állami Vagyonügynökseg müködéséröl* (Report on the activity of the SPA), Nov 1990
12 See, for example, Milanović, 1990.
13 For details see Mora, 1990.
14 See, for example, Stark, 1990; Milanović, 1990; Frydman and Rapaczynski, 1991.
15 See Stark, 1990.

Bibliography

Frydman, R., Rapaczynski, A. (1991), 'Privatization and Corporate Governance in Eastern Europe: Can a Market be Designed?' in G. Winkler (ed.), *Central and Eastern Europe. Roads to Growth,* forthcoming.

Hoch, R. (1990), 'Részvénytársaság és reform' (Share company and reform), *Kozgazdasagi Szemle,* no. 1.

Kopatsy, S. (1969), 'Onallo tulajdonosi szervezetekrol' (Independent organizations in the role of owners), *Pénzügyi Szemle,* no. 3.

Matolcsy, G. (1988), 'A vagyonerdezeltseg kulcsa' (The key to interest in asset value), *Figyelö,* 7, April.

Milanović, B. (1990), 'Privatization in Post-Communist Societies', Washington DC: The World Bank.

Mora, M. (1990), 'Az állami vállalotok al-privátizaciója' (The pseudo-privatization of state enterprises), *Gazdasagkutato Intézet.*

Sarkozy, T. (1986), *Egy gazdasági szervezeti reform sodrában* (In the current of an economic organizational reform), Budapest: Magreto Kiado.

Stark, D. (1990), 'Privatization in Hungary: From Plan to Market or from Plan to Clan?', Cornell Working Papers.

Szalai, E. (1989), *Gazdasági mechanismus, reformtörekvések es nagyvállalati érdekek* (Economic mechanism, reform and the interests of big enterprises), Budapest: Közgadasági és Jogi Könyvkiadó.

Tardos, M. (1997), 'A gazdasági verseny problémai hazánkban' (Problems of economic competition in Hungary), *Közgazdasági Szemle,* no. 2.

Voszka, E. (1991), 'Tulajdom-reform' (Ownership-reform), *Penzügykutató Intézet.*

Index